I0816022

BISON
BOOKS

Our Regenerative Future

SERIES EDITORS

Stephanie Anderson
Sonja Trom Eayrs

"In Kathryn Wilder's new offering, *The Last Cows*, there are cows, several kinds of cows, and horses, especially the author's beloved ride, who is her companion throughout the story. There are also elk, cougar, coyotes, bears, piñon jays, dogs, and there are fences, lots of fences to be mended, taken down, and repaired. And there is every kind of extreme weather, a rattlesnake, and a near drowning, all of this around the herding and care that take place on a cattle ranch run by the author and her sons. . . . What I didn't expect was an ecological journey of fine attunement to the land, to the elements, to the living inhabitants of the ranch area, and a penetrating spiritual awareness that can happen with the grueling everyday work that it takes to care for and run a cattle ranch in Disappointment Valley. This important book is anything but a disappointment and builds on Wilder's legacy of conscientious storytelling."

—JOY HARJO (Mvskoke), twenty-third U.S. poet laureate

"Kat Wilder knows cows in the way that leads her to write in an unlabored eloquence that expands bovine to define wild landscapes and deep love for a hardscrabble way of life. Disappointment is Wilder's valley of contentment, and her writing will become the fortunate reader's joy. *The Last Cows* sings with a sense of westernness that lends itself to a longing for her arid country."

—J. DREW LANHAM, author of *The Home Place: Memoirs of a Colored Man's Love Affair with Nature*

"Kathryn Wilder is a wonderful writer with some crazy good stories to go along with it. Reading this passionate book is a pleasure. Wilder is writing about a life that's very different from most lives—and decidedly not an urban one. These stories of a woman on the land are so damned refreshing. *The Last Cows* is captivating, courageous, and full of love."

—JANISSE RAY, author of *Wild Spectacle: Seeking Wonders in a World beyond Humans*

"*The Last Cows* presents amazing, gritty detail of cattle ranching from the unique perspective of a woman's life experience. Ride along with Kathryn Wilder and her three-legged ranch dog in her Toyota pickup or with her trusty horse, Savanna, and immerse yourself in amazingly detailed descriptions so clearly written that the reader can visualize being in one of the truly wild places left in the West."

—BOB WEST, author of *Twenty Miles of Fence*

"In beautifully crafted language, Kathryn Wilder gives us a genealogy of place that reminds us that the pulse of the earth—of all her creatures—was once indistinguishable from our own. Each hoofbeat, each fluttering wing and flash of fish, reminds us that we *belong* to the earth. Rooted to an ancient family, we are saplings struggling to survive. *The Last Cows* offers shade and life-giving water. Read each line as you might trace the tributaries of a river on her way to the ocean. Destiny, and our future, demands no less."

—**PAGE LAMBERT**, co-founder of Women Writing the West and author of *In Search of Kinship*

"I just unsaddled and I've been thinking all morning about what to say about Kathryn Wilder's new book. Agriculture is not homogeneous, a truth that applies especially to ranching. With her stories of family history that include her love of cows, land, and wild things, Wilder brings to life an important examination for the times we live in. I think her words are exactly what our world needs right now."

—**AMY HALE**, award-winning author of *Rightful Place* and *Ordinary Skin*

"For me, one of those who disdains cattle grazing on public lands while still enjoying my rib-eye ritual, Kathryn Wilder's *The Last Cows* is complicated. Did my meat come from the bull that charged her, sending her flying across rocks, soil, and cheatgrass? Or Bandito, with the black rings around his eyes? Now I cannot separate my steak from its story, which I want to know."

—**BROOKE WILLIAMS**, author of *Encountering Dragonfly: Notes on the Practice of Re-enchantment*

"Part personal story, part history, *The Last Cows* is an altogether compelling book. Kathryn Wilder brings the reader into her world of cows, cowboys, relationships, life changes, and more cows. She weaves historical accounts into her contemporary experiences to create a layered story that makes you want to reflect and keep reading at the same time."

—**JOLYN YOUNG**, author of *Never Burn Your Moving Boxes*

The Last Cows

On Ranching, Wonder, and a Woman's Heart

Kathryn Wilder

University of Nebraska Press
Lincoln

Acknowledgments for the use of previously published material appear on pages 264–65, which constitute an extension of the copyright page.

⊂⊃- brand is registered to Cachuma Ranch Co. LLC.

The University of Nebraska Press is part of a land-grant institution with campuses and programs on the past, present, and future homelands of the Pawnee, Ponca, Otoe-Missouria, Omaha, Dakota, Lakota, Kaw, Cheyenne, and Arapaho Peoples, as well as those of the relocated Ho-Chunk, Sac and Fox, and Iowa Peoples.

Publication of this volume was assisted by
a gift from an anonymous donor.

For customers in the EU with safety/GPSR concerns, contact:
gpsr@mare-nostrum.co.uk
Mare Nostrum Group BV
Mauritskade 21D
1091 GC Amsterdam
The Netherlands

Library of Congress Control Number: 2024048556

Designed and set in Bulmer MT Std by L. Welch.

For Lacey Park Lausten
& Lucas Allen Lausten
that they may know, when it's time,
some of their family backstory

And for wildness, always

There is a language beyond human language,
an elemental language, one that arises from the land itself.

—Linda Hogan, interview in *Listening to the Land*

Leave this muddy water and seek clarity.

—Rumi

Contents

Illustrations

The Last Cows

Prologue

Tumbling

Endings come.

—David Lavender, "Rancho Los Alamitos" manuscript

Disappointment Valley, Colorado, 2023

As I approach my seventieth birthday, I find myself looking behind me as well as ahead, because a question looms: What will I do with the rest of my life? Followed by: How long can I keep this up? Keep my cows? If the higher *They* would tell me my off-date, planning might be easier. Instead I am left to figure this out on my own.

In southwestern Colorado, I run a working cattle ranch with my elder son, Ken, and the help of my younger son, Tyler, and Ken's wife and children. Here the land tumbles out of the San Juan branch of the Rocky Mountains onto the Colorado Plateau, melding with southeastern Utah, northeastern Arizona, and northwestern New Mexico as if no artificial lines separated states, only a movement of geology oblivious to the mapping and geography that created the Four Corners.

The cattle are my day job. Sometimes I live in a cabin above a creek in Disappointment Valley, doing my part of the ranch work while Ken takes care of his part at the headquarters near Dolores, and wherever else he's needed. The Bureau of Land Management tells us when our cattle can go onto our winter grazing allotment and when they come off—days on a calendar marked, known. The U.S. Forest Service does the same with our summer grazing permit. The days in between these on- and off-dates fill with activities prioritized by urgency—horses ridden, loved, and cared for; cattle checked, doctored, moved, removed; fences checked, fixed, built.

Often I also tumble from the mountains to the desert, loosely following a pattern of seasons. Following our cows. Or following the trails of wildness toward a story. In winter and its shoulder seasons I tend to do this afoot. Summer into fall I'm ahorseback high in the mountains. That's our ranch—pieces of desert linked to a mountain summer pasture by a watershed like stories linked together by a life.

I grew up with ranches in my background. Rancho Los Alamitos, among the first ranches in my family's lineage, was built where the Native village of Puvungna once thrived—Puvungna, a sacred place of emergence and gathering for the Tongva people of Southern California. Their creation story begins at a flourishing spring on a hilltop near the Pacific Ocean, where a village blossomed. From there the people spread up and down the coast, inland, and across the water to the southern Channel Islands, living in more than a hundred villages in a vast area called Tovaangar, *world*. For thousands of years Tongva occupied this region. Then came Spanish exploration and colonization, and thus began for the coastal tribes the years of displacement and death resulting from disease, forced relocation to California missions, enslavement, and starvation.

The Spanish Crown took the land and gave grazing rights, to which it had no right, to patrons such as José Manuel Nieto of the Gaspar de Portolá expedition; Nieto's provisional "land-use permit" included Puvungna and three hundred thousand surrounding acres and became Rancho Los Nietos. An erasure. The Mexican government replaced the Spanish government in 1822 and distributed Mexican land grants—deeds to the land—and in 1834 Nieto's descendants received five land grants partitioned from Rancho Los Nietos. From Puvungna. Nieto's eldest son soon sold his portion, Rancho Los Alamitos. Nearly fifty years later, my great-great-grandfather, having dabbled with his cousins in buying cattle, sheep, and land since he arrived in California from Maine in 1870, leased Rancho Los Alamitos, and then purchased it in 1881. The spring on the hill is still called Puvungna.

My great-grandfather, raised on and then running Rancho Los Alamitos, acquired another ranch, Rancho el Cojo, in 1913 and the adjoining Rancho Jalama a few years later, both located in Santa Barbara County, where the

California coastline elbows from its east-west slant to stretch north at Point Conception. Named by a Spanish explorer sailing past in 1602, La Punta de la Limpia Concepción—Point of Immaculate Conception—already had a Chumash name, Humqaq, *the Raven comes*. Humqaq has long been considered a stepping-off point by local Chumash, "where our souls leave this earth [for] the afterlife," says Brian Holguin, Indigenous archaeologist and descendant of the Santa Ynez Band of Chumash Indians.

Point Conception, then, is a land of beginnings and endings, as the Cojo turned out to be.

Memories of Rancho el Cojo span my first fifty years: eight miles of California coastline, cattle, *horses*. I remember foreman Floyd showing my big sister and me how to milk a cow in the old barn that still stands. And my family having breakfast at the long wooden table in the cookhouse, me eating pancakes and peeking at the cowboys seated at the other end of the table. I remember the Appaloosa stallion, Cojo Mapachi, foaled at the Cojo just months after I was born in Berkeley. (*Cojo* means "lame" in Spanish—the stallion was named for the ranch, not an injury, while Rancho el Cojo was named because of a Chumash chief in the area who walked with a limp.) Cojo Mapachi went on to sire Cojo Rojo, who literally starred *under* Marlon Brando in the 1966 movie *The Appaloosa*.

I remember gathering cattle on the Jalama, stopping on a high point beside the ranch foreman, whose hand circled his head as if he were swinging a lariat as he told me that every bit of land we saw was part of the ranches—the north-facing hills of chaparral, deep canyons of poison oak, the ridgelines of coast live oaks, the slope to the sea.

The Cojo had a summer program for family youth, like a ranch internship. I applied, but the ranch-company president said no. I was a girl. And, he said, I could do better than being around cowboys and doing grunt labor. Plus he thought boys and men might feel concerned about bathroom etiquette.

When I told the foreman this, he said, "I don't care if you're a man or a woman, as far as I'm concerned you should use the facilities on the other side of the hill." Meaning, find a tree or a bush and keep out of sight.

Sorting through old papers recently, I found an unsent letter addressed to: *To Whom It May Concern* (probably me). I had apparently written the letter while under the influence—in it I describe a conversation with a friend in which I tell him about the rejection, my whiskey scrawl full of misspelled words (puek, oficially, sence). I didn't say that I was in trouble, that I'd hoped working at the Cojo might straighten me out.

"I must create a new plan," I wrote. "I *know* what I want to do. What kind of life I want. But how to get what I want . . ."

To my friend I'd said, "I'm going to marry a rich cowboy and own a ranch. Or I'll find my own ranch and then I can do anything I want. No men around to tell me it's not my place."

"Or you could marry a poor cowboy and just be happy," he said.

And that's what I did.

1

The Last Cows

Even now a man with bowlegs and Wranglers
will get a second look from me.
—Linda Hogan, *The Woman Who Watches Over the World*

Central Coast and Santa Ynez Valley, California, 1980s

"Don't ever fall in love with your cows," Keith said. We sat on our horses one summer morning on the coastal ranch where he worked, looking over a pen of heifers weaned a couple of months before. "That's the best piece of advice I can give you about the cattle business."

"Oh, I wouldn't do that," I said. "Love a cow?"

He got first pick, then I would get a turn. But only one. My introduction to owning my own herd of cattle would begin with one heifer. Keith and I weren't married yet.

"Why not?" I asked. The smell of salt spray drifted on the breeze.

"You never know when you'll have to sell 'em," he said, yawning. "If it's a dry year, or she doesn't get bred or she loses a calf, or the market goes way up and you just can't pass up the opportunity, she goes to town." Meaning the sales yard, the slaughterhouse, the meatpacking plant, the supermarket.

In cattle terminology "cow" and "cattle" are interchangeable in only one direction: all cows are cattle but not all cattle are cows. A cow is a mature female. A heifer is a young female, from birth to motherhood. First-calf heifer means a heifer is either with a bull, is already bred, or she has calved but hasn't quite grown into cow status. Replacement heifers are those heifers selected to keep and breed, who will eventually replace some of the older cows.

I eyed the heifers, mostly Brahma crosses, blacks and reds, and some Santa Gertrudis, white markings like spilled milk on their faces, legs, and bellies. I tried to remember everything Keith had taught me—straight back, good angle from hip bone to tailbone, not too high-headed, no whites of the eyes. My horse shifted beneath me.

As the sun climbed up the morning, Keith squinted under the brim of his straw cowboy hat. "Choose carefully," he said.

I watched a dark heifer circle the outside of the herd then push toward the middle, her ears nearly as long as her face, her legs long too, like a colt or a deer. A sheen of red outlined her neck, chest, and belly and ran down the insides of her legs. She had a small Brahma hump above her withers—the red there too and along her backbone—and suggestions of dewlaps at her throat and brisket.

Keith picked a pretty red heifer, one with not much Brahma showing and a splash of white above one eye that looked like a question mark.

"Well?" he asked.

As I took off my sweatshirt and draped it over the corral fence, the heifer moved deeper into the herd but soon her head rose above the others, her ears twisting back and forth, one eye on Keith, one on me.

"That one."

"You're sure? She's a little high-headed. There are a lot of other heifers here."

"Yes. She's the one I want."

Keith didn't tell me that day the other reasons you might have to sell your cows. Like when your husband decides he wants to buy more farming equipment but has to make a payment to the bank first. Or when he decides there's no money in the cattle business and if he sold off more cows he could get better established in his side business of specialized bulldozer work, where he thinks there is money. Or the other reason: because someone tells you that you have to.

On a fall afternoon some years later, I walk up a dirt road that wraps around the side of a mountain, my dogs at my heels. Technically I'm trespassing, having climbed over a locked gate to get here, but from the gate on up the mountain to the national forest, ten thousand acres of this land used to belong to my great-aunt, whom everybody called Sister, and her husband, Ed: Cachuma Ranch, another ranch in my background.

1. Three sisters: Katharine (seated), Deborah, Sister. Courtesy of Rancho Los Alamitos Foundation, RLA #95.36.

My great-grandparents Fred H. and Florence Bixby had five children, the first three "the girls": Katharine, born in 1899; Elizabeth (Sister), born in 1900, the family so sure she would be a boy that they hadn't thought of girls' names and called her Sister forevermore; and my grandmother Deborah, arriving in 1904. "Girls they might be, but they would grow up learning to help around the ranch just as though they were boys," wrote family friend David Lavender in a hand-edited manuscript I found among the old papers. Boys did come to the family: John in 1906 and Fred in 1910. By then the older two girls were already cowhands.

Much history about this family has been written, including by the eldest child, Katharine, who wrote *Trip with Father* "for Deborah . . . who asked me to resurrect our sketchy little diary, ransack my memory, and write this down for her grandchildren as she herself would not be here when they grew old enough for her to tell them about it." Our grandmother, knowing she was dying, asking her sister to give us this gift.

In *Trip with Father*, Katharine tells of the three sisters, at sixteen, fifteen, and twelve, riding alongside their father in 1916 from San Francisco to Rancho Los Alamitos. The girls debated with their father (Fred H., as our family still refers to him) about what to wear while riding five hundred miles, as he considered pants on women "immodest, unbecoming, and unfeminine . . . and embarrassingly conspicuous." To make such a trip in the teens of the last century was in itself "unfeminine" and "conspicuous," but the girls didn't care. To ride alongside their father—how many girls have had that unfulfilled dream? Despite his disapproval, the girls, "thanks to a boost from Mother," wore their "nice stylish beige linen riding habits," which qualified as pants but flared and tapered modestly. Most importantly, the girls could straddle their saddles as they rode a total of 522 miles along dirt roads connecting distant ranches, and sometimes cross-country. Everywhere they went, people knew their father.

At one time president of the California Cattle Men's Association, also president of the American National Live Stock Association, inducted into the National Cowboy Hall of Fame posthumously in 1958, Fred H. Bixby owned or partnered on dozens of ranches in California and Arizona from the early to mid-1900s, among them the Moqui Ranch in northern Arizona where the family first met Ed Janeway.

From boarding school in the San Francisco Bay Area, Katharine went on to earn a degree from Vassar College, and my grandmother graduated from University of California, Berkeley, but Sister didn't go to college. Instead, she worked for her father, "doing some secretarial work, but mostly riding," as she wrote in a school newsletter.

Sister and Fred H. had a standing argument about whether polled or horned Herefords made better animals. Neither won the argument, but Fred H. let Sister run her own (horned) herd on 4,600 acres called Little Cojo, while he managed the rest of the Cojo and the Jalama. She lived and worked on the Cojo, eventually marrying ranch foreman Ed Janeway, five years her younger. Not only was he an employee of her father's but the handsome, rough-around-the-edges Arizona cowboy was a quarter Cherokee, his grandmother a full-blood from the land at the beginning of the Trail of Tears. While Sister cared what the family thought, in her early forties she didn't need permission to marry the man of her choosing.

I'm told that Ed was an expert horseman. He could bring the best out in an animal with a few words, a gentle touch on a horse's face, or by communicating through his hands on the reins and his legs against the stirrup leathers. I imagine that Ed's skills with horses held all the romance a woman who loved animals as Sister did would ever need.

In my place of trespass, I perch on a rock overlooking a series of low, smoothly rounded hills crossed with barbed-wire fences. A long strip of fenced land, which I can't see but know well, runs upcanyon all the way to the public-land boundary. It includes 7,200 acres of Cachuma Ranch backcountry and Cachuma Creek watershed. Just out of sight sits a reservoir, "Lake" Cachuma. A tunnel housing a huge pipe cuts through the rugged mountains so the city of Santa Barbara can siphon water from Cachuma Creek and the other tributaries that used to flow into the Santa Ynez River. The river still tries to run along the bottom of the reservoir and sometimes gets let out into the riverbed at the base of the dam.

When Sister and Ed bought the ten-thousand-acre ranch, much of it was wild. Tractors, non-native seed, and irrigation tamed some of it, and then, through the rights of eminent domain, the government took the tamed part. Those two thousand acres of lake bottom used to hold the haying fields. "That land raised good alfalfa," my Uncle Ed would say, "the best land on the ranch."

When they felt they could no longer manage it, Sister and Ed sold the 7,200 acres of backcountry to the elite, exclusively male riding group, Los Rancheros Visitadores. The 580 remaining acres included the headquarters—barns, corrals, and houses—where Sister and Ed lived until he died, and where Sister lived alone until she died.

That's when the president of the ranch company, which Fred H. had started in the 1930s, sold Cachuma Ranch to Steven Seagal's ex-wife, Kelly LeBrock. Sister and Ed's possessions—their silver-trimmed saddles, Navajo rugs, original Frank Tenney Johnson paintings—went to museums or family members. Living in Arizona at the time, I didn't know people were going to the ranch and taking what they wanted. Later an aunt sent me two of Sister's belt buckles, and I have a mental picture of what became of the house: I was told the Hollywood personality tore down some of the adobe at the front—adobe the newlyweds ordered up back in the '40s, handmade in the old Mexican style and shipped by truck across the Central Valley from Bakersfield. Uncle Ed said the adobe was so heavy that a semi could only haul one or two layers at a time—a big rig pulling a flatbed with a short stack of bricks on it. Bricks three feet wide that made windowsills you could sleep on, turned to rubble.

My perch among the yellow grasses of fall—no rain has come yet to this part of California—is the closest I've been to the ranch since before Sister died. She got Alzheimer's disease, no longer knew me, and I couldn't bear it. Sister, the elder in my world—mentor, friend, matron of honor at my wedding—was the only woman left in the family who had lived a life similar to mine. Who understood. As she drifted into her private world, I pulled away. And then moved away.

Dusk settles over the dry hills, the western sky flaunts a bright orange hue, and I feel the ache of regret. Sister would understand my sense that part of me belongs to this land. As part of me belongs to the Cojo and Jalama. I long to speak with her. With no way to reconstruct the past, only acceptance is left. Which may mean letting go.

In the sun's afterlight something in the field below gleams white, and I stand to get a better look. Lured by shapes glowing under ebbing twilight skies, I head downhill and climb another fence, making the final trespass onto the remains of Sister and Ed's Cachuma Ranch. The dogs scoot beneath the barbed wire and scurry ahead to sniff at the old bones. I pick up a heavy cannon bone, which runs from knee to fetlock joint, and it occurs to me that these could be from the team of Shire mares belonging to Sister and my grandmother, or to the mares' descendants. Sister kept those mares on the ranch after my grandmother died, until one by one the original team of eight Shires died, and then so did their offspring. Along with other family relics, the wagon pulled by the team owned by Sister and my grandmother resides at the Parks-Janeway Carriage House at the Santa Ynez Valley Historical Museum.

Some of the Shire mares lived more than thirty years, their bones now utterly white in the approaching night. I pick up one at a time, awed by the weight, length, and thickness of each. And a skull, nearly as long from poll to front teeth as my arm. Wrestling another from the base of a pungent white sage, I see the bullet hole between the eyes and understand that Ed and his foreman had turned the hillside near the white oak into a boneyard, a graveyard, a burial ground. Except they didn't bury those horses or the big ol' longhorn steers. They left them for the coyotes, bobcats, bears, and birds, the bones now scattered like the past across the hills.

My grandmother Deborah was raised at Rancho Los Alamitos and the Cojo. The family would take the coastal train to central California, where it would stop at the Concepción depot in the middle of Rancho el Cojo (mail, and sometimes horses and cattle, also got shipped to and from the ranch this way). A ranch hand waiting in a wagon would take the family down to the headquarters set in a valley encircled by smooth, grassy hills. The valley's mouth, once open to the ocean, had been filled in and topped with railroad tracks, separating the barns and ranch houses from the pounding sea.

Like Sister, Deborah was quite the horsewoman, but the boarding school in Northern California took her away from full-time ranch life. After meeting a Harvard Law School graduate and practicing attorney from Council Bluffs, Iowa, Deborah settled into married life in Berkeley. She couldn't shake her love of horses though—of all animals—and in 1938 her husband found a small ranch on Mount Diablo where she could keep her horses and ride into the hills with her dogs and bring her children on weekends and for a full month each summer.

This wasn't a real ranch—at 170 acres it couldn't sustain itself, which in Deborah's upbringing was the definition of a ranch: land that could raise enough livestock and crops to feed the working families and, some years, to pay the bills. The acreage on Mount Diablo, part of another early land grant, had failed its previous owners, which is why it came up for sale.

My father and his siblings grew up in Berkeley and spent a lot of time at Mount Diablo, the Cojo and Jalama, and Rancho Los Alamitos. While others in his generation learned to ride at a young age, my father, the first-born of his siblings, had horse and hay allergies and didn't take to much of anything about ranch life. Despite being misunderstood and shamed for his "weakness," he did bring us to all the ranches when we were little.

My parents met at Berkeley High. They had my older sister, Terry, in Ithaca, New York, my father finishing college at Cornell. When he gradu-

2. Deborah (author's grandmother), about fourteen, on her palomino. Courtesy of Rancho Los Alamitos Foundation, RLA #68.1.1080.

ated, the small family drove back across the country to the Bay Area. My younger sister, Peg, and I were both born in the same Berkeley hospital as our mother and her mother.

For a time we lived on a cul-de-sac in a suburban neighborhood, a creek looping around behind the houses, and we went to "the mountain" often—much closer to the Bay Area than the Cojo—three little girls bundled into the backseat of our father's Volkswagen Bug. If the road turned muddy, we got loaded into the bed of an old green flatbed truck that had wooden slats as sides. We clung to those sides as the truck slipped and slid around mountain curves.

My grandmother's house on Mount Diablo fit the land, the living-dining room jutting out over pasture grasses and a plunge toward the oaks, large windows on three sides showcasing the view. Through the kitchen door, a covered, red-tiled porch began, its huge barn doors usually opened to the breeze. A hammock that could hold us three sisters hung in a corner, and I remember swinging in it high toward the ceiling.

On the other side of the big porch a short, red-tiled hallway led to our grandmother's bedroom. Though a curled, sleeping metal fawn complete with spots held the door open, I rarely ventured into that room. The hallway ended at steps also tiled with the red squares I want to think were Saltillo—handmade terracotta tiles from Saltillo, Mexico—but I'm not sure. The steps led to an elevated, splintering, redwood-plank walkway that passed in front of a screened-in sleeping porch, which held multiple single beds, their curved metal frames set against a back wall. Our feet pointed toward the walkway and a view of fog rolling in over the hills, bringing with it a severe chill. I remember shivering in my bed until an adult—my uncle?—checked on us and gave me another blanket. I don't remember my parents sleeping anywhere at all.

After my grandmother died, I looked into her bedroom at Mount Diablo. The bed made, everything in its place. She was fifty-five, I wasn't yet five, my little sister just four months old. On a wall of the sleeping porch I found a denim jacket hanging from a nail and wore it overlarge around me in the chill, thinking it was hers. Her.

My mother's father, renowned painter David Park, died of bone cancer at age forty-nine, sixteen months after my father's mother died from breast cancer metastasized to her liver. What I remember most of what was undoubtedly a horrific time for my parents are my mother's best friend's husband's hands forcing violation into my jeans, my grandmother's death creating a void in me that filled with another kind of horror.

From the house on Mount Diablo, a path through gray pines led to an unheated, spring-fed pool; beyond that, a small barn with stalls that opened to corrals, and horses and chickens and, for a while, an orphaned fawn in a chicken-wire pen. The screen door from the kitchen and the screen doors to the sleeping porch were made of wood. Wooden screen doors banging meant people coming or going, and I stuck like pine pitch to the goers if they headed toward the barn or pool. I already knew where to find comfort: in water or with horses, not people.

Across the road and down the hill from the barn and corrals an arena stood on leveled ground. I don't remember riding in the arena, but I remember watching my uncle galloping on horseback from one end to the other and leaning down out of the saddle to swoop his cowboy hat up off the ground. He could do the same with a handkerchief. And I do remember riding. On Robin, a flea-bitten gray, his speckles like freckles, following my grandmother's beloved gelding, Benedito, along forest trails. I remember the rich smell of horses, and of hay and manure baking in the sun. Sometimes I would slip away and sit on a bale of hay to watch the horses eat, their sweet alfalfa breath a tonic. I might even take a nap in the warmth and safety of horses.

As children, my sisters and I visited Sister and Ed with our parents. Sister had a walk-in aviary. I remember the sounds of wings, and birdseed and bird poop spattering the dirt floor. Peacocks roamed freely outside the aviary, shivering their feathers into brilliant blue fans near the pepper trees or screeching with the guinea hens from the valley oaks down by the hay barn. Uncle Ed's dog bit me in the forehead one time when I bent down to say hello and startled her awake. Neither Ed nor Sister rode anymore, so I didn't get to see the horsemanship for which they were both known. But I do remember seeing retired Cojo Mapachi at Cachuma Ranch. Sister also had Welsh ponies, and the big Shire stallion and mares in corrals built of heavy lumber like the ones at Rancho Los Alamitos, where Fred H. had raised the prized Shires.

My older sister, Terry, and I lived in Santa Barbara in our twenties and visited Sister often. She still had aviary birds, peacocks, and guinea hens, but fewer horses, and Ed had a plethora of cats. One afternoon I sat in the straw with Sister as her last Welsh pony rested her head in Sister's lap, the mare's breathing pausing and resuming until she shuddered the last bit of life out—the first time I'd seen an animal larger than a deer die, and I had no words for my great-aunt Sister, born fifty-four years before me, sibling of a grandmother I longed to know.

In my late twenties I lived for a short time at Cachuma Ranch. Keith had taken a job working for a rancher who leased what was by then called "the Janeway," the 7,200 acres of Cachuma Ranch backcountry. Keith and I were to live in a double-wide trailer on a bluff that dropped down through gray pines to the seasonal Cachuma Creek, where a roping arena and working corrals sat among the oaks. It was that record-wet spring of 1983, and the creek rose and flooded all the crossings and we couldn't get past Sister and Ed's to the double-wide on the bluff, so for a month Keith and I stayed in the guest cottage at the back of Sister and Ed's house. I rose in the early mornings to drink delectable cowboy coffee with Ed—he would add coarse grounds to warm water in an enamel coffeepot and leave it to boil for four minutes; after a couple of cooling minutes, Ed would add cold water through the spout, further settling the grounds, and it was ready to pour. Evenings the four of us ate dinner together, Ed and Keith swapping stories of wild cattle and broncy horses. (Author Stella Hughes included some of Ed's escapades in *Hashknife Cowboy: Recollections of Mack Hughes.*)

At the small kitchen table, we would watch Sister's peacocks torment the pile of Ed's cats outside the window—that pile often three cats deep, even in summer. If Sister left the room, Ed would grab the buggy whip he stashed behind the kitchen door, and the peacocks would flash with color as they ran and flew to the branches of the nearest pepper tree. Ed's eyes would twinkle, and Keith and I could only grin back.

When we got all the way moved into the trailer, we ran the boss's cows on the open hillsides up near the national forest and in the canyon that drained the Cachuma Creek watershed into the creek and then the "lake." Sister and Ed, our nearest neighbors, lived three miles down the dirt road; the next people lived miles away if you rode cross-country, no roads between us.

I would visit Sister and Ed often, Sister and me talking of cows and ranching and family but not of men—I didn't tell her how the thrill of riding over the hills after cattle sometimes turned on me. Sister and Ed came to our brandings, sitting on hay bales in the bed of a pickup that Keith would back up to the corral fence, and one time Keith and I took Sister to a branding at the Cojo. I worked the ground, branding calves, and then roped, while Sister sat on the top rail of the fence so she could see, and I paid more attention to the work before me than to her until we drove away. But even then I didn't think to ask her how it felt to be back at her old home ranch. If I could have that time over again, I would spend it asking Sister about her growing-up years on Rancho Los Alamitos and the Cojo, and about my grandmother, but I was married then and in a hurry, keeping up with Keith the force that ruled my days.

I loved staying on the bluff, often alone, watching weather and wildlife, our horses, the cattle. Hot summer afternoons and crisp fall mornings, the screen door banging when I went out to do chores, wind picking up through the gray pines carrying the smells of pitch and white sage and cow manure and youth . . . in my memory it was so like Mount Diablo, blacktail deer whispering through the pines, those trees, their long gray-green needles like a woman's hair, not the short, curly hair of Sister and my grandmother but something freer, the loose branches of those trees and their long needles moving like the manes of horses running, like my own hair blowing behind me as I ran through the years between childhood and adulthood.

Eventually I had company safely harbored in my womb, but peer pressure had us leaving the Janeway—the baby due in January, what if we had another wet year and the creek rose and we couldn't get out? We moved to a ranch closer to a town and hospital. We'd still see Sister and Ed often, and after I had Kenney, to whom we gave Ed's middle name, I would take him to visit. Sister eighty-four, Ed almost eighty, Ed would prop Kenney on his knee and giggle at this wriggling great-great-nephew who bore his middle name, Lafayette.

Sister died at almost ninety-three. Ed died seven years earlier, a year after Kenney was born. A big man, heavy with sadness and alcohol, he had a stroke one night, sitting on the bench outside their adobe home with a couple of cats and a dog Keith and I had given him, whom Ed named after my husband. Most of his cats—he usually had a dozen or two milling and mewing and mating around the place—were too wild for petting, but often a couple of them would get gentle enough to rub up against Ed's legs and allow the slide of his hand down their backs. Coyotes killed them on a regular basis, but Ed didn't seem to notice. He loved them indiscriminately. He talked to them all, fed them canned cat food in the early mornings, and scared the raiding peacocks off. With his cats around him, Ed felt okay. The way Sister did with the peacocks and guinea hens, her great Shire horses and small Welsh ponies, her cows. Animals filled up the lives of those two the way work used to, the way children would have had they married younger than middle age, the way family might have had they not married at all.

I imagine a gray tabby rubbing against Ed's Levi's-clad leg that evening as he sat on his bench watching the sun lower itself from the day. Sister sat with him for a time, then got up and busied herself in the kitchen, and Keith-the-dog trotted into the field to roll in horse manure, and after they departed the cat jumped up on the bench and bent her head to the reach of Ed's hand. She was small—they didn't get very big, whether from inbreeding or lack of longevity I don't know—and Ed called her Kitty. A deep sigh ran through him as he looked over land tired from years of overuse by cattle and horses, deer—they didn't allow hunting—and feral pigs. It was the first of March and the color had already faded from the hillsides, cattle chasing the green faster than the grass could grow. He knew he hadn't made a good rancher, not culling on a regular basis—he didn't like selling cows or calves—so he overgrazed then fed hay half the year.

Perhaps Ed felt the cat purring under his rough hand as he spoke to her, but the words came out funny. He tried again. His hand grew heavy; the cat's purr ceased; he tried to lift his hand. He tried to call his wife. He tried to stand, the cat scrambling away and watching from around a corner. I imagine Ed pushing himself up off the bench, not noticing that the sun had dropped, that the sky flooded with a pink so soft he might have cried over it on another day, not noticing that what he hit when he fell was the cement of their covered porch. Hers, really, but he didn't have to think about that anymore.

From inside the house, Sister heard the cry that was supposed to be her name and dismissed it as an anti-peacock yell. But the thud made by Ed's body could not be categorized as anything other than something wrong, and Sister rushed outside to find her eighty-year-old, 250-pound husband collapsed on the porch, his face smashed into the cement, one arm bent oddly beneath him. Keith-the-dog, having run up at the sound of the cry, licked Ed's face, and Sister nudged her husband with a hand on his shoulder. His eyes closed, his breathing light but still in and out, she pushed on him and tugged on his free arm. When she hurried into the house to call for help, Keith-the-dog lay down beside his master and the cat crept up and brushed against Ed's fallen leg.

As soon as allowed, I visited Ed in the hospital, sitting close to him, holding his hand, talking into his ear, watching his face for signs. His hand heavy in mine, he didn't wink, grin, grunt, or flinch with recognition, that day or any other. The stroke affected the right side of his brain so he had no use of his left arm and leg and couldn't talk—which didn't matter, as he remained comatose until death caught up with him five days later.

When an aunt called to tell me Ed was gone, my instant tears confused her—we'd known it was a matter of time. I didn't say that my favorite cowdog, Cotton, had also died that day, nor did I try to explain what I felt for my great-uncle Ed, the old geezer who called my dogs turd-hounds, laughed when I got bucked off, and giggled when he was drunk, and who gave me his name for my son. Nor did I give voice to what I knew that old man felt for me.

Ed wanted to be cremated. Sister and I knew that, and in one sense the formality of the act, arranged by the family, and the lack of ceremony—there wasn't one—honored Ed's wishes. No one questioned why he desired cremation, but here's the story: Sister and Ed purchased the ranch along Cachuma Creek near Santa Ynez, and when the government took the two thousand acres of good bottomland to make Lake Cachuma to water Santa Barbara, the couple moved to a ranch near Paso Robles. Fred H. managed that ranch, which had an adobe home, barns, and corrals, and Sister and Ed arranged to purchase it. When the government decided to dam the Nacimiento River, it returned the purchase price and drowned the house and barns and corrals, which sent Sister and Ed back to the short-sheeted Cachuma Ranch. Two ranches in one lifetime, and Ed told me he wanted his ashes scattered over the reservoir called Lake Cachuma, over his old haying ground, the best land on the ranch. He wanted the last word.

3. Ed, Sister, and friend. Photographer unknown. Courtesy of the author.

A couple of years before Ed died, Keith wanted to sell Sister and Ed our cows. From more than a hundred we were down to ten, including my first cow, Ruby, her red-black coat sleek and shiny over her rolling muscles, my brand on her left hip. Ruby and nine others. Our last cows. I said no. I pleaded, begged, threatened. I wanted the cows, the work. But Keith had a payment to make. My only consolation: they moved to Sister and Ed's, where I could visit any time.

The foreman rigged up a water trough ten yards from the house—an old porcelain bathtub placed on the other side of the fence and filled with a hose that drew water from the house plumbing. Through the large picture window Sister would watch the cows come to water, their cute Brahma-cross calves dancing around their legs, bucking and butting heads, white froth covering their mouths as they nursed. On warm days Sister would top the trough off herself. She called Ruby by name, as I did, and Ruby would raise her head, flick her big Brahma ears back and forth, and look at Sister with one eye, her weight on her outside legs, leaning away.

Ruby never got less than half wild, though some of the cows acted like big ol' puppy dogs. Out in the field they'd walk up to Sister and let her scratch them behind the ears, or Sister would reach through the board fence and rub their faces, Ruby tall in the background, waiting her turn to drink. But she would answer in body language when Sister spoke to her: *Ruby*.

When Keith and I still had a decent cow herd and lived on the coastal ranch, we'd wean the calves in either May or June—depending on how much rain we'd gotten and when the grass headed out, the maturing seedheads signaling the end of the growing season—then trailer them to a field a few miles up the highway. The cows would mill around the corrals, their bags taut, bawling for their calves. The younger mothers stayed the longest, thinking that since they'd last seen their babies there surely the calves would return to that spot, while the older cows, understanding the futility of it, wandered out toward the back of the pasture and better feed. We had just weaned Ruby's second calf, and I noticed that Ruby had gone missing.

Driving up the highway a couple of days later, searching, I saw movement along the shoulder of the oncoming lanes of traffic, a big dark shadow slipping through sagebrush near the edge of the road. I hit the brakes and yelled *Ruby* through the open window. She jerked her head around, looked right at me, and trotted across the road to the center divider.

"Shit, Ruby," I said, pulling over to slow traffic, and she fixed those big browns on me and held me with her half-wild, half-mad, half-sad look, and then she crossed the near lanes of highway and trotted on as if she had someplace to go and someone to see. Emergency flashers flashing, I followed until she pressed through the brush on the shoulder and veered off with the fenceline. She crossed the frontage road, paralleled the fence, and hopped over a loose wire.

I didn't understand how she got out of the original pasture, managed to find water and not be seen for several days, and knew in which field to find her calf. But when I pushed Kenney out into the world and held him to my breast, the understanding hit me with that first release of colostrum. Keith said Ruby didn't make a good cow—her calves' weaning weights weren't high enough for him—but I knew better. I knew Ruby was the best damned cow we had.

What Keith neglected to tell me that day so long ago when I picked Ruby out of that bunch of heifers was the main reason not to fall in love with your cows: because it cracks your heart open like an egg when they go, and all you have left to hold a marriage together is slippery yolk and tiny bits of shell.

As night comes, I make a sling of my sweatshirt and load up a pelvis and two polished white cannon bones. Hoisting the load over the barbed-wire fence and stepping over in the dark, I snag only one leg of my Wranglers. Bones on my back, I follow the dogs through moonshadow to the second fence and the road, and as we trek to the truck on the far side of the locked gate, I remember the rest of the story.

When Ed died, the ranch company president gained power of attorney and started running Sister's life. One day a phone call came, no warning, just an order to the foreman: sell the cows. Today. They brought slaughter prices though they still had a few good calves left in them and people would have paid good money because of Keith's reputation as an excellent cattleman, and everyone knew Sister's cows came from us. But no one knew they would sell that day. Not even Sister. To slaughter they went, including my Ruby, who weighed over 1,200 pounds and brought near brood-cow prices anyway. But it wasn't about money. It was about Ed being dead and Sister getting Alzheimer's and her nephew having control.

The foreman was forbidden to tell Sister what happened to those cows. Her cows. My cows. The last cows. Cows who would not leave skulls under a sprawling old oak tree on a hillside, would not leave bones behind for me to find like rays of moonlight on a darkening night. I was told that for the three years between the selling of her cattle and her death, Sister, no longer able to grasp the passage of time, sat in front of that great big picture window day after day, waiting for the cows to come to water.

2
Another West

And then there is California.

—Edward Abbey

Santa Cruz Island, Northern Channel Islands, California, 1989

The faces around the campfire—rough, stubble-bearded, weather-cracked skin under low-setting cowboy hats—look as if from another time. Beef stew simmers in a cast-iron pot set on a crude frame above a second fire, steam carrying the fragrance of onion and wild sage to the night sky. Some of the men still wear chaps and spurs. A whiskey bottle tilts up and a few swallows travel to the belly of a tired man.

As the bottle gets passed around, a tall, thin cowboy appears from the shadows with his guitar. Someone offers him the one chair. He sits and pulls the chords of "Strawberry Roan" from the instrument as easily as milk from a seasoned dairy cow.

Beyond the faces, a clear, sparkling sky. Horses grazing nearby. The mouth of the valley opens to the sea, and the sounds of the surf receding over sand and stone mix with the cowboy melody. The only indication that this is 1989 and not 1889 is the presence of two pickups hidden in darkness and three women who also wear jeans and boots, tap the whiskey bottle, and do not cook. The music and voices surging and ebbing like the waves, the smells of stew and salt air, the horses' soft blowing, and the men's faces are timeless.

Santa Cruz Island, one of the four northern Channel Islands that parallel California's central coast near Santa Barbara, is, at sixty-two thousand acres, the largest of the Channel Islands. I lived in Santa Barbara County an entire summer before the fog lifted and I actually *saw* Santa Cruz Island, a ridge of sharp peaks accentuated by deep canyons twenty-three miles away. When viewed from the air, the island looks like a flightless chicken, its body six and a half miles wide, its neck and tail feathers narrowing to widths of two miles. It faces east, paralleling the unusual east-west trending coastline.

Santa Cruz Island was called Limuw by its Chumash inhabitants, meaning *in the sea*. Chumash ancestors were the first human occupants, dating back at least thirteen thousand years. According to Chumash creation stories, the people originated on Limuw. When their numbers grew beyond what the island could support, a deity built a bridge of rainbow and urged people to cross and populate the mainland. Instructed not to look down as they walked the rainbow, some dizzied in the swirling fog and fell into the sea. They became dolphins, which still play in the surf today.

In 1805 a Spanish padre estimated that two thousand Chumash lived on the northern islands. He reported the next year that a measles epidemic drastically reduced the population. Colonizers removed the remaining inhabitants, the last Santa Cruz Island Chumash baptized on the mainland between 1812 and 1815.

In 1989 my husband and his friend Pete signed a contract to remove the last cattle from the island. Another group had conducted roundups in the spring of 1988, shipping off a few hundred animals, but the wisest and fleetest cattle remained, an estimated fifty head.

Keith, Pete, and a handful of additional cowboys tried a gather their first day, but as they pushed twenty-five head across an open flat it turned into a scatter, each animal intent on escaping in a different direction. The cattle had the advantage—they knew every nook and cranny—and they were cunning, racing up a sidehill, hiding in a brush patch until the pursuing cowboys passed, then backtracking toward freedom. The cowboys snared ten head that day, along with an immeasurable amount of wisdom—likely gleaned by both cowboy and cow.

On the days following, the cowboys rode as a group to a designated area, then spread out to surround unsuspecting cattle. The men moved their horses slowly, pushing the cattle toward each other. A man would ease into the herd, swing his lariat in a slow rotation, and send the loop out over an animal's head. If the bunch broke, which was more like *when*, it was every man for himself. Each time they captured a few, a few others escaped, the cattle growing more desperate and sneakier after every run.

In 1830 Governor José María de Echeandia sent Mexican prisoners to Alta California to help colonize the territory, transporting thirty of the most incorrigible to Santa Cruz Island along with the first known cattle to arrive. The prisoners soon escaped aboard handmade rafts. The cattle stayed.

Frenchman Justinian Caire acquired the island in 1869 and formed the Santa Cruz Island Company. He imported purebred Rambouillet Merino sheep, and by 1875 at least sixty thousand sheep roamed the island, with fifteen thousand killed for the hide-and-tallow trade in that year alone. Two years later, twenty-five thousand sheep were killed due to lack of feed. Land management in those days meant grazing as much livestock as you could until the feed ran out.

The sheep had free range on thousands of acres, across rugged peaks, and into canyons that cut to the sea like the crevices between fingers. As the cowboys in 1989 could attest, gathering sheep for shearing and slaughter would have been no easy feat.

Caire died in 1897. His wife and heirs continued to run sheep and cattle. Disagreements eventually led to the majority of Santa Cruz Island—54,500 acres—selling to oilman Edwin L. Stanton. The eastern end remained in the hands of the Gherini family, also Caire heirs, who continued to raise sheep, descendants of which could be seen from the air until the 1990s—white puffs of cotton floating along the ridgetops.

Stanton introduced polled Herefords, the forebears of the elusive red whiteface cattle the cowboy crew encountered fifty years later. Upon Stanton's death in 1963, the island officially got passed to his son, Carey Stanton, who had lived on Santa Cruz full-time since 1937. He continued the cattle operation, and in 1978 entered into an agreement with The Nature Conservancy to ensure preservation of the land and its native ecology. When he died unexpectedly in 1987, TNC assumed control of 90 percent of the island, and the cattle, introduced and invasive, had to go. The Gherinis still ran sheep on the eastern end.

Keith and Pete were familiar with the island's wild, rugged nature and, as well, with the ways of wild cattle, having cowboyed on many California ranches, but these cattle descended from a long line that had occupied Santa Cruz Island for decades, and they didn't want to leave. I wondered if the island Chumash fought removal the way the cattle did, and if they were shipped to the missions like cattle to the stockyard.

The cowboys had to provide all supplies except water and the two relic pickups. This included crew (cowboys, cook, drivers); sixteen horses and the saddles and tack to go with them; an abundance of lariats; hay and grain to last sixteen horses fourteen days; enough food and drink for the men (they ran short of the latter); bedrolls, clothing, and personal necessities (cigarettes and guitar for the cowboy singer); and kitchen supplies (cook tent, cookware, flatware, dishes, tables, soap, lanterns, etc.).

They loaded all this onto the *Vaquero II*, a barge designed for seafaring cattle, as my two young sons and I watched from the pier. We could see into the barge from above: the horses, half of them saddled, tied to a railing in the open barge bottom, cowboys securing lead ropes and checking cinches. Some of the horses braced against the ocean surges, their legs spread wide. I felt a little nauseous. From a large pile of all brands of gear, more cowboys and the cook/driver and photographer/driver handed off duffle bags and boxes of food for storage below deck. Keith looked up at his kids, waving his cowboy hat.

"I want to go with Daddy," four-year-old Kenney said. Tyler, one and a half, snuggled in my arms.

"I know," I said to Kenney, and I did know. I also wanted badly to go. But the island cattle were as rough and wild as the country—no place for young children—and with Keith gone I couldn't leave horses, dogs, cattle, and kids for ten days at a time. Someone had to stay home.

Two other women and I did manage to arrange for a long weekend away, and Pete's fiancée, Karen, pushed her Bronco II down Highway 101 toward the tiny Camarillo airport as if the Bronco were a racehorse. We didn't want to be late, to be left behind, again. A saddle filling the passenger seat, the backseat down to fit more stuff, Cheri and I sat cramped among duffle bags and sleeping bags, rope bags and grocery bags, the other two saddles our backrests, cases of beer supporting our feet. Cheri cradled fifths of whiskey in her lap. Her husband, Larry, was known in Central Coast California as a top hand, and Cheri was one of the two best women ropers I knew, her sister the other.

After we untangled ourselves and stepped out onto the blacktop, we found that the race to the airport was unnecessary—our Channel Islands Aviation flight was delayed, the plane having just returned from an emergency flight to the island to pick up an injured man.

"Do you know who?" I said.

"An old cowboy with a beard."

We looked at each other. None of the cowboys on the island were old, and after ten days with no running water or electricity they must all have beards—we remounted the Bronco and hastened to the hospital to find out whose cowboy it was.

To our relief, he didn't belong to any of us, though he was crew. He'd separated his shoulder when his horse fell with him. His right arm taped to his side, his thumb hooked into his belt for support, he was scratched and bruised and adamant about returning to the island.

"Hell, nothing's broke," he said, and that settled it.

Somehow four passengers and all our gear fit inside the small plane. The landing strip looked like tundra leading toward a cliff edge and the sea, but the plane stopped in time. A driver waited in one of the old trucks, surprised to see the taped-up cowboy, who called shotgun. Cheri, Karen, and I joined the gear in the truck bed and bounced the dusty miles to camp, where our men and the other cowboys circled the campfire.

They had scoured the massive Laguna Canyon area for days, trying to capture every ounce of beef living within the perimeter of the major drainage. Most of the cattle had seen neither man nor horse before and were as tricky and wild as the terrain. Upon sight of a mounted cowboy, they would break into a run or move stealthily toward a clump of island scrub oak, where they might hide for hours. Or, like wizened old bucks, they'd sneak up the hill, moving between stands of chaparral until they neared the top and could escape over the horizon.

The four northern Channel Islands used to be one large island, Santarosae, and much closer to the California coastline. Long before humans arrived, plants and animals traveled to the islands by wave, wind, and wing. In 1989 The Nature Conservancy documented forty-three species and subspecies of plants found only on the Channel Islands, with ten endemic to Santa Cruz. One tiny succulent, the Santa Cruz Island live-forever, grew on cliffs and rocky outcroppings and nowhere else on Earth. Of the endemic island birds, perhaps the best known was the island scrub-jay, which couldn't fly to even the nearest neighboring island. The island fox, endemic to the Channel Islands, was, at four pounds, the smallest fox in North America. The island spotted skunk was smaller than mainland skunks, and there once existed a Channel Islands pygmy mammoth, which estimates say stood four and a half to six feet tall. In search of food, Columbian mammoths swam the six miles to Santarosae; over the next twenty thousand years, the sea rose, islands separated, food sources diminished, and the smaller mammoths survived until the megafauna die-off.

I would get to see island scrub-jays and an island fox, its delicate feet, grace, and curiosity more closely resembling the characteristics of a cat than a mainland fox. But I wasn't there to gawk. I was there to cowboy as part of Keith's crew.

The cowboys are tired down to their dirty socks, and time is running out, along with supplies. Feeling all fresh and flirty despite our dusty arrival, we manage to infuse some energy into the crew, or perhaps it's the return of the injured cowboy or replenishment of the bar that does it. The island is in the songs and stories passing around the campfire with the whiskey bottle—these are cowboys and cowboys tell stories, from traditional ballads to cowboy poetry to campfire yarn—the story of the morning's wreck the latest in the growing folklore.

An every-man-for-himself day, as the cowboy chased a yearling heifer down a rocky slope, his horse stumbled and went down. With no time to push himself free, his horse landed on top of him, smashing his shoulder into the ground. The guitar picker, racing after a cow, came upon the scene first—he saw the cowboy waving from beneath the horse, thought all must be well, and rode on. A buddy showed up next and stopped to push the 1,200-pound horse off his friend—usually a horse will fight to right itself; apparently this one needed a rest.

The guitar picker tells us that when he rode into camp later, he said to the cook, "What do you suppose the range etiquette is in this situation, anyway—do you save the cattle or the man?"

The injured cowboy laughs with everyone else, but in the crackling firelight I can see my husband growing somber, the weight of the day's failures on his shoulders. He tells us that seventy-six head wait in the holding field three miles from Prisoners Harbor (from which the prisoners had escaped in the 1890s). Each calf, yearling, cow, and bull had been roped, its forelegs tied together, its hind legs tied together, and then pushed up a ramp into the bed of a pickup. Rolled onto its right side so its rumen wouldn't get squished, the bovine then traveled miles of rutted dirt road unable to move except to lift its head to the view if so inclined.

"We spotted nine this morning," Keith says. "I know there's more. In the next two days we have to catch them, get them to the holding field, and then drive them all to the harbor." There we would load the cattle onto the barge.

I look at the faces—not a single man is willing to stop short of that goal, even the cowboy with his arm taped to his midriff.

Something cool brushes the back of my hand. I lift the bottle to my lips, punctuating the reality of the twentieth century, for surely no wives were present at a cowboy campfire like this a hundred years ago. I glance at Cheri. She smiles and winks.

The next morning begins slowly, with a six-mile uphill ride before we get anywhere near where the cowboys last spotted the cattle. We set a trap—our horses hidden behind hillside chaparral and in a side canyon—and as the cattle come our way we are to step out and start herding them. Inevitably, they break and scatter. When someone shouts, "Every man for himself," we race up and down the brushy slopes, ropes swinging, cowboys whipping and spurring until they get some of the animals roped. The pickups arrive, the men push and pull hogtied cattle aboard, and the drivers haul them to the holding field.

The following day, we start where someone last spotted four two-year-old heifers, all prior escapees. Keith gives us our positions and tells us to wait, eyes and ears on the alert. Karen, the cowboy singer, and I are staked out at the edge of a deep canyon that broadens as it reaches toward the sea. Cheri and Larry ride to a hill somewhere behind us, and two other cowboys ride one way while Keith and Pete trot off in the opposite direction.

Time drifts slowly by. Occasionally we hear a faint shout; once we spy dust across the canyon. The singer leaves to ride up the ridge to see better.

All of a sudden we hear someone crashing through the brush, though we can't see him. "Did they go down the canyon?" Larry hollers.

"Who?" Karen says. We've been watching for four monotonous hours and have seen nothing but that small dust cloud. "What should we do?" she asks me.

I look into the canyon, at the steep sides and loose soil. Handing Karen my horse's reins, I commit one of the worst sins a cowboy can when gathering cattle: I leave my post. Plus, I leave my horse—I don't want to end up with him on top of me in the steep canyon. But if the cattle are heading down, I reason as I begin the slide and tumble, someone has to stop them.

Breath and heart drowning out all other sound, I skid to a stop in the *V* of the deep ravine. My breathing slows and that's when I hear it, Keith yelling to Larry: "They're rimming around." Then, "It's okay, Kat's over there."

I sit down hard on a rock and put my head on my knees, waiting for the storm to hit. I picture the heifers busting by Karen, who is ill-mounted and holding my horse to boot. Then I hear it—the thundering, "*Where the fuck is she?*"

The quiet tells me that the whole crew has gone in pursuit of the heifers, so I slowly pick my way through shale and stone on the more gradual east side of the gulch. Not eager to face anyone, I stop again to catch my breath and notice dust far off on the opposite slope. Peering, I spot splashes of red between clumps of sage. If they cross the canyon, they'll be gone for good—no fence or natural barrier exists in that direction for literally miles.

Running, slipping, sliding, tripping, I race along the east side, the canyon getting wider and deeper in its descent toward the sea. Thinking that if I get hurt down here they won't find me until the buzzards do, I keep going until I draw abreast of the cattle, still on the other side, perhaps a mile away. They slip and slide too, blind to everything but escape. I yell. Holler.

Scream. Wave my arms and jump up and down and make other desperate cattle-stopping noises.

It works.

I'm so far down in the groove of the earth that I can't see any horses or cowboys. Nor can they see me. I feel panic creeping in, but what's the point? I wait, panting; the heifers do the same. I suspect we're all thinking the same thing: How the hell do we get out of this mess?

When silence settles, I holler a loud "Hello?" And again, with all the diaphragm power I can muster, knowing that if wind isn't blowing sound can carry across distance in country devoid of automobiles and air traffic.

In the stillness of the afternoon, Larry hears me, then finds me with his field glasses. "What are you doing way down there?" he yells.

We establish a broken communication of hollers and arm movements, and he in turn indicates to the others the location of the heifers. Keith rides down the wrong ridge. Randy follows Larry's voice and mine down the right one.

From across the canyon I guide Randy to the heifers—he still can't see them but can now see me. He rides partway, then ties his horse to an island scrub oak and proceeds on foot. When he gets below the heifers, he urges them back toward the rim of the canyon, though they don't need much urging, wanting out as badly as I do.

The only way out for me is down, across, and up, and I reluctantly begin the journey. Then comes Randy's voice: "I'll leave my horse here for you."

"I'll kiss you later," I call, but he doesn't hear me.

Three of the heifers get roped that afternoon and hauled to the holding field, and one escapes, again. We have a sober supper that night. Even the guitar picker can't cheer us up.

The boat will arrive the next day. Twenty bovines remain on the loose, one with my name on her, and we have yet to move the captured seventy-nine head the three miles from the holding field to Prisoners Harbor. Keith and I walk tiredly to our separate bedrolls.

Early the next morning the drivers haul all the gear to the harbor while the rest of us ride to the barbed-wire holding field near the ranch headquarters built so long ago. Keith's plan: he and two others will wait near the gate to get in front of the herd and lead it down the dirt road, riders dropping off in various holes, and Cheri and I will bring up the rear.

Once inside the pasture, Larry, Pete, and I ease our horses around behind the cattle and begin gently nudging them toward an open but not clearly visible gate. A few lead cows walk through, and Keith and a couple of cowboys turn them down the lane, but the rest of the herd passes the opening and balls up in the corner, milling, turning, not seeing the hole as they circle until they can't stand it anymore and they break, heading toward the back fence. I thrust my reins forward and lean low over my gelding's neck, urging him into a run. I can see big, deep holes almost hidden in the tall grass and tell myself *don't think, just ride*, and I do, spurring my horse in a race with stampeding cattle, and we get to the back fence ahead of them, several of us do, hollering and waving our coiled ropes, and half the cattle turn, the other half busting through the fence as if it doesn't exist, wire popping, bulls and cows and calves running madly away.

We have to stay with the part of the herd that turned, which we push again toward the ill-designed gate, some cattle going through, others turning back. Six of us are left, riding back and forth, hollering, yelling, doing whatever we can to turn them. A bull charges the cowboy singer's horse, almost knocking him over. Cheri races toward a corner, but the cattle beat her, flattening the fence. Larry yells to us—a few more have gone through and he's going with them. Then the singer, too, has gone. Only Cheri, Karen, Randy, and I remain. Fighting for control. Yelling *hyah, hyah* as more cattle bust through the fence. I stay with a big Hereford cow and her calf, getting ahead and turning them, but she breaks around me and heads toward a different fence and I leap off my horse so I can jump the fence and turn that cow on foot; three running strides in the tall grass and I trip, fall, hit something hard with my knee, roll out of my horse's way, and hear the twang of wire as the pair leaps to freedom.

"Come on," Cheri yells, "hurry!" and I climb back on my horse, ride after another renegade cow, ride for forty-five more minutes, no time to feel, spurring my gelding's sides, I've dropped my rope, use my romal; *turn you bastards, turn!* Five head stop. The rest have vanished through the gate and down the road or through the fence to open range.

Cheri rides over. "Are you all right?"

I lean down to look at my knee, my Wranglers ripped seam to seam, no blood anywhere, just pink flesh and white bone. "Do you want to see?"

"No," Cheri says quickly. "Can you make it okay?"

I tell her I'll stay with the cattle. "You're sure?" Randy asks, and I nod, though I'm not at all sure. They leave, and my horse and I watch the last five head jump the fence one by one.

I head down the road in the direction all the cowboys and some of the cattle have gone, but the adrenaline rush has passed and with each jarring step pain cuts into my knee. I turn my tired horse toward the ranch headquarters—a fine old house and barn, cookhouse, and guesthouse, that's what I remember, anyway—and stop near the main house, both my horse and me dripping sweat and panting. A blond woman about my age steps outside.

"Can you help me?" I ask. "I need to wrap this so I can catch up to my husband."

She walks over, looking not at my face but at my torn jeans. "Why don't you get down?" she says, her voice kind.

"I'm afraid I won't be able to get back up." It's my left knee. We mount and dismount on the left side. I made it once. Twice is doubtful. "Do you have an ACE bandage? Will you wrap my leg to the stirrup so I can trot after them?"

"I'm an RN. You need to get down so I can take a better look."

I swing my right leg over, putting my weight on my left leg, bend my knee for the step down, and fall backward into her arms. My horse disappears, and I'm lying on a picnic table. The nurse holds a cloth and tweezers in gloved hands. Her husband stands at her shoulder.

"There's cow manure in here, and foxtails," she says. "We've radioed for a plane to take you to the hospital."

"*Please* help me back on my horse. Keith will be mad if I don't show up to help."

They exchange a look. And load me into the pickup and drive me to the tundra runway. This time it's just the pilot and me. All I have is what I'm wearing—torn jeans, short-sleeved blouse, boots, belt with a buckle I won with Keith, underclothes, turquoise earrings Keith gave me. My wedding ring. No wallet or identification, no insurance card.

Airplanes can't go to hospitals. The pilot radios ahead for a taxi while I strain at the window, searching for cattle and cowboys heading for the pier somewhere beneath us. The blue ocean takes over. I wait for the cab alone and end up in the ER, where a doctor says I landed just right on a sharp stone that cut into the bone at my knee and nearly severed the tendon. "There's serious threat of infection, even gangrene," he says. "We have to go into surgery *now*."

"My kids," I say. I'm supposed to pick them up that evening. I call the friend who has Kenney and Tyler. "I'm at the hospital. Will you please keep them another night?"

Waking to a circle of unfamiliar faces, I feel even more alone than I did in the bottom of that canyon. It's ten at night when I call my mother from the recovery room. "I'm okay, but I'm in the hospital. They did emergency surgery on my knee. I wanted someone to know." She packs a bag right then, readying to leave at five in the morning.

From a drugged sleep hours later I hear hushed voices, then a shape in a cowboy hat stands over me. "Out of seventy-nine head we shipped twenty-three," Keith says. "They're on a truck to the sales yard and everyone else is headed home."

"You didn't have to come," I say. Our ranch is miles in the other direction.

"I thought you would want me to." For Keith, his visit to the hospital in the middle of the night was an expression of love, but I didn't see that then.

After three more trips, the crew gathered a total of ninety-nine head, twice as many as The Nature Conservancy estimated. Every single animal had to be roped. The last one—the last two-year-old heifer of that bunch of four—eluded the men for three days before she fell captive to Pete's rope. Ultimately the cattle, like the Chumash, had little power against those who voted them off the island.

Keith told me that as the heifer trotted down the chute onto the *Vaquero II*, a grim silence replaced the usual sounds of cowboys yelling and rawhide slapping leather. The men knew they had written the final chapter for the cattle of Santa Cruz Island, thereby ending the era of a magnificent island cattle ranch. They knew they might never again see such nimble heifers and wise old cows, whose will to survive was as indomitable as the tiny endemic Santa Cruz Island live-forevers. The cowboys sipped whiskey and talked quietly in the night aboard the *Vaquero II* as it crossed the channel. One by one they lifted the bottle and saluted the receding island. It no longer felt like 1889.

I didn't yet foresee that in several months I would leave the ranch like that heifer leaving the island—a one-way trip. Believing deeply that my kids should live with their mother, I fought hard when Keith challenged me for custody, but the court determined that at three (Tyler) and six (Kenney), the boys would live with their dad, his new wife, and her children. I hit the bottom of my life then, yet I kept fighting—the attorneys, mediation, and court scenes spanned seven years. I took Tyler back after he'd lived with Keith for three years but couldn't get Kenney—a court-appointed mediator, observing Keith and Kenney in Wranglers, belts with silver buckles, cowboy boots, and cowboy hats, said it was clear that Kenney had bonded to his father and should stay with him. Tyler, in clean T-shirt and jeans, could continue living with me.

I also didn't imagine that in several years my sons would accompany Keith on boats and in helicopters as Keith worked to fulfill a contract to eliminate thousands of sheep from Santa Cruz Island. He and his crew, including my two young sons, would remove 9,500 head. It would take them a year and a day. The stories that unfolded wouldn't reach my ears until decades later.

3

The Colors of My Familiar

The sense of place is a lasting, marvelous, and painful
gift, for the child who absorbs the love of place
has also been given the pain of severance.

—Helen Park Bigelow, *This Is Where I've Been*, a work-in-progress

---

California, New Mexico, Arizona, 2007–12

The ocean rolls out before me; behind me lies the land, lupine and sage spreading north and east toward hills speckled with cattle and coastal brush and crowned with live and white oak. I stand in the updraft at the dividing edge between land and sea, salt air and soil mixing in my senses. To my left, the Channel Islands arc across the horizon, San Miguel and Santa Rosa fully visible, while two hundred feet below, in a protective cove we call the rookery, northern elephant seals lounge and snore and shuffle and fight, the big bulls ramming the smaller ones away from dozing or nursing females. California sea lions and Pacific harbor seal adults and pups also haul out on rookery sands, and western gulls swoop up with the wind. On the northward leg of their ten-thousand-mile round-trip migration, Pacific gray whales navigate the waters around this western point of California coastline on their annual journey to summer feeding grounds in the Arctic. Beyond the sea of life within my visual range, the sun wavers west, its light also a division as the Earth spins toward darkness. I lean into the wind, feeling, as I often do at edges, the possible fall.

I don't even think to imagine that this is my last visit to the Cojo. Although this ranch has been in my family for a hundred years, not thousands, it's part of the historic makeup of five generations, but the threat will go through, the ranches sold, and all those bearing my great-grandfather's genealogy, and mine, will be banned from the premises. Like the Chumash people and the cattle forcibly removed from Santa Cruz Island, only our stories will remain.

In 2007 the company president negotiated a deal to sell the "Cojo-Jalama Ranch" to a Boston-based hedge fund. (Sister had persisted in calling the ranches by their two names—you either referred to the Cojo or the Jalama—but time and family lumped them together.) Discussions took place prior to the big decision: meetings and opportunities to write letters and offer ideas about how to make things work while giving the older generation a break. We—those of my generation and the next—took this seriously and discussed it at length. We had good ideas, putting our combined strengths and experiences to use.

Kenney had worked on those ranches since he was fifteen. He knew them better than most family members other than a cousin who had hunted in the backcountry since childhood and my uncle who has ridden those hills since age nine when he went on his first cattle drive.

During Kenney's initial summer at the Cojo, he lived with three other boys in what we called the schoolteacher's house, because that's where schoolteachers lived when teaching ranch kids in the old days. Kenney stayed there the next summer as well, part of the youth program (for boys only) established at the Cojo years before. After high school he worked full-time on the ranches and had his own small house on the Jalama. He had his own dogs and horses and girlfriend then too, and an old pickup he bought from the Cojo and named the Salmon Beauty.

I wanted desperately to keep the ranches in the family for Kenney, my cowboy son, and Tyler, my surfer son, and for the land itself, and I fought with all I had, which was only verbal ability, firsthand knowledge of the cattle business, and a passion for the environment. My sisters and I spoke of returning the land to the Chumash, which the older generation wouldn't for a moment consider, and we suggested giving the whole place—almost twenty-five thousand acres—to The Nature Conservancy. Others of our generation offered similar ideas, reflecting similar ideals. But none of us had enough shares in the family company for a vote that counted.

As it turned out, after Sister's death the company president and his brother owned a combined 51 percent of the total shares (though the final vote to sell was closer to 80 percent). I suspected that the requested meetings, letters, and ideas were designed to make us feel better about the predestined sale as the family traded land for money I didn't think anyone needed.

What my small branch of the family needed was continuity. Heritage. Not California's government or economy or millions of people but that beautiful golden land that birthed and raised us. I'd first carried my sons to the Cojo in my womb; now we weren't allowed to return. The sale tore Ken apart, his heart and history ripped right out of his young body. Tyler went to Cojo Bay by boat and surfed and walked the beaches up to and across the high-tide line.

Soon after the sale, the development company sourced by the hedge fund started grading roads, digging dozens of wells, and clearing house sites, damaging and removing native habitat with resulting damage to Indigenous sites and remains. No wonder the buyers didn't want us there—no witnesses—but people on the neighboring Hollister Ranch saw and reported the activities to the California Coastal Commission, which issued more violations to a single property for unpermitted work than ever before. But the damage was done.

My grandmother's place on Mount Diablo was gone as well: through eminent domain the state took it for park service personnel to use, eventually abandoning the beloved house, then burning it, and all that remains today are three chimneys, a few red tile steps, the cracked and empty pool, and memories, though my memories of my grandmother are few.

Of Sister I have many. I have this: Sister, eighty years old, my matron of honor in a light-blue suede dress and lapis necklace and earrings; the wedding held on a green lawn backed by the blue Pacific; a gray whale breaching as Keith and I spoke our vows. Afterward, Ed Janeway danced his wife across the grass, swinging Sister around in his strong arms as she giggled like a schoolgirl, her eyes matching her dress and the ocean and the sky.

Ten years after the Cojo and Jalama sold to the dishonorably intentioned hedge fund, the ranches will sell again. This time a wealthy couple will put up much of the money to enable The Nature Conservancy to purchase the twenty-four-thousand-plus acres—what my sisters and I suggested, except we said give, not sell, to The Nature Conservancy if not the Chumash. I will wonder after the second transaction if The Nature Conservancy will allow descendants of coastal and island Chumash visitation to the lands that birthed them.

The ranches first sold in 2007. In December of 2008, Rebecca, my best friend for forty-three years, died, and within the next eighteen months, so did both my fathers.

The currents at Point Conception, where cold northern waters collide with the warmer southern flows, create a wildness of water both fearsome and compelling. I stood at the edge, felt the pull, and eventually followed it from Maui to New Mexico. Ken, having graduated from Colorado State University weeks after his grandfather died, came to visit me at my cousin's house in Taos. We were both looking for what to do next. I found a small casita beside a Rio Grande tributary. Two months later Ken landed a job on a northern New Mexico ranch eighty-five miles away: ninety-six thousand deeded acres on the western edge of the Great Plains.

Ken and I started a new relationship as grown-up son and mother after twenty years of living apart, Ken on ranches with his dad in Santa Barbara County, me in northern Arizona, the Sierra Nevada, southeastern Utah, and Hawai'i. Now we lived in the same state.

Spring started showing in the cottonwoods along the rio that ran past the casita, long, drooping catkins floating like cotton on the breeze. I had survived a record-cold winter and found myself hungering for something in addition to warmth and sunshine.

I'd hung a small painting by Redwing T. Nez, with whom I had written a children's book years before, on an adobe wall. In the painting, massive sandstone formations, desert varnish streaking their faces, cut down to a dry riverbed bottom. Through the cold months I'd watched the colors change the way redrock does, from the deep reds of morning shadow to paler muted tones under the noonday sun, receding back to the tempered pink of twilight, and then shadowed nightfall. I wanted to climb inside that painting. I appreciated my house and the canyon and river but yearned for redrock country, so I signed up to volunteer with the Grand Canyon Trust, an environmental advocacy group whose mission was to protect and restore the Colorado Plateau.

With no idea about what to do with my life beyond writing, and no job to return to, I decided to visit Redwing at Bitahochee Trading Post in

Arizona on my way to the volunteer weekend. Tall with hair to his waist and laughing brown eyes, Redwing pushed open big rolling doors in his warehouse-turned-painting-studio, letting light in through the thin membrane of plastic that prevented wind from applying dirt to fresh paint. We sat in folding chairs and caught up on our kids, marriages, and divorces, my border collie–Aussie, Cojo, lying beside me. Then Redwing showed me around outside: a restored hogan, originally built in 1950; the older trading post; and an even older building waiting for designation as a national historic site. The tour ended at the base of Bitahochee.

Bita, meaning "edge"; *hochee* (hochii), meaning "red." The fact that it is spelled in different ways reflects the challenges white people experienced when trying to force Athabaskan languages into English spellings. *Chii* is "red" and pronounced "chee," like Cheetos. A pair of *i*'s (ii) originally represented the sound; to simplify for white readers, someone changed it to the Cheetos spelling. Redwing translated: Bitahochee, *red streaks on the edge of the butte*. Backed by the browner hue of a volcanic core—the neck of a volcano that remains after wind and water have eroded the original mountain away—the deep-red rock fell into formations reminiscent of childhood sandcastles at the beach. Dribbles of red sandstone.

Redrock and hoodoos, dramatic volcanic formations, an elemental lifestyle in which little more than a thin membrane separates a person from the land—I felt dizzy, my lives spinning around me. Cowboying in California. Long floating river days in the Southwest. Hawai'i, 'nuff said. And I had just spent below-zero-degree days inside layers of clothing and thick walls, with Cojo giving comfort and warmth to my feet and spirit.

Leaving Redwing's easy laughter, I headed northwest across the Navajo Nation, Naabeehó Bináhásdzo, which, at twenty-seven thousand square miles, is the largest reservation in the United States and the most populated. Yet many people on the rez still have no electricity or running water. Heat comes from woodburning stoves. Redwing had water but it was undrinkable, the pipes unsafe. He boiled it on the woodstove for cooking and drinking.

After crossing the Colorado River on the new bridge, I turned right to Lee's Ferry, the put-in for river trips through the Grand Canyon. I'd been down there, deep inside the earth, working as a swamper—riding on baggage boats to bail in the big rapids, sometimes rowing, doing the onshore labor beside the licensed river guides. I loved the hard work. The river itself. Any river.

Cojo trotted to the edge of the Colorado in his offbeat gait. I found him on Maui when he was eighteen months old and named him Cojo for the ranch and for his permanently crooked front legs, the result of getting run over as a pup. He'd come with me from Maui and now drank from the river as I put my hands in the cold water and brought it to my face. From the filtering Glen Canyon Dam fifteen miles upstream, with no major tributaries between the dam itself and the put-in, the river smelled clean and clear and nothing like the silty, storied waters downcanyon, which hold the traces of origin: limestone, sandstone, basalt, Vishnu Schist. I wanted to immerse fully into the river, but I had a date with the Grand Canyon Trust.

Turning off the highway again, this time south toward Kane Ranch, I expected to meet other volunteers to monitor the Trust's grassland restoration projects. No one was there. Finding cell service, I discovered that I was a week early.

Feeling completely stupid, I sat on the porch of the old ranch house and allowed two tears to fall. Then the quiet washed over me. It moved in waves across the miles between the Kaibab Rim behind me, the Vermilion Cliffs to the north, the Echo Cliffs to the east, and the invisible Grand Canyon. No buildings existed within my view other than the house whose porch Cojo and I occupied, the barn, and a couple of outbuildings. No other ranches. No towns. Nobody but Cojo and me. But we couldn't stay on that porch for a week.

Returning to the distant highway, I headed east. Though I now doubted my judgment, I chose not to backtrack 450 miles only to return days and another 900-mile round trip later. Marble Canyon Lodge, an aging, single-story motel near Lee's Ferry in which I had stayed before, had a room. Each morning I headed into the desert with Cojo. Each night I wrote about it.

I first saw this part of the Arizona Strip—the stretch of land between the north rim of the Grand Canyon and Utah—thirty years before, when Keith, my then husband-to-be, and I drove to the Southwest in search of a ranch on which to begin our new life. We approached the Colorado Plateau through the Virgin Gorge—fitting, as that was my first trip to the Strip. At twenty-five, I had lived in California and Hawaiʻi, but with the exception of shopping in Reno I had not ventured east of the California state line.

We looked at three ranches: one on the Arizona Strip, one deep in the Bradshaw Mountains, one in the Chiricahua Mountains in southeastern Arizona. I wanted the first ranch. The one on the Strip. In House Rock Valley. Too much money if you needed the calf crops to make the bank payments (which we did), but that didn't stop the longing. Decades later, as I waited for my volunteer weekend to begin, I drove dirt roads in all directions, looking for that ranch.

Back at Lee's Ferry in the afternoons, I did strip and dip, wading into a small eddy, bracing the forty-six-degree water from the bottom of the dam, dunking quickly, the water tightening my chest and skin. Even the top of my head hurt. I started to feel awake.

C⊃-

This time on the correct day, Cojo and I sat again on the porch of the old ranch house, looking east across House Rock Valley and the Arizona Strip. On the miles-long dirt road in, I had followed a cowboy driving a three-quarter-ton Dodge pickup pulling a gooseneck stock trailer, two saddled horses and two bulls inside, until he pulled over to let me to pass. Then we both turned up the same long driveway to the Kane Ranch headquarters. I headed toward the house while he parked near the barn. Unloading the horses and tying them to the fence, he gazed off across the valley at five additional cowboys riding in, and I found myself thinking about the odd coupling of cowboy and environmentalist. Though an environmental organization had purchased Kane Ranch, three generations of a ranching family rode that day, gathering the low country into the twelve-thousand-acre Kane Pasture, where the cattle would graze until the Forest Service said they could head up to the summer grasses in the national forest on the Kaibab Plateau.

The ranch manager—the cowboy in the three-quarter-ton Dodge—drove off to turn the trailered bulls out with the cows. Telling Cojo to stay, I drifted down to the barn to visit with the ranch manager's father, patriarch of the operation, who sat in the shade after riding in. His grandchildren, their horses tied to the fence with the others, splashed and giggled as they tried to catch goldfish in a water trough.

The grandfather pointed to some cattle I couldn't see. "It doesn't look too far over there but when you start across ahorseback you realize it's a long way away." Squinting through heatwaves, I finally spotted the cattle.

"Up on the Paria Plateau," he said, "on the 220,000-acre BLM allotment that's part of the Two-Mile Ranch owned by the Trust, they can run 1,500 cow-calf pairs, and a thousand down here." He explained that the Forest Service and Bureau of Land Management designated how many animal unit months, or AUMs, the allotments could handle, and Grand Canyon Trust chose to run fewer head to give the drought-ridden range a rest. "Right now they don't run enough cows to make a trail," the grandfather said.

"We only cowboy ahorseback," he continued, "and rope our calves to brand them. If a ranch uses a calf chute that means they can't rope and their horses ain't any good."

Like my ex-husband and my son, he and his son were old-school cowboys. Yet they worked for an environmental advocacy group. I didn't understand.

The granddaughter came squealing up with a big goldfish in a coffee can, her brother right behind her. After showing their catch to their grandpa, they ran back and dropped the fish in the trough. This was the kind of scene I had imagined with my own children and their father: handsome ranch headquarters, good quarter horses tied to the fence after gathering cattle, the kids playing in the horse trough.

"Where does the water come from?" I asked, water a most precious resource in vast, dry country, second in importance only to children.

He gestured toward the Vermilion Cliffs. "It gets drawn from springs and piped under the highway. Here the water comes from springs in the canyon behind the house."

Built in 1877, the sandstone slabs cut from nearby cliffs and stacked, puzzled, and mortared together by an earlier Mormon ranching family, the house now hosted Grand Canyon Trust personnel and volunteers. The Trust acquired the Kane and Two-Mile Ranches in 2005. Perhaps the best thing about these ranches of a few deeded acres and hundreds of thousands leased from the federal government by Grand Canyon Trust and run by generations of Mormon cowboys is the puzzling-together of philosophies to better manage the land. I wondered if my marriage might have fared differently had Keith and I shared this brand of creativity.

The cowboys declined an offer of lunch or a beer after work. "If I had one beer I wouldn't stop until my face hit the dirt," said the grandfather. I had to laugh—we had forgotten the Mormon doctrine.

As the last of the volunteers drove in through the gate, I wanted to ask the grandfather if I could come help gather cattle in the fall. But I hadn't been on a horse in too many years, and there's protocol in cowboy culture: you don't invite yourself. Instead I turned away from the glimpses of my earlier life.

After introductions and lunch, we divided into small groups. Due to having knee surgery two months earlier (it was coincidence, the doctor said, that arthritis and bone spurs and bone fragments haunted the same territory of my knee injured on Santa Cruz Island), for perhaps the first time in my life I didn't volunteer for the heavy labor. Instead I watched others wrestle stones into place for a native garden in front of the house, three people per stone. Another group weeded around sagebrush and fourwing saltbushes, the only native plants within a perimeter of post-and-rail fence. Those volunteers worked on their knees, so I gravitated back to the porch, joining two women making square PVC "hula hoops," they said—meter-by-meter quadrants to measure the vegetation transects we would inspect the next day.

In 2006 Grand Canyon Trust chose a site of poor soil—heavily impacted due to its proximity to corrals and water—to fence off and seed with ricegrass, needle-and-thread, bottlebrush squirreltail, and Sandberg bluegrass. A year later the Trust no-till-drill seeded (seeding without discing or plowing the land) a nearby area with the same combination of species—experimental attempts to reintroduce indigenous grasses. We would count the native grasses and Russian thistle seedlings, the latter commonly known as tumbleweed.

After supper Cojo and I returned to our temporary shelter at Marble Canyon Lodge, where I showered and lay back on the bed, tired from the sudden social contact after a quiet week but not beat up physically—the tactic of underdoing seemed to work.

In the morning I cut down from 89A to the worksite following a mental map laid out for me the night before. I didn't get lost, the roads moving south toward sources of water for the cattle as the land itself moved in low undulations toward the north rim of the Grand Canyon.

The group already at work within the fenced acre, some counting, others replacing the strings that marked transects, I joined the latter group, and when we finished tying the last knot, we joined the counters. At first I was just recordkeeper, an easy task: ____ Russian thistle; ____ this kind of native grass, or that. It was immediately clear that the invasives overpopulated the indigenous by the thousands, wreaking havoc on the land.

Some of the volunteers moved off with their square PVC hula hoops to the drill-seeded site, and I was left to prostrate myself to the thistle, finally getting down on my knees at the edge of six-by-six-foot transects to count tiny seedlings. These took my eyes a while to even see, the tiniest plant not half an inch tall, with less bulk than a new blade of grass. At dinner my transect partner and I received a round of applause for counting the most Russian thistle, a dubious honor: with his 100 and my 194, we tallied nearly 300 tumbleweeds growing in the last six-by-six-foot plot. Three hundred plants that would grow round and stickery, then dry and blow across the valley, leaving seeds in their wakes.

Cowboys know good feed and water from bad—despite the depiction of the tumbling tumbleweed as a symbol of the West, they know it as a big, round, rolling, worthless weed that grows anywhere and outcompetes native grasses. Still, they would not get down on their knees to count it, even in an effort to unravel it from the web of life on the rocky soil. And the botanists on board, their faces inches from the earth, magnifying glasses scrunched to their eyeballs and butts raised like defensive beetles as they identified native seedlings, would not climb on horses to push cattle across the hot, dry desert, even in hopes of stomping out tumbleweeds. Yet this relationship worked—in the same way that my two sons are brothers regardless of their different lifestyles—because of common territory. Parents, in my sons' case. In the case of Grand Canyon Trust and the cowboys, the common ground was the land itself. And they had that most necessary ingredient for a successful union: the willingness to listen and to learn. The basis for growth and change.

At weekend's end I sat again with Cojo on the porch of the old ranch house, thinking about the Arizona Strip and the trip with Keith to look at that House Rock Valley ranch for sale; hunting in the valley with my second husband, Smith, years later; camping at Lee's Ferry after rallying against the dam, also with Smith, ten years after that; and running the river in between. And here I was marking another decade with a trip to the Strip, House Rock Valley, the river, finding myself thirty years later at the same ranch that had brought me to the Southwest in the first place.

That's right, *I found it!* At the end of a dirt road—deep ruts in the fine red sand—the Trust's Two-Mile Ranch was the very ranch I fell for on that trip with Keith in 1981. I stood outside the house Keith and I had hovered inside as we talked with the couple selling the place after they showed us the features of the headquarters—two houses, tack room, bunkhouse, shipping pens, shop—Keith already knowing it wasn't for him, me dreaming beyond the practical problems of low weaning weights and little water. The rancher drove us on back roads that crossed the state line into Utah, showing us water troughs and dirt tanks, proudly pointing out the potholes in the redrock: "Those'll water five head for three days when it rains."

I wanted it; I wanted to make the change and face the challenges and gaze up at the red cliffs in the long afternoon light. Keith said no.

He drove us home by way of Flagstaff, and for some reason as we dropped west out of town we talked about speeding tickets. I had collected them for years; Keith said he'd never gotten one. It wasn't but a minute later that lights flashed behind us. This set the tone for the rest of the trip home—he refused to take the sixty-mile detour so that I could see the south rim of the Grand Canyon, and I pouted clear to California. Yet even without the Grand Canyon, I fell hard for that country—a sky as vast as the sea, rocks the color of my heart. That's where I went when I left Keith—to the Colorado Plateau—and now I was back, watching the light move across the Vermilion Cliffs that spanned the northern skyline. The cliffs ended in the northeast, where they seemed to stair-step steeply then roll into Marble Canyon. My brain strained to remember the geologic layers, the Echo Cliffs and Redwing's painting their mirror.

In no hurry to leave, Cojo snoozing near me on the porch, I slipped into further reverie.

⊂⊃-

Several times a year my mother would come down from the Bay Area to visit us at whatever ranch we lived on. She had a special bond with Kenney, her first grandchild. Once he started walking, they would mosey around the ranch looking at things—leaves, acorns, cows. Actually, *walking* is an understatement. That kid never did learn to walk. He crawled fast as a little racecar, stood up at eleven months, and ran. Kenney said his first word with my mother: *orsey*. Horsey without the *h*. He said his first "sentence" with me one day as we checked the cows during calving season: *baby cows*. Tyler's first word was *deers*.

This visit (before Tyler, before Keith sold our cows), my mother's arrival meant I could go with Keith in the morning to help the neighbors gather three hundred Brahma-cross replacement heifers. Keith and I left the house early, Kenney still asleep, my mother at the dining room table with her coffee. We saddled our horses in the dawn.

The neighbors' ranch, a rolling thirty thousand acres of grass, chaparral, and gray pines, ran up to the national forest like Sister and Ed's neighboring Cachuma Ranch. Five of us rode from headquarters, spread out, and started pushing small groups of heifers toward a big open field bordered by a steep, sage-covered hillside and the dry riverbed below. I rode point to the left of the herd on my good bay quarter horse, his hooves stirring the early morning dew on dry summer grasses, releasing the smell of the California I knew.

Both of us relaxed yet watchful, we knew the heifers could break at any time. As a tall brindle heifer with a small Brahma hump and dewlaps took the lead, her long ears pivoting, I felt a sharp pinch in my abdomen and stiffened for a second in the saddle, causing my responsive horse to jump. That's when the heifer made her move, trotting toward a side canyon, followed by others. I grabbed my right side, momentarily off balance, as my horse accelerated into the lope he expected me to want him to do. Collecting the reins to stop the run and the pain, I heard Keith yelling as if I were one of the dogs, "*What the fuck are you doing? Get around 'em!*" I gave the gelding his head, squeezed with my knees, and we bounded over rocks and brush up the side of the hill toward the mouth of the canyon, my cowdog Cotton running ahead and getting to the lead heifer first, jumping at her and biting her nose. She shook her head, turned, and they circled back to rejoin the main herd.

I pulled my horse up, clutching my side, feeling white with pain. Feeling Keith's glare. Leaning forward, I rubbed my horse's neck and whispered "good dog" to Cotton.

It was just a moment, and it passed. We got the heifers to the corrals without further incident, and neither Keith nor I mentioned anything as we headed back to my mother and bright little Kenney, not yet a year and a half old.

I cooked catfish for supper. A neighbor had given them to us, and with my mother visiting, cooking the catfish seemed the right thing to do. I ate a few bites. After dinner, Keith prepped Kenney for bed—normally Keith would sit in his chair with the newspaper as I cooked, fed us, bathed Kenney, and put him to bed. Sometimes Keith would sit reading the damned paper, Kenney standing next to the chair shaking Keith's shirtsleeve, saying, "Daddy, Daddy," and from the kitchen door I'd say, "Keith, *he's trying to talk to you*."

That night Keith had Kenney giggling in the bathtub. After he yelled, "Where are his pj's?" it got quiet at that end of the house.

My mother and I filled the dishwasher, then sat at the round oak table. "I think I'm pregnant," I said.

"I wondered what was up. You seem . . . distracted?"

"I'm six weeks along, and the doctor's not sure—he couldn't feel anything. But I feel it."

"And you want this?" she said.

"Oh, yes, very much." I hoped another baby might change things.

After everybody went to bed I puttered around, enjoying the quiet. In the shower, letting the hot water wash the day away, I felt fine. But when I lay down in the big Cal-King bed, pain sliced into my side.

"Keith, wake up—something's not right."

"What," he murmured, rolling toward me, "horses out?" He resumed snoring.

I pushed up from the bed and shuffled to the bathroom, making myself throw up the catfish I decided was the cause, which made no sense because the first pain struck hours before I ate, but I wanted a reason: catfish, appendicitis, not the baby—no blood. Hovering at the sink to brush my teeth again, I dropped the toothbrush, sank to my knees, and crawled back to bed, not fast like Kenney, pulling myself up over the edge and in. Pain stabbed me again.

"Keith, *wake up*."

"What?"

"*Get my mother.*" This time he leapt up and scurried down the hall in his skivvies.

My mother appeared. When she sat down on the bed, I screamed.

"Call the doctor," my mother told Keith, "*now*."

Long before cell phones, the telephone lived in a different room, and Keith ran to it. Soon he had the doctor on the line. My mother helped me out of bed and down the hall, bearing my weight as Keith held the phone to my ear.

"Where does it hurt?" the doctor asked.

"My right side. No, no blood."

"Put your husband back on."

The doctor told Keith to get me to the hospital *right away*. No time to wait for an ambulance, Keith hurriedly dressed and carried me in just my bathrobe, T-shirt, and underwear down the porch steps to the pickup. My mother staying behind with sleeping Kenney, Keith raced to the hospital an hour away. I lay across the bench seat, feeling every pebble in the road, the princess and the pea. My head bouncing on Keith's solid thigh, I watched his set jaw as he devoured the miles.

At the emergency entrance, men waited with a wheelchair. "You need to sit up and slide over," one of them said.

"No," I said, but I sat up. And passed out.

Coming to as they propped me in the wheelchair, blacking out again, no blood getting to my head anymore, they took my blood pressure—sixty over forty—and put me on a gurney; lying down, I could squint my eyes open. I could see a nurse—"I know you're hurting honey," she said, "but we can't give you pain medication until we know what's wrong."

The doctor, who had told me he couldn't feel the fetus, appeared. "We have to find out where the blood is coming from," he said. But there'd been no blood. When he pressed on my stomach, which rose from my ribs like a wino's, I screamed. In the operating room they slid me from the gurney to an operating table, and the doctor aimed a huge syringe topped with a long needle toward my thighs. "You're hemorrhaging internally," he said. "Your abdomen is full of blood, and I have to get a blood sample." He pried my legs open, the syringe he held entering my vagina, the needle piercing the uterine wall to get blood from my abdomen, the pressure of touch beyond any hurt I've ever felt, and I wanted the pain to stop, I didn't care how, just *stop*, dying for it to stop . . .

Keith told me later that from the waiting room down the hall he could hear my screams, and then the doctor rushed past him with a vial of my blood, saying, "We have to stop the bleeding *now* or we're gonna lose her."

The nurse gave me a shot, Darvon; I couldn't tell her *no, morphine*, and I puked into the silver moon-bowl—*Darvon makes me sick, morphine okay*—and went out again.

The ectopic pregnancy had taken place in my right fallopian tube, where it grew until the tube burst from the pressure and ruptured a main artery that filled my gut with blood. The tube and pregnancy disappearing in the mess sucked from my abdomen, the doctor saved my life and my right ovary. He ordered transfusions—three units of blood—wanting to give me more but stopping on the side of caution, HIV and AIDS at the forefront of medical minds at the time. 1986. They weren't yet concerned with hepatitis C.

In order to heal I couldn't lift anything heavier than ten pounds, which meant Kenney—I couldn't pick up my adorable, quick, confused little boy. Thin and taut ("He's all sinew and muscle," said a friend when Kenney was six months old, and he hasn't changed), he still weighed almost twenty pounds. A bag of dog food, a saddle, bales of hay all weighed more.

Keith agreed with my mother that I should convalesce in the Bay Area. Cousin Nancy flew down to help with the drive. I hugged a pillow to my belly as I climbed into the backseat of my mother's car, Kenney small in the car seat beside me. A five-hour drive to my younger sister's house, where Kenney and I would stay, my mother coming over in the daytime, Peg home after work—they would take care of Kenney, my job to rest and get stronger.

As soon as we could, Keith and I started trying to make the next baby. It wasn't happening, my pre-ectopic chances cut in half by the vanished fallopian tube. The doctor gave me a test in which he put dye in my uterus and watched onscreen as it leaked out my tubes into my abdomen. Cramping and fleeting pain followed the dye flooding out the tubeless side, but the left side was blocked. It looked as if I couldn't get pregnant without more surgery.

Tyler showed up as a shadow in my womb three weeks later—the test had apparently cleared the blockage. So I had a second healthy baby boy almost three years after Kenney. Tyler, nine pounds, fourteen and a half ounces at birth, his face swollen and bruised from the journey, was pure joy in a house so cold, no money to heat it, Keith gone on a job for days, my mother there (again) to help with my newborn and rambunctious Kenney, her getting sick as we could not stay warm, but I had this soft, round baby, black hair framing his face and milky-blue infant eyes, so easy to love. I kept trying to love his father, who worked away from home more often than not, leaving me with kids cattle cowdogs and horses, a bear in the front yard one day, and all those rattlesnakes. I fed the cattle and horses through the winter with Tyler in the car seat in the cab of the pickup, Kenney and me in the bed kicking off flakes of hay as we circled the field in granny-gear, no one driving until we headed toward a fence, and I'd swing off the bed

4. Tyler, one, in saddle, and Kenney, four. Courtesy of Christine Photography.

through the open door and turn the steering wheel, trusting Kenney to hang on back there.

That was my marriage, for the most part just the boys and me.

Cowboys don't do therapy. When I went to see a therapist after Tyler was born, I lied to Keith, snuck money from our account, and paid cash. I told the therapist I kept hoping that Keith would start spending some time with our sons and me, but when I begged for Sunday afternoons with the family—like, all four of us—Keith said he had to work. I hoped things would change.

"Hope is a noose," the therapist said.

Wisps of rain crossed the sky, a few drops falling on the corrugated roof of the porch, the magnified sound interrupting my thoughts. With some effort, I pulled myself back from the past.

A few miles to the southeast across the limestone bench of House Rock Valley, Rider Canyon fell open to the Colorado River, House Rock Wash, and House Rock Rapids, which I had run several times in my life as a river girl. Aside from Rider Canyon, and a rim of redrock highlighted for a moment by streaks of yellow light, nothing showed of the ditch that has an average width of ten miles and depth of more than five thousand feet. Rays of sunlight slanted through a gap in the clouds—pukalani, we call that hole in the clouds in Hawaiʻi. To the south, rain fell but misted away before touching earth. Virga.

A ball of rainbow floated above the valley the way they float over the ocean in Hawaiʻi—ʻonohi, a rainbow fragment. I wondered what it was called in Navajo. The wind grew colder as the sun shifted west and the rain pretended to fall. The weekend at Kane Ranch had ended, but whispers of want had grown louder. Driving away with Cojo from House Rock Valley thirty years after I first ventured there with Keith to look at a ranch for sale, my heart flushed with a strange emotion. If Keith hadn't said no to that ranch, what would have happened differently in those thirty years? Would I have stuck? *Would I have been able to raise both my boys?*

4

Desert Friendly

Criollo Cattle Could Save Ranching

—*Moab Sun News* headline, June 2, 2022

New Mexico and Colorado, 2012–15

Although related to blue jays and Steller's jays, piñon jays have different characteristics. They fly in huge flocks—as many as five hundred birds. They don't scold; instead, they call out when en route, like migrating Canada geese, more to check on each other's whereabouts than as a forewarning of their imminent arrival.

At the cabin in the ponderosa pine forest near Flagstaff where my second husband, Smith, and I lived, piñon jays watered at the dogs' water trough, which Smith set outside a sliding glass door near my desk. Calling from afar, then descending abruptly in earthbound sweeps of varying shades of blue, the jays landed on ponderosa branches, hopped to the edge of the trough, and dipped their beaks to water. From the other side of the glass I could study the smooth-feathered, crestless-headed birds in their varying shades of dusty denim-blue, which matched my own worn blue jeans.

When living in Utah, I would hear the calls and look up to see a moving cloud of piñon jays far above. In New Mexico years later, I didn't see—or hear—piñon jays in the canyon by the river. While one-seed and Rocky Mountain junipers grew large, only a few stunted piñon pines grew in the sandy soil. Since these jays thrive on the seeds within piñon pinecones, this may have explained their absence, my canyon not their habitat. Which brings to mind another favorite bird of the Colorado Plateau: the canyon wren. I kept waiting for its call, the scale of notes descending to the very depths of a person.

Unfamiliar shale defined this canyon. The tributary flowed into the Rio Grande, which flowed into country also unfamiliar: Texas. Mexico. The Gulf of Mexico. I had only lived west of the Continental Divide—perhaps, like me, canyon wrens and piñon jays did not know this place as home.

From six years old to high school graduation, Kenney had lived with his dad in California. (Tyler lived there for five of those school years; the rest of the time he lived with me.) Days after graduation, Kenney flew to Zimbabwe to work for four months on a cattle ranch and game reserve. Robert Mugabe ruled at the time, and I was terrified. But Keith had said yes the previous year when Kenney went for a month, and he said yes again. When Kenney returned (safe and sound, thank the gods), he went to work on the Cojo and Jalama ranches while attending a two-year college, eventually transferring to Colorado State University. Academia was something I knew about, both as student and teacher, and Ken turned to me for guidance. Slowly we started rebuilding our relationship based on this connection. Different roads led us to New Mexico.

I found that at the ranch where Ken worked, piñon jays flooded the sky above the fringes of piñon-juniper woodland at the edge of the open prairie, large flocks swooping, soaring, calling, reminding me of life on the Colorado Plateau. In Arizona. In Utah. And when Ken invited me to help gather cattle, I remembered how that felt—horse and rider, cowboys and cattle in a movement like water flowing downstream. Ken, tall and lean with stunning hazel-green eyes that can flash with laughter or anger, sat a horse as if he were born to it. Years before, my aunt Nat had written in a happy-birth card, "He, your fine son, is so *big*—properly so; he's a rancher's son, and son of a girl-cowboy. He'll sit a horse well." And he does. Like his father, and my grandmother.

Astride a borrowed horse, watching my son, it occurred to me that Ken and I had not cowboyed together before. When he was an infant I pushed him along in a blanket-padded wheelbarrow as I fed the horses, and when I started going down to the arena to lope a few circles I'd do the same, hoping he'd fall asleep and I could ride longer. At three and a half weeks old, Kenney went to his first branding—Peg had come to the ranch to help, and she carried him around in a Snugli while I roped. "You should take a break more often," someone joked as I swung my loop and caught almost every calf at which I aimed despite pain and milk-full breasts.

Women at these brandings were happy to watch another's child—especially a baby—so that the mother could rope or work the ground, and by the time Kenney turned six weeks old he had gone to five brandings and made the local newspaper as the youngest person on a horse on a Cowbelle trail ride (carried by his mother).

Team roping competitions worked the same way—women sharing kids while the mothers roped. But I found cowboying itself more difficult—I couldn't, wouldn't, pack Kenney into steep, rough country, riding under oak branches and trotting through rocks and sagebrush. While I'd ridden into my eighth month of pregnancy, carrying my baby outside of me seemed more dangerous. It was hard to say no to cowboying, and to Keith, but I had someone else to care for who was more important than my husband or myself.

Now, as Ken and I rode side by side pushing cattle, our relationship felt fragile and new. Perhaps too eager in seeking more time with my son, and more cattle work, I started looking at small ranches around the Colorado Plateau, sometimes with Ken, sometimes without him.

Two days at least away from his job, Ken couldn't join me when I went to see a place in Colorado. The ranch sat *on* the Colorado Plateau, near the seam of the Plateau and the San Juan branch of the Rocky Mountains, forty-nine miles from the Four Corners Monument on the Navajo Nation that marks the point where Colorado, New Mexico, Arizona, and Utah meet (you can touch all four states at the same time). Nostalgia might weigh more than practicality. I arranged to buy the property and named it Cachuma Ranch, for Sister and Ed. For Ken.

Some of my big ideas simply tanked the first year, and I found myself alone with my animals on 171 acres: dogs, cats, horses, and, soon, cows. It would take another two years for Ken and his family to join me, which would then draw "Unk Ty," as devoted an uncle as I ever saw.

Meanwhile in New Mexico, Ken observed neighboring ranchers running some mostly black Corriente cows, which they crossed with black Angus bulls. The Corrientes, cheaper to buy and raise than Angus, did well in the high desert and on the plains, and at weaning time the black calves brought decent money. Ken found a good deal on some Corriente cows and easily convinced me to say yes. I wanted to say yes to anything he wanted.

Ken and I had both known of Corrientes for decades. When Keith ran the coastal ranch, every couple of years he would order a truckload of Corriente steers out of Mexico for his boss. The ranch had a wonderful roping arena, and Keith's boss would drive up from LA to practice team roping. We practiced too, our friends congregating at the arena on many a summer eve.

Those half-starved steers came off the trucks looking small and thin, which they were. Their overall size belied their age, and we would look at their heads, the thickness and size of their horns, and the length of their tails to guess. Definitely not yearlings, they could even be three years old and still weigh four hundred to five hundred pounds (our calves averaged more than six hundred pounds when we weaned them at six to eight months). The Corriente steers would grow and fill out on good grass and hay but wouldn't get big enough to balance out their heads and horns. Like bison, they looked tilty.

The cows Ken found were someone's backyard animals, hence their gentle nature, especially Lightning, whom Ken named for her slow, plodding ways, usually at the back of the herd, so gentle we could scratch her forehead and around her horns, rub her neck. I could stand next to her and rest my elbow on her shoulders. Later, the grandkids would ride her.

This small herd fit perfectly on the 171-acre spread of fenced and cross-fenced horse pastures, where I could move the cows on foot (though I preferred to do so ahorseback) and feed them easily by myself in the snowy winters, throwing two-wire bales into the bed of the pickup and driving to the feeding area, carrying the bales a short distance, and spreading flakes by hand. Of those initial cows, we still have all-black Lightning and a blue roan cow—black with white hairs mixed in, giving her a blueish tinge—whom we call Roanie (fitting though unoriginal).

Now we needed a bull.

A few head of cattle do not a rancher make. Even my tax guy thought I was in this as a hobby. But when Ken brought his wife, Kathy, six months pregnant, and yearling daughter, Lacey, to live at Cachuma, he went to work and found an outfit that leased Colorado summer pasture for their Corriente cows and bulls, which wintered in New Mexico. They had a yearling bull for sale.

Down on Cherry Creek, about forty-five minutes from Cachuma, Ken and I helped gather the cattle. The fences in disrepair, a Corriente-longhorn

5. Kathy on quad (Lucas arrived ten days later). Photo by the author.

cow knew all the holes, as well as the hollows in the willows along the creek in which to hide her week-old calf—so many holes to block in a pasture we didn't know, but we got the pair in with the rest of the cattle. Afterward, we sat on our sweating horses while the couple selling the bull looked over the herd. With trucks on their way to haul the cattle back to New Mexico, the woman said, "Would you be interested in taking that pair? I don't want to ship that young calf."

We had a stock trailer and didn't live far, but Ken looked skeptical—the cow had just shown us she could be a problem.

"Yes," I said, before we could discuss it. And then I asked, "What about that one?" gesturing toward a small black, brown, and white cow with upright horns like a dairy cow, very unlike the wide, twisting horns of the other that showed the longhorn influence. The paint cow had a black bull calf at her side. "Could we buy her too?"

Scowling at me from under the brim of his hat, Ken looked like his dad.

"Why not?" the woman said, without consulting her husband. "Sure," and we sorted off the two pairs and the yearling bull who would become our herd sire, whom Ken would name Ferdinand. The bull was a deep reddish-brown that would darken to black, with a red dorsal stripe along his spine. He looked like the Ferdinand of the book I read as a child, which I read to my young sons long before the animated movie came out. Some things do come full circle.

When we rode off to get our rig, Ken said, "Mom, you don't just do that."

"What? Ask about buying a cow? She said yes, didn't she?"

His stern cowboy etiquette could not curb my joy at the additions to my small herd.

Ken first learned about Criollo (cree-o-yo) cattle in New Mexico at Holistic Management International meetings (HMI is a not-for-profit organization working globally through regenerative agriculture toward "healthy, resilient lands and thriving communities"). As the ranches near him became more interested in raising and selling grass-fed beef, people talked about this heritage breed, Criollo, predecessor to Corrientes and Texas longhorns. Grass-fed beef is higher in the good stuff than grain-fed beef—beta-carotene, omega three fatty acids, antioxidants, vitamins, minerals—and Criollos, a desert-evolved beef breed, make lean, tender, marbled, healthy steaks.

Balanced, beautiful, hardy, and agile, Criollos can be directly traced to the original Spanish cattle from the Andalucía region of southwestern Spain. On Christopher Columbus's second voyage to the Americas, which sailed from 1493 to 1496, he carried cattle alongside horses and other animals. In the early 1500s, conquistadors moved cattle to the continent; in 1539, descendants of those cattle entered what is today the United States. Between 1540 and 1542 Francisco Vásquez de Coronado included five hundred head on his gold-seeking expedition into today's New Mexico. In 1572 Criollos from stock that hadn't yet ventured north were introduced to the state of Chihuahua, Mexico.

Don Juan de Oñate drove several thousand head to northern New Mexico in 1598, these cattle still bearing Criollo genetics. He let them roam freely, and they dispersed into smaller groups in search of feed and water. Some became the ancestors of the mavericks of the 1800s, which contributed to cowboy lore.

Meanwhile Oñate, known for his fierce treatment of Native people, attacked Acoma Pueblo in 1599, destroying the pueblo and killing five hundred warriors and three hundred women and children, enslaving survivors aged twelve and up. To prevent escape by men older than twenty-five, he ordered a foot amputated from each of them, though it has been argued that he "only" amputated toes.

When I lived in New Mexico, a 1991 bronze statue of Oñate reigned in front of the visitor center in Alcalde, and I learned that in 1998, a small group of civil disobedients snuck through the night to sever the right foot of the statue. The sculptor repaired it. The left leg was painted red in 2017. Following the trend of removing monuments, in 2020 the Oñate bronze moved "temporarily" to a safer place.

Oñate died in Spain in 1626. In a completely unrelated event, the next year the last aurochs died in Poland. Aurochs, German for *original ox*, is an extinct species of Pleistocene megafauna and likely the wild ancestor to all cattle. Aurochs calves, born a reddish-brown, would turn night-black as bulls, with a dorsal stripe of a lighter color running along their spines, light-colored muzzles, and long legs. Bulls reached six feet in height at the shoulders, with horns spanning thirty inches, and could weigh 1,500 to 3,300 pounds. Aurochs cows were smaller, measuring five feet tall at the shoulder. Also horned, with similar markings, the cows would stay a dark reddish-brown.

In 1627, the year the last aurochs cow died of natural causes in Poland where the final herd had lived since 1601, far across the water Jesuit missionaries introduced Criollo cattle to the Raramuri people in remote Sierra Tarahumara (Copper Canyon) in Chihuahua, Mexico. Isolated family groups learned the benefits of these cattle as milk, beef, and draft animals. For nearly four hundred years, Raramuri Criollos lived exclusively in the desert mountains and canyons of Chihuahua, continuing the adaptations to arid lands that began in southwestern Spain.

Ed Frederickson and Alfredo Gonzalez of New Mexico State University's Jornada Experimental Range near Las Cruces, New Mexico, heard about the Copper Canyon cattle and went in search of them. Deep in Sierra Tarahumara, Gonzalez saw cattle "walking on the canyon walls," as Alisa Opar reported in a *Pacific Standard* article titled "Drought? Climate Change? No Sweat for These Desert-Friendly Cattle." Gonzalez said, "When we saw them within people's yards, some within the houses, and children moving the cattle on the roads," he knew they had found Raramuri Criollos—not only desert friendly but people friendly too. The genetics of the isolated Raramuri herds had remained intact, and in 2005 the Jornada Experimental Range acquired thirty cows and three bulls. Thus began the Raramuri Criollo herd at Jornada.

The Quivira Coalition, a New Mexico nonprofit started by a rancher and two conservationists, "builds soil, biodiversity, and resilience on western working landscapes" through "education, innovation, [and] restoration, one acre at a time." At the annual symposium in Albuquerque, Ken and I heard Dennis Moroney speak. He and his wife, Deb, run the 47 Ranch in Cochise County, Arizona; the couple has a philosophy of matching genetics to the environment, and in 2009 they introduced Raramuri Criollo cows from Jornada to their twenty-five-thousand-acre desert ranch. Listening to Dennis speak about heritage breeds, sustainability, employing best management practices to raise a healthy animal and return health to the land, and "making a reasonable living at a family scale," I felt excited about acting on Ken's ideas about Criollos. He wanted some, and so did I—Criollos had distinct personalities and charming physical attributes (like Brahmas), and they came with a story.

Ken and I embarked on cattle-buying adventures, traveling from southwestern Colorado to ranches in West Texas and very southern New Mexico to buy Criollo cows. We (Ken) had to change a flat tire on the trailer in winds that blew sand horizontally across the blacktop—I had cut a corner and pulled the trailer over a curb. When we got a flat on a different trip, Ken cussing in the heat, we had to stop in a tiny town to get a tire patched. But I showed Ken another ranch his father and I had looked at in that year of out-of-state-ranch dreams; we got to visit with friends Pam and Nick Ewing, whom I knew from cowboying together in California before Kenney was born and when he was small; and we saw new country as we drove along rivers, through evergreen canyons, and past incredible rock formations in the Chihuahuan Desert that sweeps into Mexico.

In Texas we stayed in guest bedrooms at the ranch owners' home. Everything about the house was big: beds and bookcases and the columns supporting the upstairs. I got lost on the way to the kitchen. The couple raised pure Criollos, using side-by-sides, or "utility task vehicles," to check their cattle. The cows in a hundred-acre pasture trotted from one corner to another as the couple pointed out their genetic characteristics. Unlike the points of conformation Keith had taught me when I chose Ruby so many years before, Criollos can have prominent hip bones and a jag in their spines toward the tailbone. This, the woman said, is because some have an extra vertebra, which helps with flexibility and climbing in steep terrain (as Alfredo Gonzalez said, they can climb on walls).

The bulls in a different pasture barely glanced at us. The purebred heifers in the corral—daughters of those cows and bred to a handsome bull—skittered and snorted but loaded okay. Clearly we had some gentling to do.

The Thistle Dew Ranch on the Mimbres River in southern New Mexico raised Susieville Cattle Company grass-fed Criollo beef; from them we purchased a Criollo bull ("A Bull Named Sue," by Ken), and returned to buy some steers when we didn't have enough to supply our own grass-fed-and-finished-beef program.

As Ken walked through the steers in the pen, I eyed the cows in the holding field. After we sorted the selected steers off, I said, "What if we got some cows too?" We picked out three Criollo cows, two with calves at their sides and another heavy with calf.

At a gas station on the way home I accidentally locked the doors to the pickup as I stepped out; diesel motor rumbling, cattle restless in the trailer, we sat on the running board for an hour waiting for rescue by AAA. Fortunately the overhang above the pump kept us all in the shade, and fortunately the cow didn't calve.

We had kept the Corriente cows we already had, and on another New Mexico ranch we bought some additional Corrientes from cowboy singer Randy Huston, with whom Ken had cowboyed and roped. This was the easiest trip, yet despite previous mishaps I loved the overall process of buying cattle with Ken. Looking, consulting, pointing out desirable characteristics, agreeing on which cows to take home. Sharing the driving, talking on the road, planning our herd, learning from my son. Learning *about* my son as he shared stories of working on the Cojo and Jalama ranches. And earlier stories of gathering thousands of sheep off Santa Cruz Island, Kenney thirteen, Tyler ten, both strapped into a small, open-door helicopter as the pilot buzzed the cliffs. Ken also had stories of going with Keith to gather wild cattle, his father once telling Kenney to climb a tree and stay up there as Keith and Larry chased an angry, horned Hereford bull, and the bull chased them. Kenney, ten, sat in that oak tree for three hours, holding his horse's reins from above. Finally Keith and Larry got the bull roped and tied to a different tree, and Kenney could climb down. He said cold rain fell as he lay in his bedroll in the trailer that night, listening to the bull thrashing against the ropes. Peeking out, he could see drops springing through the air when the ropes tightened. They eventually broke, and Keith and Larry had to rope the bull all over again.

Sometimes my stomach ached with laughter, sometimes with alarm, and sometimes with longing—traveling with Ken and listening to his stories illustrated how much I'd missed.

C⊃-

The Criollo heifers, cows, and the bull, Sue, all carried the genetics of Raramuri Criollo cattle. Small, horned, and athletic, some were spotted like pinto ponies, or dun to deep red like the sandstone formations of the Southwest; some brindle; some a dark reddish-brown with a lighter stripe down their backs and a light muzzle—"mule nose," people call it. Savanna, my grulla mare, is gray with a black dorsal stripe along her spine from her withers to her tail, and black horizontal stripes on the backs of her knees. These "primitive markings" trace back to the early horses; with cattle, primitive markings can be linked to aurochs.

I love the color variations. But as Dennis Maroney says, "Spots are not an advertisement for high-quality feedlot cattle, and consequently, if they have spots or horns, or, worse, if they have both, that's not the way to sell them." Which is why he sells grass-fed Criollo beef. And why we do too.

Years ago a doctor told me I needed to go grain-free. I quickly noticed the difference between grass-fed and grain-fed beef—not only the taste, but on my digestive system. Turns out it was all the additives given feedlot cattle that bothered my stomach. Now I am a happy almost-paleo, devouring our beef like my grandkids, who gnaw on the bones like cavepeople.

Descended from hundreds of generations of desert cattle, Criollos graze grass when it's available and are heavy browsers, munching on greasewood and fourwing saltbush as a matter of choice in our corner of Colorado, or prickly pear and mesquite in southern New Mexico and Arizona. Dennis Moroney has watched his cows stick their tongues deep into cholla cactus and lick the cholla bud out to eat it. This browsing behavior makes them a more versatile and hardier desert breed than any other, except their Corriente relations. But Criollos are a beef breed, unlike Corrientes, the latter selectively bred for thicker horns and even lighter weights for rodeo events, or Texas longhorns, bred for their huge, long horns. And the Raramuri Criollos first seen by Ed Frederickson and Alfredo Gonzalez were practically family pets. I have sat in the middle of the herd and watched every single cow around me buckle her knees and fold her hind end down, landing with a whoosh of expelled air. This demonstrates familiarity and trust—they know me. I have also stayed with one or two cows while the others went off to water or graze, the remaining cows, and me, the calf-sitters. Usually the babysitter is a single cow, who might have fifteen calves with her. I like that they let me calf-sit once in a while.

As we started conducting our own unofficial experiments with our Criollo cows, the government prepared for the federally funded Sustainable Southwest Beef Coordinated Agricultural Project, a "five-year USDA-NIFA funded project that promotes ranch and rangeland resilience in the Southwestern US" using heritage Raramuri Criollo cattle, the hands-on aspect of which would commence in 2019 and run through 2024.

One of the five ranches selected to participate in the program, the 4,500-acre Corte Madera Ranch in Southern California added a few Criollo heifers and a bull to their herd of black Angus cows. Then as drought conditions increased, they went to all Criollo cows. The four additional ranches included the Jornada Experimental Range and the Chihuahuan Desert Rangeland Research Center, both in New Mexico; Evergreen Ranching and Livestock in South Dakota; and Dugout Ranch in southeastern Utah.

Almost a neighboring ranch in this part of the Southwest, where going to visit a friend could mean a one-hundred-mile drive one way, Dugout Ranch first came to my attention when I moved to Moab in 1998. The Nature Conservancy had purchased it the year before. The ranch borders Canyonlands

National Park at the heart of the Colorado Plateau, where arches and spires and deeply iron-reddened rocks grace the skyline.

In 1891, as a nineteen-year-old boy, the "Mormon Cowboy," legendary rancher Al Scorup, started putting together a herd of cattle. He and his older brother, Jim, slept in caves and cow camps for years as they moved cattle from one little oasis of water and grass to another in the deep, hidden canyons of southeastern Utah. By 1910 they had thousands of cattle, including mavericks—unbranded cattle they roped, branded, and therefore owned. Al Scorup and his brother joined forces with two Moab brothers to buy Indian Creek Cattle Company in 1918, which included Dugout Ranch. Their first year, three feet of snow fell in November, followed by more snow, killing 1,500 head and starving the rest to hide-over-bone and dimly pulsing veins. Jim Scorup died during that time, of heartache, Al surmised, as Jim's wife predeceased him before they could ever actually share a house—twenty-six years of cave dwelling and hard riding was, for Jim, meant to culminate in living in a real home with his beloved bride and children.

The Scorup Somerville Cattle Company holdings ran for 150 miles on the east side of the Colorado River. By 1927 Al Scorup and company had permits to run 6,800 head of cattle on national forest land, more than any other U.S. Forest Service permittee, which didn't include what they ran on deeded land. Or the vast numbers of sheep. Starting as a nineteen-year-old boy with a grubstake of a few dollars and some flour and beans, Scorup eventually ran cattle on "a million and a quarter acres of staggering desolation between the San Juan and Colorado rivers, a vast triangle of land that even today is not completely mapped," wrote David Lavender (who once worked for Scorup) in *One Man's West*, originally published in 1943.

In 1967 five-foot-two, eyes-of-blue Heidi Redd and her husband, Robert Redd, moved into a room in the back of the cook shack on Dugout Ranch. Although Heidi came from a non-ag background in Blackfoot, Idaho—skydiving brought her to Utah, where she jumped 198 times—she took to the ranch in the wild red lands of Indian Creek and Canyonlands immediately. After some trading within the Redd family, she and Robert came to own 5,207 deeded acres—a small portion of Indian Creek Cattle Company resources; the rest, about 350,000 contiguous acres, consisted of BLM, Forest Service, and state land. Here Heidi made her home and carved out her own legendary life.

During Heidi and Robert's first year, three feet of snow fell in an unusual snowstorm, killing 350 head—the same way a snowstorm hit the ranch almost fifty years earlier during Al Scorup's first year. By 1989, at the end of Heidi and Robert's marriage, the ranch ran about 900 mother cows, down from 1,400; in contrast with Scorup's 1.25 million acres and 6,800 head, or the 2,500 AUMs the Kane and Two-Mile Ranches could run, the Dugout Ranch numbers seem modest, or, perhaps more appropriately said, in tune with the environment.

When Robert agreed that Heidi could buy him out over time, the ranch in its entirety became her responsibility. A single mother of two sons, Heidi monitored the land, feed, water, cattle, the tourists coming down the now-paved road, and the rock climbers and campers who would increasingly change the landscape. She spent many days on horseback, and soon her sons did too.

In the mid-1990s, after several years of pressure from developers wanting to purchase the Dugout to build condominiums and golf courses, Heidi contacted The Nature Conservancy. It took two years, but ultimately the Redd family supported the sale of the ranch to The Nature Conservancy, the only way to ensure that no development would take place. Heidi has said that accepting the reduced price (about $2 million less than the appraised value) was one way to give back to the land. She retained the cattle, the brand, the government permits, and has lifelong use of her home and the surrounding acres.

In 2009 The Nature Conservancy bought the Dugout cattle for research purposes, creating Canyonlands Research Center in 2010. TNC hired Matt Redd, Heidi's eldest son, to run the ranch and cattle operations after Heidi's official retirement in 2015, with Matt's wife, Kristen, heading the CRC outreach and education programs. In 2018 Matt would purchase ten Criollo cows from Jornada Experimental Range. Right away his observations of the cattle would support what Ken and I had witnessed with our Criollos over the past several years: browsing, covering the country, tolerating heat, traveling long distances to water, ease of calving (due to the low birth weights of the calves), protective mothering, and consuming far less feed and water than the popular European breeds.

5
Birth of a Ranch

We all have to respect each other, and not think our own use is the most important. It isn't climbing, it isn't ranching, it isn't running marathons, it isn't any activity. It's the landscape itself that is the priority.

—Heidi Redd, Dugout Ranch, Utah

Dolores and Disappointment Valley, Colorado, 2015 into 2018

A brief exchange with Amy M. Hale, an award-winning author who has written several excellent books about life in the West, including a favorite novel, *Winter of Beauty*, got me to thinking. When I told her that I ranch too, Amy offered that she is not a rancher, she cowboys for a living.

"That's better than cowboying for free," said I. I didn't mean to sound glib. I was serious.

Amy worked on a fifty-thousand-acre ranch in northern Arizona and rode for day wages, sometimes for weekslong stretches, while I wasn't cowboying nearly enough—whether paid or unpaid. At this point our "ranch" consisted of some deeded acres and several leased pastures on private ground, our cows so gentle we could easily move them on foot—they came when called and followed us from one pasture to another in the few places where fields adjoined.

That is not cowboying. Is it even ranching?

One day I started chores when the sun peered over the mountains of La Plata at seven in the morning. While Ken went to check steers on a lease three miles away, I fed the cattle and horses at headquarters. When Ken still hadn't returned, I texted.

He called. "The steers are out. Kathy's on her way." I followed after quickly changing from manure-stained Wranglers to clean ones, as I had a rare lunch engagement for which this mishap would make me late, but I still wanted to go.

On foot Ken and three-year-old Lucas, who has the brown hair and luminous brown eyes of his mother, had tracked the two-year-old steers and found them bunched together under a juniper. The steers had stayed out all night and, like wayward teenagers, they knew they had done wrong but didn't know how to make it right. Ken and Lucas pushed them toward a corner near their home turf and Kathy held them there while Ken cut the fence and I walked across two pastures carrying flakes of grass hay and calling the steers. They balked, one bolted, and when the first gangly, deep-red horned steer found the hole, the rest followed him right up to me.

Not cowboying.

Despite arriving late for lunch with my friends, I had to leave the lunch early to meet Kelleen, our vet: the kids' two small mustangs needed attention. That done, Ken and I jumped into his waiting pickup and headed to the processing plant an hour and a half away to pick up beef—after an equipment breakdown our beef was finally ready, and we needed to get restocked for the farmers' market early the next morning. Still an hour from the ranch, Ken got a call that a neighbor's dog had chased the same steers through a different fence. And he got a text: on a lease fourteen miles farther away, cows had gotten out.

After we unloaded hundreds of pounds of frozen and boxed beef, Ken went to the closer lease while Kathy, the kids, and I did afternoon chores, which now included doctoring my granddaughter's sweet mustang mare for moon blindness (equine recurrent uveitis, a condition of temporary and fluctuating blindness that can lead to permanent blindness), and a cut on Lucas's little mustang's foreleg. Ken drove up as I finished and, sun at the horizon, we raced off to the other lease. In the twilight I tripped through the thick grass and the marks in the irrigated pasture that guide the water to the lower end of the field, where I opened a gate while Ken pushed the escaped bovines toward the hole. They didn't like our decision, which meant the dogs chased and bit while Ken and I ran and yelled before the cattle acquiesced.

Not cowboying.

Gate closed, fence checked in the near darkness, we drove back to the ranch, where Kathy would have the kids ready for bed and leftovers for Ken. I fed my dogs, ate a salad, and went to bed myself, where I went to work on my other job—writing—which I can do anytime, anywhere, as long as my eyes stay open. Which they didn't, for long.

Amy Hale writes of long days in the saddle, sleeping in cabins at line-camps or on the ground for many nights in a row, trailing cattle through rain and mud. *That* is cowboying.

In *My Ranch, Too: A Wyoming Memoir*, author Mary Budd Flitner writes of ranching in Wyoming for her seventy-something years, moving hundreds of cows from summer pasture to winter range, feeding by draft horses and feed wagons when the trucks can't reach the cattle in the deep winter snow, throwing flakes of hay to the cows in thirty-five-degrees-below-zero weather. *That* is ranching.

Heidi Redd has lived on Dugout Ranch since 1967. Retired from full-time ranching, she still cowboys with her son, moving Criollo and Angus cattle from summer to winter ranges and back again. *That* is ranching *and* cowboying. "Lucky for me," Heidi says in her 2024 book, *A Cowgirl's Conservation Journey*, "retirement did not mean giving up my saddle or missing out on the action."

While I coveted days ahorseback, checking cattle from my seat in the saddle instead of on foot, I did the necessary work, whatever it was that day; I simply didn't think of it as ranching.

In the California ranch country where Keith and I lived, wives often cowboyed with their husbands. I went everywhere Keith went on a horse; with our dogs we could get the work done, until it came to branding season. A favorite time of year, neighbors gathered, and women worked in the corrals beside the men, roping, flanking, castrating. Keith taught me to do everything but castrate (though from watching, I knew I could do that too).

On the New Mexico ranch where Ken worked, brandings also drew friends and neighbors, and Ken "neighbored" on the surrounding ranches when they gathered and branded. I was the only woman I saw on a horse in the corral. In Colorado, without neighbors we knew or friends in the cattle business, we were reduced to me being the only person roping while Ken branded and castrated. Kathy, small and tough, could flank if she needed to, and she also did the vaccinating and supervised the kids.

On this late spring day, cows bawl and mill around outside the corral. Inside the pen, bawling calves cluster in a corner. My mare, Savanna, stands calmly amid the noise and commotion as people bustle over the calf I just roped and brought to them. The calf flanked and down, Tyler holds the back legs and my friend TJ kneels on the neck as Ken brands. TJ, an Army brat who grew up all over, has now lived in the West and worked with mustangs so long that her wind-blown hair and sun-touched skin suggest *wild horse woman*, which she is. Lacey and Lucas, twenty-one months apart and as close as ranch kids get when there are no other children in the neighborhood, stand nearby with the nut bucket, and Kathy has syringes ready. Smells of blood, singed hair, and dust texture the air.

I sit in the middle of it, my saddle as comfortable as a good chair, and rub my hand along Savanna's neck—my hand with its barbed-wire scars and thinning skin, fingers long and more slender than my body has ever been, but strong too—all my life I have been strong except sometimes—the busted fingernails and calloused palm showing work and persistence but not the softness felt on a newborn's head or a lover's cheek. The mare's smooth coat, warm with try, fills that same palm of my hand that holds all the years of my life.

Beyond the corral, irrigated pastures undulate toward Sleeping Ute Mountain, which angles up out of the land. The southern skyline holds Mesa Verde's high buttes, and to the east La Plata still shows seams of snow above timberline. The cows know it's too early for their calves to get weaned, which happens in the fall in Colorado; they also know their calves are being manhandled and the mamas protest loudly. I feel for them as their bags tighten with unspent milk, but I can't linger long in empathy, or memory. Slipping rope through the honda of my lariat, I build a loop, hold it out, and feel the weight of it. Savanna moves, anticipating.

"Go get another one, Mom," Ken says.

Flipping my braid of dirty blond over my shoulder, out of the way, my left knee presses Savanna's left side, turning her toward the huddle of calves as I plot our next move. Lifting my arm, swinging the loop in a slow circle above my wide-brimmed cowboy hat, feeling the smooth momentum, I let the loop slide through the air—and miss, the calf bouncing away.

Mare patient, family patient, they watch and wait for me to bring them another calf, which I do. Of course I do. I must. When that loop sails out and encircles a neck, my left hand, gripping reins and coils, keeps Savanna steady while with my right hand I hold the rope high as the calf startles then jumps and bucks. Jerking the slack out of the rope I go to the horn, dally, and head toward fire and family, the calf trotting behind me as if I'd been doing this all my life without a twenty-year gap between go-rounds.

So I do it again, but between the catches are the misses. The wind starts up. Tiredness shows in the faces of my grandchildren. My boys, on foot, also tired of waiting, swing their own loops at a small calf and catch it and pull it to the fire by hand.

My boys. Young men in their thirties, brothers with tall bodies and taut muscles working and laughing as if they are three years old and six, wrestling each other, not the calf. I may have chosen directions that were not always best for my children, or for me. Yet those directions led me to the middle of a corral in southwestern Colorado, my children the young men to whom I'm dragging calves. The three of us together again.

Savanna waits to see which way my legs will guide her, which calf we will follow next. Each calf a life, a story, which I know almost as well as I know my own children's birth stories—I know their mothers, the days they were born, which calf I saw get dropped to the ground, which one I found still wet in the willows, cow licking calf as if that was all there was to do in the world, no bull around saying follow *me*.

My knees squeeze and Savanna moves toward a light-red heifer I watched get born in the willows near a pond. Lifting my arm into a swing, I throw and catch and dally and gently pull the calf to the fire. My sons smile.

"Nice loop, Mom," Ken says.

I smile too and allow the feel-good.

My world on this day: horses and cows, family and work. The work of a cowboy, but under my skin I feel a scratching like scabies: a real cowboy would catch far more than miss, the way I used to.

In southwestern Colorado, few ranches have contiguous parts. Many ranchers truck cattle up to summer range and back down to winter pasture—summering in subalpine forests after the snow thaws, and wintering in the

6. Kat and Savanna at a branding. Photo by TJ Holmes.

desert, often on Bureau of Land Management public lands, often in Utah. Or they feed cattle at ranch headquarters if they don't have winter range. That's just how it works here. When Keith and I ran cattle, he had pastures leased all over the place (though none on public lands), so piecing together a ranch was a familiar strategy for my sons and me.

7. Tyler surfing on the Animas River, Durango. Photo by Tyler Lausten.

It began with the 171 acres—a ranch designed for horses not cattle, we would modify it over the years and discuss whether to keep it or sell. Meanwhile, it gave us a headquarters where Ken and his family had a house, and another house took care of me, and sometimes Tyler. (A natural athlete like his brother, Tyler follows water. Winter means swells in California; spring and early summer can mean surfable river waves in Idaho, Montana, Wyoming, and Colorado, if winter provided enough snowfall and rain.) We had two income-producing rentals, barns for horses and equipment, an arena and round pen. I boarded horses, then didn't. We put in fences and repaired broken ones. Ken and Tyler built cattle pens.

Meanwhile, by happenstance, I wandered into a valley called Disappointment and fell quickly in love: with its mustangs; with a 160-acre inholding that shares a perimeter fence with mustangs; with an off-grid cabin that sits on a cliff above Disappointment Creek and overlooks creek, cottonwoods, canyon, sagebrush, piñon pine, and juniper, with views of the Glade, Groundhog Peak, the tip of Lone Cone, and the dramatic sandstone formations rimming the upper valley. To the west, La Sal Mountains of Utah hold the horizon. Piñon jays fly overhead. Sometimes I see mustangs from the cabin's kitchen or bedroom windows.

I soon found that what I call the mustang cabin nourished me the way I imagine Mount Diablo nourished my grandmother, though our needs were likely differently spawned. I felt as if I needed the quiet, peace, and time *away*, and Disappointment Valley and the mustang cabin are *away* from everything: forty-five miles away from headquarters in summer when the dirt road over the mountain is open, eighty miles in winter when I have to drive around, forty-seven miles from a gas station or store. I needed *away* to write and to soothe my sometimes-troubled soul. For a long time, drugs did that. And now that I have lived without drugs for a much longer time, sitting on the cabin porch listening to the quiet, or watching water move, or cattle or turkeys or deer, gives me a deep and necessary calm. As does watching mustangs, their family-band bonds, their flight-or-fight instincts at work, how they survive. This way of being *away* may be my best teacher yet.

Upvalley from the mustang cabin, a section—640 acres or a square mile—had been for sale for half a dozen years. Equipped with a Nature Conservancy easement, it angled and cut back on itself and crossed the road and bordered a BLM wilderness study area, fenced in some places, not in others. A mile and a half of Disappointment Creek meandered through the section, yet no one wanted it because you can't hunt on it. Which was fine by me.

A similar situation presented itself with what we call the Nichols Wash pasture downvalley near Slick Rock. Also listed for several years, the 1,425-acre parcel didn't sell because the oil company owners had not bothered to secure agricultural taxes even though neighbors' herds had grazed that land for at least thirty years. With the backing of an agricultural bank, we got it for a song and documented ag use with the previous lessee's records and the ones we generated the first year. Taxes dropped by thousands. (Landowners in Colorado are known for buying a few head of livestock for their thirty-five acres in order to qualify for ag taxes. Our intention was to use the pasture exclusively for cattle, which we do.)

Working on 2,225 noncontiguous deeded acres enfolded within hundreds of thousands of BLM acres topped with national forest, I felt safe and home and *away*.

Disappointment Valley, as the story goes, was named by a party of surveyors in the late 1800s. From the hills above the valley the men saw a winding green trail of cottonwoods, which meant water. They hastened down to the trees only to find a dry creekbed.

The valley stretches over about forty miles. Lone Cone, a singular peak rising 12,618 feet above sea level and visible from a hundred miles away, marks the valley's tapered beginning as well as the westernmost reach of the San Juan Range of the southern Rockies. From Lone Cone's base, the valley slopes west-northwest, rimmed by huge buttes, high cliffs and fins, and cracked and broken rimrock, its southern perimeter the long line of mountain called the Glade. Fifty-five hundred feet above sea level at its low end, Disappointment Valley disappears into a redrock canyon and the Dolores River near Slick Rock, the valley abutting redrock layers typical of southeastern Utah: Navajo Sandstone topping the Kayenta Formation, Wingate cliffs below.

Sharing its geologic makeup with a dozen valleys in the Paradox Basin—nearby Big Gypsum, Dry Creek Basin, and Paradox Valley in southwestern Colorado, and Spanish and Castle Valleys in Utah, among others—Disappointment Valley embodies the phenomenon of collapsed valleys. These valleys formed from the weight of overlying rock formations squishing the plastic salt domes of the much earlier Paradox Formation. Liquid escaped, the Paradox Formation settled, and the layers on top fell in. Like a failed cake. These valleys host creeks that run from the mountains to the Dolores and Colorado Rivers. The Dolores River turns north past Dolores-town, rounds to the east of La Sal Mountains, and merges with the Colorado River in Utah north of those peaks.

If Santa Cruz Island looks from above like a flightless chicken, a map of the Dolores River watershed—which contains the different aspects of our ranch—might look like a dancing pig. Its snout in Utah at the confluence of the Dolores and Colorado Rivers, its ears the canyons siding West Creek, San Miguel River its backbone, with Telluride (I'm sorry to say) at its rectum. La Sal Creek joins near the sternum, and Big Gypsum and Disappointment Creeks spill into the guts of the Dolores. The West Dolores could drain into the bladder some miles above the town of Dolores, where the Dolores River turns and follows the belly of the beast north.

Within that pig, Lone Cone might be a hipbone, where the headwaters of Disappointment Creek form; Groundhog Peak may be the other hipbone. A ridgeline that parallels Disappointment Creek could be an intestine (Ken might say it's the bowels).

I like the pig dancing on its short, stumpy canyon legs.

The stories of the earliest people in Disappointment Valley are carved in stone. "The whole valley . . . was occupied for the last 13,000 years," says Fort Lewis College archaeology professor Jesse Tune. He and nine students spent six weeks in Disappointment documenting archaeological sites as well as sites of major looting. Tools such as a thirteen-thousand-year-old Clovis spearpoint indicate that people lived here as hunter-gatherers at the end of the Ice Age. Did they leave with the megafauna die-off or did they continue adapting and evolving with climatic changes, the forebears of today's regional tribes? Answers may be found in the petroglyphs and in the tribal stories.

All this country—Disappointment Valley and the nearby valleys, rivers, plateaus, mesas, mountains, and beyond; in fact much of Colorado—is ancestral Ute and Paiute land, through which Diné often traveled. In the 1850s Utes were forced onto "smaller and smaller reservations," writes Jonathan P. Thompson in *Sagebrush Empire*. The Brunot Agreement of 1873 took from the tribes millions of acres in the San Juan Mountains and on the Western Slope. The agreement included a provision that allowed Utes to "hunt upon said land so long as the game lasts and the Indians are at peace with the white people." Today, after the hunting-by-lottery seasons, Ute tribal members get special permits to hunt deer and elk on their old hunting grounds in Disappointment Valley and elsewhere—permission to hunt their homeland.

Regina Lopez-Whiteskunk, writer, activist, and Ute Mountain Ute tribal member, has deep ties to Disappointment Valley and the Four Corners region. Her great-grandfather was born in Disappointment in the late 1800s, around the time the first white settlers arrived. Whites fought Native inhabitants for land use and "ownership," a concept unfamiliar to those who had lived with the land for eons, and the valley changed.

In 2015 Regina became a member (the only woman) of the Bears Ears Inter-Tribal Coalition. She served as co-chair and worked with four other tribes. From warring in the past came contemporary peaceful ties, and Regina feels the connection between the tribes and others who share the landscape. Most importantly, she is connected to the land. As her elders taught her—her parents and grandparents, who learned from their parents, and theirs, back through the generations—a person comes from more than a birthplace. As Regina told the Bears Ears Partnership for the article "A Powerful Indigenous Woman's Step into Leadership & Healing," "home" includes a person's history, ties, lineage, and family. This shows me that part of what I'm doing here, by reaching back into family lineage of place and purpose, is defining my home.

In the first documented European exploration of the territory, Juan Antonio María de Rivera kept minimalist journals of his company's horseback-and-pack-mule travels into southwestern Colorado, studied and elaborated upon by author Steven G. Baker and translator Rick Hendricks in *Juan Rivera's Colorado, 1765*. Rivera meant to reach the Rio de Tizón (Colorado River) and cross it in search of the people of Teguayo—mystery people who wore heavy beards so were presumed white. Fearing competition for hidden riches, the Spaniards wanted to investigate.

Rivera's trek started in Santa Fe, New Mexico, in July 1765. The company got to Big Bend on the Dolores River (then a camp where different tribes congregated, eventually a white-settler community, now under "Lake" McPhee). Paiutes in camp stressed the heat (the desert temperatures topping one hundred degrees in July), and Rivera and company returned to Santa Fe, regrouped, and set out again in more merciful October.

Before he headed south, Rivera had secured guides for the next trip. From Big Bend what would become the Old Spanish Trail headed northwest toward Moab, an easier route, but on October 6, 1765, Rivera's Paiute guides followed another trace (the Navajo-Uncompahgre Trail), which headed across the river and up to the Dolores Plateau. Under heavy skies the company crossed the high, flat land of little water, making camp at either Bradfield or Black Snag Springs. Rivera called the area La Soledad.

They had to drop off the plateau somewhere, and it appears that they descended near the confluence of Dolores River and Disappointment Creek, where the company encountered several paralyzed Ute women on the banks of the bigger river. In his journals Rivera calls the river Rio de los Dolores. (In the 1776 journals of Fathers Atanasio Domínguez and Silvestre Vélez de Escalante, they refer to the river as Rio de Nuestra Señora de los Dolores—the River of Our Lady of Sorrows.) Rivera's company camped that night by Disappointment Creek, which Rivera named Rio de San Francisco. The next day, heading east-northeast, the party crossed Disappointment Valley, probably stepping very near our Nichols Wash pasture as they headed toward the "pass of San Francisco" (Gypsum Gap) to Gypsum Valley.

They made it as far as the Gunnison River near Delta, but Rivera and his men turned around before reaching the Colorado River or seeing the people of Teguayo. His thin journals aided Fathers Domínguez and Escalante on their better-known 1776 expedition.

Rivera's writings offer a visual of southwestern Colorado valleys when Utes, Paiutes, and Diné moved over the land long before the presence of white people, cattle, and sheep. Rivera wrote of "beautiful valleys" and said of Dry Creek Basin, "How pleasant its valley and beautiful swamps with several springs that flow due west." He commented on the abundance of grass, wood, and shelter in addition to water. How different from today.

The history of white settlers in Disappointment Valley began in the 1880s. A menagerie of marriages, divorces, cheating, gambling, and gunfights followed the early arrivals, some of which is documented by Wilma Crisp Bankston in *Where Eagles Winter: History and Legend of the Disappointment Country*. Lizzy Embling, the first woman rancher in the valley, arrived in 1881. At less than five feet tall, with a strong English brogue, Lizzy blacksmithed and raised dairy cows in Rico when the mining boom began. Wed to William Embling after a previous marriage in England went bad, Lizzy married off her daughter from that earlier union to one Henry Knight. Before the cold struck, Henry Knight took Lizzy's cows to winter in Disappointment.

Back in Rico in the spring, Henry's wife made him sleep elsewhere. Lizzy's husband apparently sheltered another woman. Lizzy took her cows back to Disappointment Valley, and Henry went to help her. When Lizzy brought legal charges against William Embling, Embling filed for divorce, and Lizzy married Henry Knight, her former son-in-law, twenty days after the divorce was final. Together they raised Edith, Henry's daughter and

Lizzy's granddaughter. Lizzy and Henry's union lasted until Lizzy's death in the valley in 1914.

Her original cabin and the homestead still stand, maintained by Marsha Bankston (Wilma's daughter) and designated a Centennial Farm by the state of Colorado. Lizzy Knight was buried in Lavender Cemetery, on a peaceful knoll that overlooks part of the valley where our cows graze in winter. Among the headstones of valley residents from the late 1800s to early 1900s lie the graves of infants and small children—a picture of what women went through and the harsh conditions of the time and place.

When the California court system ordered that my children would live with Keith, for a while I didn't want to survive—*and my kids were alive.* Without them I hit the depths of despair, and drugs helped me reach the bottom of my life. And then I got clean, so I could live—for them. For me. I can't imagine how the mothers who birthed and lost child after child kept on. Some didn't, dying too early, and another woman would take up the challenge of caring for the widower and his remaining children, often adding more children to the brood.

Although barbed wire was invented in 1878, Disappointment Valley didn't have fences in the days of Lizzy and Henry Knight. Families branded their own cattle, then ran them all together. In summer Disappointment cowboys would drive the herds up to the mountains in the Groundhog area, Beaver Creek, or the Glade, and gather them in the fall, sorting some off to go to market and herding the remainder back down to Disappointment to winter. BLM has no records of exact numbers of cattle, though in the Tres Rios Field Office in Dolores, records tell of sheepmen annually running thousands of sheep from the high end of the valley to the low end, leaving the land as shorn as sheep after shearing. Many native grasses known by the first people of the valley and later seen by Rivera didn't grow back.

My nearest neighbors, Cliff and Cindy Bankston, live five miles up the dirt, gravel, and rocky road from the mustang cabin (sometimes the road is fixed with fist-sized and larger "gravel," which, when the smaller stuff washes away, leaves tire-eating rocks). The sixth generation of his family to live in Disappointment, Cliff descends from the original white settlers: through Edith Knight he is related to both Lizzy and Henry Knight. Through his family generations back he knows the stories of some of the fighting against Utes that took place. They were eventually forced out of the valley. Cliff still ranches and farms at the old homestead. His sister and brother have properties that border his, the section we acquired was once Cliff's, and his brother owned the "rock chimney," a local name for the inholding wherein sits the contemporary mustang cabin. Near a low ledge above the creek I found the rock foundation of the old homestead, including the stone threshold, but no evidence of the chimney at one time visible from the road.

Cliff, my elder by several years, decided to let go of his BLM Salt Arroyo Allotment, which wraps around his place, adjoins the section, and runs west toward the mustang cabin. Winter pasture. Ken and I took it over, paying Cliff an agreed-upon price and transferring the permit to Cachuma Ranch through the BLM office. Cliff, who had watched his son and others of Ken's generation turn from agriculture to jobs that pay better, was happy to see a young man ranching, and perhaps he was happy to see a woman ranching as well. We got the 11,003-acre winter allotment, our properties and Cliff's interconnect, and Cliff has become a good friend.

Some people refer to grazing on public lands as welfare ranching. Here's how the system works on Bureau of Land Management land: First, you purchase a ten-year grazing permit from the previous permittee for thousands to hundreds of thousands of dollars, depending on how many animal unit months, or AUMs, the permit allows (an AUM is based on a thousand-pound cow with or without a calf at her side). You must have "base property" to attach to it—enough deeded acreage to handle the cattle in the off-season. BLM decides how many AUMs a permit will run, as well as the on- and off-dates, based on studies of forage—the grasses, their growing seasons, the kinds of soil, average rainfall, history of use, all of that. In other words, BLM uses science to determine the carrying capacity of the land.

The Bureau of Land Management works with you during your ten-year contract. In drought years BLM can tell you to run fewer head, or none, or adjust grazing dates. This doesn't retroactively impact the purchase price of the permit—you could buy a ten-year grazing permit for five hundred AUMs and not be able to run any cattle for two of your ten years. The contract can be pulled at any time—if you overstock or understock, if your cattle trespass repeatedly onto the neighbors' land because you don't maintain your fences, or for any number of other reasons. BLM can reassess the carrying capacity and cut your AUMs permanently. Since the permit holder and real estate market determined the value, BLM doesn't care what you paid for it, or if you get your money's worth. It cares, theoretically, about the health of the land.

The purchase is a one-time transaction. The annual grazing fees may change but remain cheap, and this is why people call it welfare ranching: the government determines that fee. I've seen it fluctuate between $1.35 per AUM to $2.10. Multiply that by five hundred AUMs and it might cost around $5,000 a year to run cattle for that season—in grazing fees only. Now add to that the payments to the bank, plus interest, for the money borrowed to acquire that permit. The longer you have the permit, the lower that will average out, but it's money out of pocket that no one I ever knew on welfare could have paid. Still, the purchase of the permit was thousands—or more likely millions—*less* than if you bought deeded land of similar acreage and forage.

You're responsible for maintaining fences. And for hauling water if the water sources go dry. You may have to rent or own a bulldozer to access fencelines, or to clean out ponds. Which means you either rent or own a lowboy trailer to haul the dozer.

Dare I mention time? You have to check miles of fence before turning cattle out and throughout your stay. You have to monitor herd health and rangeland conditions and look for wayward cattle—yours or the neighbors'. For some ranchers once a week might do, but too many things can go wrong and I'm with my cows several times a week.

You can also factor in other expenses, though many of these are the same whether your animals graze on public or private land: what you pay truck drivers to haul cattle; the pickups and trailers you need to check cattle and move smaller numbers around; and horses, tack, feed, medicine, brand inspections, fence supplies, and equipment.

At the end of ten years, if all has gone well, you sign another ten-year contract. But you don't pay another purchase price—that was a one-time deal. The longer you have the permit, the better deal it was. And you can always sell, maybe for more than you paid.

On the other hand, if you have a lease with private landowners, you don't have to pay big bucks in advance. And the landowners will often share costs of fence maintenance; they may even fill water troughs or break ice. You negotiate this into the price of the lease, which the landowner and cattle owner might together determine along with cattle numbers and grazing dates. You still cover maintenance costs of cattle, hauling, and vet and horse expenses.

The financial difference between running cattle seasonally on a private lease or on a government lease may come down to a few dollars per AUM. But, again, you don't have to pay millions to purchase the land. Having a grazing permit on public lands is a privilege, not a right. As Heidi Redd has said, "It's ridiculous to put up a fuss" about the rules and regs.

And there's this: the number of AUMs doesn't change if you run bigger cows, smaller cows, or some steers (which weigh less than mature cows), which contributes to why ranchers started raising bigger cows. If you pay the same per month for a 1,000-pound cow or a 1,400-pound cow, and your total AUMs remain the same, why not run the bigger cow? She will theoretically produce a calf with a higher weaning weight, which will bring more money. And, right now anyway, the government doesn't care if you have 850-pound cows or 1,400-pound cows—the price per AUM is the same.

Not so the impact on the land. Bigger cows need a lot more forage and a lot more water.

I believe in the ethics of low-impact grazing. I know it's better for the land. But ethics and finances don't always mix. As a rancher—if I am a rancher—making decisions like what kind of cattle to run can cost me, if I lean toward ethical over commercial. Which I do. As Criollo cattleman Dennis Moroney says, financial pressure on farmers and ranchers can lead to prioritizing quantity over sustainability. My ethics could cost me right out of the cattle business.

Sadly, debt and drought (and perhaps moral conundrums) contribute to the emotional stress and high suicide rate among Colorado ranchers and farmers.

6
Labor

Let me live into love.

—Rosemerry Wahtola Trommer, "Untamed"

Disappointment Valley, Colorado, 2018

Male cattle are born bulls. At a young age a lucky few might get chosen to remain bulls, but most are castrated, becoming steers. In the commercial cattle world, these steers usually get turned out on pasture for a season after weaning and then taken to the feedlot, where they're fattened for ninety to 150 days on a mixed high-energy ration often containing genetically modified corn, grains, hay, silage, minerals, and vitamins, with growth hormones and subtherapeutic antibiotics given to them regularly in their feed. The feedlot steers, 1,400 to 1,500 pounds of live weight at harvest, carry those growth hormones and antibiotics to the dinner table.

Because it takes longer for Criollo grass-finished steers to reach a mature weight, our steers (hormone- and antibiotic-free) have nearly twice the lifespan of feedlot steers. Weaned, pastured separately from their mothers until spring, we then turn them out together as yearlings—cows, yearling steers, two-year-olds, and those going on three. I've seen Money (whose left side bears two large dollar-sign brands, hence Ken's name for her) with her three-year-old heifer-turned-cow, two-year-old steer, yearling steer, and current calf, the family of five lounging in the spring sunshine like a band of mustangs (unlike a bull, a mustang stallion stays with his band to protect it and keep rivals away, whereas bulls roam the countryside, going from cow to cow in search of those entering estrus). Criollo cows have the same strong mothering instincts as mustang mares, and they like having their kids around.

Money's horns and the white spots sprinkled throughout her light red coat indicated longhorn influence, but we had needed more cows so we bought her along with Curlie, Bobbi, and Rabbit's mother. Money's calves have Appaloosa butts, except Marshmallow, who is white all over (we don't usually name the steers, but Lacey couldn't help herself). Money has modeled the fertility and protective mothering for which Criollos and their descendants are known. The first in the herd to lift her head when an intruder approaches—coyote, dog, horse, me—Money watches with a look that says, "Don't even think about it." Because of her thick, tipped horns, people say she looks like a rodeo bull—their horns get cut off at the ends so they don't spear fallen riders or pick-up men or horses. "Money-Money," I call, and she relaxes a bit, but if a predator were to approach her calf or the herd, I have no doubt Money would use those horns.

Some of the division of labor between Ken and me came about naturally. I love calving season, genetics, and keeping records of who did what when, and it has fallen to Ken to take the steers to the processing plant, where butchering happens and the meat gets stamped with USDA approval for public purchase. The facility we use is Animal Welfare Approved based on annual inspections and certified for humane livestock-handling techniques. I went with Ken the first time. Since then he has taken care of this alone.

Some tasks we do together, like the other day when, on our hands and knees and then on our bellies like soldiers, we pushed through a thick stand of Gambel oak. Commonly called scrub oak, the native, deciduous trees spread liberally around the Four Corners region. One of the first plants to recover after fire, Gambel oak can grow to thirty feet tall, and it grew in abundance where we needed to work—on the south side of the canyon, the north face—where years of detritus held moisture. The opposing canyon sides smelled as different as they felt, one dry, exposed sandstone showing geologic age and wear and garnering the sun's warmth, the side we needed to ascend pungent, shed leaves and twigs mixing with dark, fertile earth and smelling like soil, not dust or stone.

Truly one step forward, three back, my feet slipped constantly downhill, oak branches snagging my braid. Pushing a circle of barbed wire in front of me, with a free hand I clung to roots that held tightly to their own struggles.

When Ken reached firm footing, he grabbed the wire I held and pulled me up to relatively solid ground, though the angles of our ankles remained precarious. Then the bucket with fence pliers, clips, staples, and the rusting cans I find everywhere slipped, tipping to its side as it rolled, and I had to slide back down to retrieve those supplies and claw my way back up.

So it went as we strung and tightened wire along the old, thick metal T-posts graciously left by an earlier fence-builder. After we completed that stretch of fence, we stashed our tools and explored. At the canyon rim, a large chunk of Dakota Sandstone, eroded at its base by water and wind, made a protective overhang, and traces of black curled up the underbelly of the rock like smoke. Which perhaps it once was—stains left by early campfires, possibly of the people who populated this land for eons before Spanish conquistadors came through, followed by cattle ranchers and sheepherders and bad guys like Butch and Sundance.

First a cowboy, Bud Parker, as he was known in these parts, worked for a Paradox Valley rancher who summered his cattle on the north side of Lone Cone. The cattle drifted to the south side of the mountain, which put Parker in the vicinity of some Disappointment cowboys summering at Groundhog. Noting that Parker was a hand with both cattle and pistol, the Disappointment cowboys welcomed him into their circle. In 1889 Parker and three men rode into Telluride and robbed San Miguel Valley Bank of more than $20,000. Parker knew the Disappointment country well by then and quickly disappeared, arriving in Utah sometime later. No one in Disappointment Valley told who gave the bank robbers food and fresh horses, but when Parker became better known as Butch Cassidy, a hint of pride showed on the faces of some Disappointment cowboys.

Yes, in our valley, this cross-section of human story. And now we have added our desert-adapted cattle to the tale.

Ken and I slid on our butts back down the steep, moist side of the canyon, clutching tools and bucket, then we crawled beneath the tangle of scrub oak to creekside, where we could stand and stretch and see again the high-desert sky.

⊂⊃-

The mustang cabin now houses me for my day job of overseeing the cows wintering in Disappointment Valley. I haul water or break ice as needed.

The morning of winter solstice, for example, I rise in the dark, hoping to get to the frozen creek before the cows do. Hefting the heavy maul, I slam it into four-inch-thick ice sheets as if I'm splitting wood, except the creek is at my feet instead of a log on a block, and my back groans with the bend and my breath comes short, and even though I did this yesterday (on my birthday—I turned sixty-four) it will take me an hour, but soon the cows will wander into this small area of riparian corridor, a "water trap" Ken and I built (with water gaps upstream and down, the cattle are fenced off from the rest of the creek). The cows will watch me, and wait, and when I step aside they will check the water, smell it, taste it, and, understanding that it's still ice cold, they will drink. And I will watch them and feel happy about these birthday and solstice gifts of water and work.

In winter I feed if I must (but only on private ground—BLM and Forest Service don't allow feeding anything but certified and expensive weed-free hay on public lands); check the cattle for health, fitness, and whereabouts; move them around; and, come spring, calve them out. Which means I watch the cows do the work, help if necessary—rare among Criollos, who typically throw calves weighing less than fifty pounds—and log the results.

When a cow gets close to calving, maybe a couple of days out, her udder gets bigger, her vulva swells and elongates, and her flanks may look gaunt—the pelvic ligaments and muscles sinking as the calf moves into position. When it's her time, the cow will usually walk away from the herd as if looking for something. The right place. She might graze and gaze for the next several hours, which may be what we call nesting (this varies from cow to cow, birth to birth). With Kenney's birth, I ironed my bathrobe between my water breaking and leaving for the hospital—not before or since have I ironed a bathrobe. Keith beside himself with angst, I felt dreamily calm, took a shower, ironed, and after a while we headed to the hospital an hour away.

The cow finds her nest, walks around, her tail switching as if at flies. We won't have flies yet, but to be sure I look at other cows' tails, which hang still. Between tail swishes, she might butt her sides, lift a hind leg and lick at her belly, and maybe she circles like a dog chasing its tail, trying to see behind her. Clearly she's getting ready, though it could still be an hour or two.

When her tail angles straight out behind her, not switching or swatting but like an English riding crop—flexible with a tassel at the end—she's for sure in labor. I note the time. Longer than an hour might mean something's wrong. I watch from a vehicle if it's cold or snowing, or sit on a patch of earth behind greasewood, far enough away that she doesn't sense me as threat.

She turns with her straightened tail and looks behind her and soon enough a bubble will appear, large or small. This is when I get nervous. If her water has broken, I give her twenty minutes before I get really nervous. My water broke at Jedlicka's, a western store in Los Olivos, as I bent down to try on cowboy boots, standing not sitting so I could reach over my belly to my feet, and whoosh the water came out and my butt looked as if I'd been riding bareback, though it was amniotic fluid not horse sweat. I turned my hind end to show the clerks, who laughed as I did, but when I wanted to try on more boots they shooed me out of the store.

The cow's bubble of sac may get larger, then disappear, and she will lie down and seem almost as if she's resting, so I train the binoculars on her back end, on the bubble, which grows or recedes as she stands again, and I may or may not see the creamy color of a hoof. That's when I get really anxious and try hard to see if it's two hooves and are they facing up or down. The hooves may also disappear and reappear. By then I'm telling the cow to *push* and groaning myself and praying and urging, and I clench my own parts against the pain or against the pushing; the cow might push the calf's forelegs twelve inches out and then I want to see the nose—such agony—and I tell her to push, *push!* She may lie down again and then stand up, tail straight out, her back rounded, and the bubble of gray-blue comes out, huge, and the calf drops to the ground, cow looking behind her again and turning around to start licking the calf who may not show movement yet or may already be shaking its head—more anxiety as I want to *know* the nose is clear of the sac. That the calf can breathe. I wait as it struggles to stand. I wait until it stands and nurses. Then I leave and want to take a nap.

⊂⊃-

In winter, second to watching the cattle comes writing and staying warm. The latter involves cutting wood. On the different properties that constitute the ranch, piñon and juniper die and eventually lie in a pile of trunk and branches. Gathering wood is part of winter for Ken, Tyler, and me. Sometimes we have three chainsaws going. Other times they cut while I carry. Together we unload and stack. We create burn piles of branches too small for cutting and burn them (my grown-up boys' favorite part) when we have snow enough for safety. Getting it all done early would deprive us of physical work when most needed—on the darkest days of winter.

At the cabin I do everything but burn—cutting, hauling, splitting, stacking—and I do it alone. It helps keep me sane, like breaking ice and checking cattle, because it forces me outside—*outside*, like *away*, a necessity for sanity in winter, where seasonal affective disorder lurks in the shadows.

Today sunlight highlights rock faces and pine tops and ravens' wings, the probing light and its warmth the glory of this high-desert country in winter. Sunlight allows me *outside*.

I put fuel and lube oil in the chainsaw. Push the bubble in four times. Set the lever on choke. Pop the safety bar down. Step on the handle with my boot and pull the cord. This is a newer chainsaw, and I don't just pull until I've flooded it—I pull halfway and let go and one of those times it will start. Which it does. I pop the safety bar off and squeeze the throttle and let the engine run for seconds and remember to turn off the choke. Then I turn the saw off, adjust my hard hat, and walk to a downed tree. My dogs have disappeared—Bow, a black-and-white, short-haired border collie–McNab, one-eared and three-legged; and Jessi, a female border collie I found after I yielded to the pain in Cojo's legs and asked my vet to put him down. These two don't like loud noises, and even when I break ice in the creek they hide.

Chainsaw on again, I remind myself before I start each cut to pay attention to the placement of my feet, the position of branch or log, the debris that can trip the sawblade, or me.

Second-husband Smith taught me to use a chainsaw—how to stand, cut, other safety tips—and he asked me to vow not to cut wood alone. But our marriage vows didn't endure, which in my mind made the woodcutting promise obsolete. Still, I think of him when I cut wood. Even when I split wood he's there, showing me—California and Hawaiʻi girl—how best to manage the heavy maul, wrists and weight working together. Us working together, until we didn't. Smith back in Montana, I cut wood alone in my hard hat and steel-toed boots, my stance wide for stability and safety, chainsaw held away from my body.

I heard the stories when I was with my first love, me sixteen, seventeen, living in the Sierra Nevada valley hugged by mountains of pine and fir and spruce, him two and a half years older than me and working in those woods—that's what the men did if they didn't ranch or cowboy. Craig told me about bucking logs—walking along the downed trunks of trees, hoping they didn't roll, trained muscles and spiked logging boots helping him balance and stick as he held the heavy chainsaw and cut off limbs to make logs for the trucks to haul.

Dropping branches around me, I watch the angle of bough and blade and think of him, thighs hard as stone, arms and chest smooth muscle, the highwater pants he wore like all the loggers so their hems wouldn't snag on a limb or bite of the saw; those black, steel-toed, spiked boots and the hard hats; black metal lunchboxes and red gas cans and chainsaws packed up mountains each day. Me the Bay Area girl living with Craig's logging family, the dad having only ever worked in the woods, a younger brother starting, mother and sister cooking and cleaning and packing lunches, and me loving them all but not the logging and hunting, downed trees and downed deer a culture away from mine—Sierra Club girl. Sierra mountain men.

I remember the stories. Stoney's blade hit a knot and bounced back, nearly severing his hand. He was out of work and drunk for months. Mike's blade caught his cuff, but he shut off the saw before it cut off his leg. Craig ran from a falling tree and tripped, a stob puncturing his thigh.

He fell on a Monday. Wouldn't see a doctor, wouldn't stay home, hiking up the steep slopes each day until something else happened. On Friday.

As he felled a large ponderosa, a limb (a widowmaker they're called) crashed without warning and Craig couldn't run, and maybe didn't have time, and maybe the widowmaker knocked him out first—maybe he didn't see the whole huge tree lean. And sway. And fall. On him. The steel-toed boots and hard hat did nothing to help Craig that day. He was twenty-one.

I think *wouldn't it be ironic if* . . . , and make myself pay attention when using my chainsaw. And make myself go outside each winter day, because I also remember the darkness into which I plummeted when Craig died. When the court and Keith took my kids. When Rebecca died, and both my fathers. As with the chainsaw, I have to be careful.

7

Shadow Side

On the first day of class, a professor in the animal science program at Colorado State University walked up to the blackboard, wrote SEX in big letters, turned to the students, and said, "It's what drives men crazy and cattle through fences. That's all you need to know."

—Anonymous customer at Mama Bear's Bakery & Books, Dolores, Colorado

---

Disappointment Valley, Colorado, 2018–19

It's already started, I think, as I tell the dogs to stay *right there*, holding my hand up, flat of the palm to them, a stop sign. Jessi and Bow settle beside a bony stalk of greasewood and my attention returns to the bull. He thinks he's hidden behind a bushy piñon pine, which in fact he almost is, both tree and bovine squat and thick, but his red-Angus color shows through the verdure like redrock, only here the Dakota Sandstone runs dun to buckskin, so he's darker.

Afoot not ahorseback, I step slowly along the fenceline, making my way to the wire gate in the corner, glancing back at the dogs and reminding them with my hand to *stay*, hoping the bull also stays put. His choices: make a run down the fenceline, away; or down into the creek bottom, away; or directly at the fence, over it or through it; or directly at me.

Bulls have bumped me before. It's not all that fun. One time a young Brangus bull threw me onto a six-foot-high wooden fence, his head hitting my butt and lifting me to the top rail, which I rolled over like a pole-vaulter, smacking packed earth on the other side. When Keith leaned down to see if I was all right, I held up my hand, the tip of a finger smarting. "I think I got a splinter."

Another time, a red Angus bull had refused to go with the cows to the pens, so Keith roped him and dallied around the trunk of a thick oak. "Come here," he said, and I stepped off my horse and snuck over, keeping the tree between the bull and me as Keith handed me the rope. "Don't let go," he said, and he rode off at a lope to get the trailer, my horse standing by.

The bull, hot, pissed off, glared at me as I tried to hide behind the tree. Several times he charged and I jumped out of the way while still holding the rope. Not soon enough, I heard the trailer rattling up the dirt road. The bull charged again, the rope on his end longer now from our dance around the tree, and I couldn't take it anymore—I let go and ran, Keith jumping from the truck, yelling, "Keep going, don't look back," so I turned my head and saw red right behind me and in that moment the bull gained on me, head lowered, and hit me in the ass with everything he had. I flew twenty feet before rolling across soil and rocks and cheatgrass, covering my head and waiting for it, but the bull had hit the end of his rope, which somehow held around the tree.

Keith jumped his horse out of the trailer, mounted, and hastily threw a second loop over the bull's head. From his horse he threaded the lariat through the slats on the side of the gooseneck. I ventured closer, wanting to get to my horse. Keith dallied, and his horse pulled the bull toward the trailer, but the bull, hot and angry, sulled up, lay down, and died. Right there by the open door of the trailer. Keith didn't check that time to see if I was okay.

Bulls in general are temperamental, unpredictable. Moody, cowboys would say if bulls were women. Bulls are only with their cows a few short months each year, which might explain their easy turn toward anger.

Now in my sixties, I'm more conscious of risk. In this remote valley, if the bull were to charge and hit me I might lie on the ground for a long time before anyone bent over me, though surely Jessi and Bow would eventually stop staying and come to see what I found so interesting in the dirt. Each thing I do out here, from woodcutting, to hoisting bales of hay, to chasing off a neighbor's bull, has a shadow side of danger, small or large. It's as if my physical vulnerability reflects that of the land—mistakes can have long-lasting impacts.

I know my own bulls. Their genetics, ages, and behaviors. And still they're unpredictable. This one I don't know, though I can guess he's not used to a woman angling around him on foot. Or talking to him.

"See the gate? Just wait; you'll get out soon enough." He watches me, his belly swollen with creek water and the hay he tore loose from my stack, the haystack now a mess.

It's not just the mess that irks me—it's the cost of time and hay and whatever other feed the bull has consumed. Yet technically it's my fault he's here. In the fence-out state of Colorado, the landowner bears the responsibility of keeping the fences up if you don't want other people's livestock on your property. Which I don't—I'm saving the feed for my own cattle. While some of the Bureau of Land Management ranges might be grazed down to dust—I heard one rancher say his cows had grazed the sunshine off the rocks—this inholding has cover and winter feed. Which is probably what first drew the bull over the fence. Then he found the hay.

Most of my neighbor's cattle have already drifted down from the high country. The cowboy, Jeff, who seasons at a headquarters thirty miles away, heads out ahorseback to gather the remnants. Each time I see him drive by with cowdogs in the truck bed and a horse in his trailer, I feel the pang of envy. I want to go too. "It's not up to me," Jeff has said when I've offered help (knowing better and doing it anyway), which means his boss has the final say, though I suspect it also means that Jeff honors the traditions in this part of the West. The few ranch women I've met may ride with their husbands, but none of them rope. If women venture into the branding pen, they're handed syringes.

And here I am, alone, afoot, dealing with Jeff's boss's bull.

Were I ahorseback, I'd be quicker. And taller. Safer. But the horses won't come out until Sunday, when we haul our cows to Salt Arroyo Allotment. I won't wait until Sunday.

Emboldened by my annoyance about the gender discrepancies that have followed ranching this far into the twenty-first century, I march to the corner, open the wire gate, drape it over greasewood instead of tucking it out of the way, and walk around behind the bull. Neither Jessi nor Bow have moved, nor has the bull, though now he sees the hole and steps out from behind his tree and through the gate onto the public lands that surround this quarter-section inholding. His tracks in the soft, dry Mancos Shale soil span inches and run deep, each of his steps a bigger impact on the land than any of the steps my cows will take.

Our horned cows average 825 pounds. With, say, fifty cows, that's 41,250 pounds of impact per month; over a five-month period, that's 206,520 pounds the land has supported. With the popular European breeds, like Angus and Hereford, or black baldies, a cross of the two, the mature cows can easily tip the scales at 1,300 to 1,400 pounds. At 1,300 pounds, fifty cows for five months equals 325,000 pounds—same land, same time frame, and 118,750 pounds more wear on the soil, the feed, the water sources. I don't know how much more grass those cows eat. "A lot" doesn't sound remotely scientific, but it is a fact: big cows eat a lot more than small cows.

As I move across this high desert I look for tracks, the braille of the soil telling the stories of who went where. Deer tracks differ from pronghorn tracks—the latter even more dainty—which differ largely from elk tracks. Cattle tracks are usually bigger and wider than elk tracks. The breadth and indentation of a bull's hoofprint in this soil will show more deeply. The same is true of the heavier cows, each of their tracks larger, deeper, than the Criollos'.

The bull, probably weighing two thousand pounds, demonstrates this as he waddles off.

"And don't you come back," I tell him.

Environmentalism, like gender equality, has been slow to make its way into contemporary ranching in southwestern Colorado. This land is *tender*. If not well managed, it could deplete to nothing but dust. Running Criollo cattle out here is an experiment. The hypothesis: if we run small cows, the soil and forage will improve. Does this justify anything?

It does justify my annoyance when neighbors' cattle trespass onto my feed.

And yet, the trespass bull is my fault: my fence. I close the gate and walk the fenceline, Bow at my heels, Jessi sniffing for the bull. Approaching the creek we push through a thicket of coyote willows, the long, silver-gray leaves drying with the season yet still clinging to the slender stems, this followed by thorny, invasive tamarisk that dares, like the bull, to invade the land on my side of the fence. Crossing the creek, shallow this time of year, I find a single set of wide, bullish, one-way tracks at a low spot in the barbed wire. The bull hulked over, found the creek, nosed out the hay, and made himself quite at home.

Back in the circle of cell service near a corner of the cabin, I text Ken: *Bull's out. Going to fix fence but it will look like a girl did it.*

After drinking water and gathering supplies, I walk with the dogs back down to the place in need of reinforcement—no way to drive there. In gloved hands I carry a post pounder, three T-posts, and a wreath of barbed wire, with fence pliers and clips in my pockets. Using the post pounder and my weight, I force a T-post into the hardened accumulation of silt from summer flash floods. The sulphury smell of water releases as the clang of metal-on-metal pierces the morning air and bounces off the cliff face. A pair of ravens drifts past. I stop pounding to listen to the whoosh of their wings pushing air. The ravens, the dogs, the bull, and I are the only creatures I *know* share this moment.

Attaching a strand of wire to the T-post, I pull the wire body tight (I didn't bring the fence stretcher—not enough room in my hands), string it to another T-post, wrap the wire around as tightly as I can, and clip it in place. As I work, barbs snagging the sleeves of my sweatshirt, I wonder why I felt the need to denigrate myself to my son. An echo of the internal conversation I'm having? Or of the past? Putting myself down before the man can?

My father, a raging alcoholic, or alcoholic rager, found love hard to show, and perhaps hard to feel. I hadn't seen him for a year. As he strode across my mother's kitchen to say hello, instead he said, "Your face is getting fat." An awkward hug followed. I was thirteen. Did he know I'd had mononucleosis for weeks? That I had decided to become a vegetarian and ate no meat or greens, just sugar? That for almost two years my mother's boyfriend had taken too long to say goodnight? And that while in Lāhainā—*O Lāhainā!*—under my father's watch, a cop caught my eighteen-year-old boyfriend and twelve-year-old me making out in the backseat of the boyfriend's car? My father's observation wasn't wrong. Just distant.

The repair does not look "like a girl did it," though it may look as if a grandmother in her sixties did. If I didn't do it, and waited for a man's help, the bull would return to gorge himself on my winter hay supply. I have to handle each thing as it comes: trespass bull, fence repair, high water, frozen water. Cutting, splitting, and stacking wood. Stacking hay.

It has begun, I think again: *winter*. Although it's actually still fall, the last of the golden cottonwood leaves clinging to their branches, resisting the change in the season (like I am), my time in the valley to watch cows for the winter has started.

Fence fixed, fencing tools returned to their stations, I sit briefly on the cabin porch, enjoying the noon sunshine. Jessi crowds my knees while Bow drinks long at the water bowl, tired from maneuvering through brush that can easily trip him. The day isn't half over—I have to unload more hay, adding to the stack mauled by the bull, hook up the trailer, and drive eighty miles to town for more hay and supplies.

The raven pair swoops in, calling as they ride the updraft off the cliff face and, wings spread like a paraglider's, float down to perch on a ledge of Dakota Sandstone. One raven struts along the edge as the other hops down a step to investigate something: the nesting site to which they return each spring.

In addition to wildlife and the cows and dogs, two horses may winter here, depending on snowfall. And, at least temporarily, there is one bull in the neighborhood. My human neighbors consist of Cliff and Cindy to the east and TJ seven miles west. With my arrival, the valley started getting crowded.

TJ lives at what remains of Cedar, once a thriving community. The 1900 census shows forty-six people living in nine houses in what is sometimes still referred to as Cedar. It had a post office and a school. The schoolteacher's house stands somewhat intact. Ruins of more buildings and corrals rest in a field northwest of TJ's two-story log cabin. The cabin, built in the early 1890s, at one time held the Cedar Post Office. It also housed the scene of one of the Disappointment Valley shootings, which involved a love triangle and one man riding up and shooting another, the second man retreating into the house and, gut shot, killing himself instead of waiting to die.

In upper Disappointment, writes Wilma Bankston, "It took the census-taker five days to count 58 residents in 16 households in and around Lavender." Lavender included the Lavender School—a rock foundation and an underground cement cistern mark the location of the schoolhouse on the section we purchased. I have pulled half a dozen metal leg-and-side pieces from the brush, what remains of children's early 1900s desks. Lots of broken glass, purpled by time, lies about. The creek runs nearby, silty, saline, and alkaline, and I wonder at the quality of the drinking water back then.

Lizzy Knight ran a store to serve people up- and downvalley, and in 1888 Henry Knight officially opened the Lavender Post Office, which he and Lizzy operated from the store. Eventually the Disappointment postal route ran from Lavender up Salt Arroyo, through Knight Canyon, today a tight, tangled mess of Gambel oak, and along North Mountain to Norwood. Our BLM Salt Arroyo Allotment includes some of this country, as well as the fenced Lavender Cemetery that holds Lizzy Knight's headstone. We have water rights to the Knight-Embling Ditch at both the section and the mustang cabin. While I could reminisce about my own family in a parallel time on a very different ranch, I like holding the stories of this place close. Stories of Lizzy Knight, who toughed it out until the end.

The allotment also includes McDermott Arroyo, where another gunfight took place. As two men pushed cattle up the valley, unbeknownst to them a third man followed. When the first two held the cattle up in a wide, deep arroyo to rest them, the third man appeared. He accused valley resident Cuck Nunn of harboring one of his cows. Cuck denied it, and Cuck's partner roped and hogtied the cow, shaved her hip with his pocketknife, and revealed Cuck's brand. But Cal McDermott, plagued by an earlier altercation, wasn't satisfied. A large man in stature and anger, he threatened the smaller Cuck, who grabbed his Winchester from his saddle scabbard and warned McDermott not to come closer. When McDermott continued his hostile approach, Cuck fired. The bullet struck Cal's side. A doctor hailed from Norwood attempted to stop the bleeding, but Cal McDermott died later that night. The name McDermott Arroyo stuck.

A chill comes over me and I realize that beneath my sweatshirt the sweat of modest labor has cooled despite the sunshine. It's time to either go inside or press on into the next task: hooking up the trailer. I back the pickup under the gooseneck hitch and when I'm lined up I get out and crank 'er down—if I'm lined up right. The ball must sit almost directly beneath the hitch, which sometimes means I step in and out of the truck several times to adjust it by inches.

It would save time if another person directed me, as well as stress on a knee that holds the stories of earlier hardships—like getting tangled in tall grass and landing on a sharp rock or getting thrown over a fence by a bull. But I was young then and fearless, optimistic, or stupid—which may all be the same thing—pain or injury not in the future I foresaw. Now sometimes the knee that did get injured and has had two surgeries gets so stiff and sore that needed sleep doesn't come for a long time. So I don't welcome the other job that awaits: dropping sixty-five-pound hay bales from the trailer and lifting them with back and knees onto the stack.

And yet I chose this. I choose it every day.

It's not all a struggle. Getting the bull out was actually easy. Just a job to get done. The hardest thing I do is hook up garden-type hoses. Righty tighty lefty loosey simply does not apply to hoses. As with tying square knots, I inevitably have to start the process again.

Much of the West is high desert, this valley no exception. Hot in summer, reaching above one hundred degrees on many June days, and cold in winter, the first freeze usually comes in October or November, the hovering-around-zero nights and into-the-teens days beginning in December, the month that usually gives us the coldest days. Sometimes in November and February we can wear T-shirts. None of this is predictable. Not anymore. Except June.

Too much of the West can now measure climate change by fire. So far in this desert we have been spared that marker, but my sons insisted on creating the recommended circle of safety around my cabin by cutting back greasewood, sagebrush, fourwing saltbush, rabbitbrush, and two dying one-seed junipers. We had already parked a 2,500-gallon water tank on a hill. That water can gravity-flow down to the horse trough or be used to fill the cisterns if the water-catchment system for the cabin isn't working (if there's no rain or snow), or get used to fight fire, until everything runs dry.

This includes the creek, the flow of which reflects the year's weather, carrying winter's snowfall toward summer if we get snow, tapering down to a trickle, then puddles, then dry if we don't. Monsoons, our other main water source, sometimes start in early July, like last year. But when they start that early, they seem not to carry into September, like last year, though two spotty rains caused flash floods. This year monsoons didn't start at all.

The possibility of drought, always hovering in this dry country, is part of why I covet and protect our feed, hauling grass hay to feed my horses instead of turning them loose to graze the native grasses, hauling hay to supplement the cows when they're on deeded land. And so I feel annoyed when I get back from town—160 miles round trip—and see in my headlights the red sheen of the red Angus bull, his big head deep in my haystack.

In the morning he stands there rooting like a pig, pulling mouthfuls of hay from the lower bales, and then pulling the bales themselves out. I watch as he waddles off to water, a trail starting in his wake as he meanders through the salt-desert shrubs on his way to the creek. He knows where to go: the gentlest slope, the low, wide bank from which his bulk can easily stand and drink. I don't chase him out this time but do walk the fenceline to look for his entrance.

The place I fixed still intact, I mosey along the outside of the fence as the bull did, his tracks broad and deep and obvious. He cornered where the fence does, turning west, just ambling, knowing what to look for. And he found it, a top wire loose enough that he reared over it and came down on my side, his tracks left behind to tell the tale.

If I kick the bull out again, he'll come back in again—he has found the perfect place to winter: free hay, close water. Only problem: me. Cell service out here—AT&T only—is spotty at best, so I tell TJ about the bull via email. Her house, set in Dawson Draw between two places of higher ground, doesn't allow her phone service—she has to drive down the road a bit to make a call—but the internet reaches her at home, and I can email from the cabin through my little black hotspot. TJ offers to help me put heavy panels around my precious hay supply.

I also get hold of the bull's owner. He'll send his cowboy, Jeff, for the bull.

That night the bull stands outside the panels, eating the remains of the hay on the ground. The next morning, as soon as it's light enough to see, the bull appears, munching on hay-scrap leftovers. And as I stand in my bathroom getting dressed—which means I'm not dressed, which means I'm naked—Jeff rides by, close enough to the window to ruin his morning if he looked. He doesn't look, thank goodness, and by the time I get outside, cowboy, horse, and bull are gone. Tracks lead over a hill to another gate, Jeff herding the bull down the road toward a set of BLM corrals where he can load the beast into a trailer. That evening, with just Jessi and Bow and me and no bull, loneliness descends with the desert darkness. Not a porch light on within thirty miles, the only other voice in my world is that of the woodstove pinging its way toward warmth and winter in Disappointment.

With my cows I moved out to Disappointment Valley full-time before winter arrived that first year of the BLM allotment, my focus on creased hills and badlands, greasewood- and sage-covered flats, treelined basins, and the native cool-season grasses that thrive despite the harsh conditions of this desert valley. I wrote and wrote and hiked all over the backcountry looking at cows and at the feed and at mountain lion and bobcat tracks in the snow (a bobcat's are much smaller), and time filled with footsteps and heartbeats and breath as weather defined my days.

That first winter, snow fell. Lots of it. With the snow too deep and country too steep for horses to traverse it safely, I did my work afoot. It was difficult and lovely. I learned the drainages from the northern stretch of valley rim to the road that defines the southern edge of the 11,003-acre pasture. When Ken came out I followed him as he shortened his strides so my boots could step in his tracks and I didn't have to work so hard breaking trail through the snow. We slid down hillsides on our backsides, my insulated overalls slick on the snow as I used my gloved hands like ski poles to steer me away from rocks and trees. At times I ascended narrow ridges on my hands and knees, afraid that if I stood upright the wind might push me over and I'd fall unfurled down a cliff face.

On days alone I tracked cows or climbed to high places and sat on my insulated butt in the snow, elbows on my knees, field glasses to my eyes as I swept still higher country for sight of something red or black or moving. Sometimes that's as close as I got to animals invisible to my naked eye. Jessi joined me for every hike. Long-haired and mostly black, her white neck and chest patches and feet blended into the snow as she bounded across it on the frozen days or jumped from the sinkholes of my tracks one to the next as the snow softened. We would trudge back down to my 2004 Toyota Tacoma where Bow, who had difficulty maneuvering through deep snow, waited. His leg was amputated after a trailer ran over him, and he lost his ear when a dog attacked him—hard to fight on three legs—and the dog ripped Bow's left ear right off.

At the cabin, I'd build up the fire and settle in to write, the dogs stretched out and snoozing by the woodstove.

8. Mother and sons, mustang cabin. From left: Bow, Jessi, Kat, Ken, Tyler. Photo by Matthew Chaves.

Disappointment Creek ran well into summer that year, thick and full. Dawson Draw, which drains country to the south of TJ's house, ran clear as a mountain stream. TJ has lived in Disappointment Valley two years longer than I have, though she lives out here full-time all the time. The ranch is next to Spring Creek Basin Herd Management Area, where, since 2007, she has documented the wild horses. Neither of us had seen a winter like that, or Disappointment Creek running like that, or Dawson Draw running at all.

When the off-date for the BLM allotment arrived, Ken and I herded the cows down to the smaller of the two pastures we lease from TJ, which makes a great birthing ground, plus TJ likes seeing the newborn calves, her photographs documentation I can later use.

When it was time, I gathered the cows and calves to TJ's pens, though one cow hid her calf and wouldn't lead me to it, instead leading me away. After securing the main bunch, I rode back out to scour the pasture. The cow watched me, and when I neared the right bush she bawled and came running and the calf jumped up and I pushed them to the pens, late to meet Ken to haul them all to the irrigated pasture closer to town. When Ken grumbled about the extra time the cow took, TJ said, "But isn't that what you want? A cow that follows instinct, hiding and protecting her calf?" Criollos acting like mustangs, I thought, smiling as Ken frowned.

We left feed behind at TJ's—which is how we want to leave any place we graze—for wildlife and for later. Another dry summer followed, though we got more rain than in the prior summer, during the deadly, "exceptional" drought of 2018.

In this part of Colorado, many ranchers summer their cattle on montane-forest public lands, while we felt lucky to have the lease on the irrigated, privately owned land. The Criollos, however, didn't appreciate the small pastures—they prefer browsing across distance to sedentary grazing. With the BLM Salt Arroyo Allotment and a winter grazing plan and strategy intact, we needed summer rangeland to balance everything out. That's the way it is here too—everybody trying to balance winter range with summer range to avoid feeding hay.

8
This Is When I Want to Cry

I can't breathe.

—George Floyd

Disappointment Valley, Colorado, Fall 2019–Spring 2020

One fall day, after fixing fence with Ken in preparation for the cattle to move to winter pastures, Ken drove us out of Disappointment through the upper valley. "I love these meadows and ponderosa pines," I told him. "They remind me of the Sierra Nevada." Ken knew I'd left home at sixteen and finished my last years of high school in those mountains, living with Craig's family.

In southwestern Colorado, ponderosas bridge the lower piñon-juniper belt and the higher subalpine region. They smell of the good parts of Flagstaff, and of the Sierra Nevada, where we called them yellow pines.

"Um hmm," Ken said, because I had said all this before.

As the truck curled up the switchbacks, my cell phone suddenly rang, surprising us both.

"I just got a call about a summer allotment for sale in the ponderosa pines," said Danny, a rancher who ran cattle on BLM lands in the valley.

"What?" I said, and glanced at Ken, who apparently had been listening to me lament about meadows and ponderosas, for he looked as stunned as I felt.

Danny, compact, jovial, with wire-rimmed glasses and hands that shook despite his easy demeanor, ran a lot of cows. He'd tell you how many, though I was taught that asking someone that question is quite rude—it's like asking how much money a person has in the bank. This is as important a rule as *leave the gate as you find it*, though the general public doesn't know the first rule and can't seem to comprehend the second, which has caused problems in the West where people make up their own minds about gates, letting cattle out or cutting them off of feed and water if they close a gate intentionally left open.

His voice staticky through the cell phone speaker, Danny told us what he knew of the BLM summer allotment, and I jotted down the name and number he offered. "Just wanted to let you know," he said, and signed off.

Within a few days Ken and I stood among ponderosa pines, but despite the eerily coincidental timing of the phone call, the ranch was too much money and we couldn't make it pencil. Ken started talking about what cows to cull and said I shouldn't plan on keeping the Criollo replacement heifers.

The 2019–20 winter started pretty well but without the snowpack of the previous year. In January, a couple of months after we had declined the summer-in-the-ponderosas deal, Danny called again. "I've decided to sell my Forest Service grazing permit up at Groundhog. Thought I'd let you know first."

Summer in subalpine aspen, Colorado blue spruce, and columbine. *Green* grass. Higher elevations than ponderosa habitat, but still . . .

Ken and Tyler drove snowmobiles into the mountains near Groundhog Reservoir to check out the property, which included a cow camp. They stepped over a gate buried in four feet of snowdrift and pushed through waist-deep snow to look at the cow camp cabin. Its door was snowed shut. They both said yes.

As COVID-19 hit we entered into negotiations with Danny, meeting outside the public lands field office, masked and jacketed, to sign papers on the flatbed of Danny's pickup. Including Groundhog, we now had nineteen thousand acres of responsibility (small holdings in the West). I kept my replacement heifers.

In January I had signed a contract of a different kind—with a Utah publishing company—and the hours around backcountry hikes filled with revision. A big deadline perched near the calendar cusp of winter and spring. One cow calved out of sync, and I probed the steep, treed ravines between the north-south trending ridgelines until I found her with her young calf, both tucked under the lacy, webbed leaves of a Rocky Mountain juniper. The rest of the cows would start calving mid-March. On March 11 Little Bit calved, followed by Ivy. On March 13 the publishing company shut down its office in Salt Lake City, the small staff dispersed, and meetings by Zoom, of which some of us (me) had not yet heard, commenced. On March 16 I sent the revised manuscript in. And our world pitched into COVID. Fear rose like a rogue wave.

Right away I was waiting for it to be over.

I think everyone in the world knows about that waiting.

"*A world within a world.*" I have just read these words when Jessi barks. Serious barking, which she does only when there's something serious at which to bark, so I drop the copy of *Orion* and head for the door, the cold of outside biting my legs as I hope the serious thing is not a stranger because I am not quite dressed. Even in healthy times people don't drop by. And my gate is closed, both to keep cattle in and people out. Which usually works. But Jessi is barking at *something*.

I hush her and sneak across the porch, step through the cacti and bunch-grassed soil toward the edge of the cliff, and peer at the broad flat of old riverbed below. Coyote willows line the creek, cottonwoods mark its course, and thickets of three-leaf sumac, seasonally ripe with berries, live there too. From my porch I have watched a black bear stripping single branches of berries with her large, delicate bear paws; out of habit I look down first, but the only movement is the creek itself in its murky brown roll toward spring.

I have work to do for which I will finish getting dressed—checking the cows, finding Ivy's calf. I will put on the same holey jeans I've worn for days. It doesn't matter. No one will see me. And no one sees me at my other job either—writing. I am as isolated out here as I usually want to be.

But now it's different. In two ways. One, the book manuscript left with its deadline, a postpartum vacuum replacing it. And two, there's that which we're all experiencing, in one fashion or another: the far-reaching message and fear of COVID-19. The suggestion or requirement to shelter in place puts an edge on life.

Apparently no one has braved my gate and almost-half-mile driveway. I look at Jessi's border collie head, her muzzle arrowing across to the other side of the canyon. Something gray-blond moves like a floater across my eyes then bounds slowly away from the sight of me in my dusty-rose T-shirt, my bare legs ashy and bruised but muscled still, my slippers muddy with snow-moistened soil. The gray-blond blur looks over her shoulder once before disappearing.

The coyote must have sat on the cliff across the canyon watching my dogs before they saw her. She didn't leave until I entered her world within a world. Does she want to play with the dogs, or does she see three-legged Bow as target? Has she sniffed for calves hidden by their mothers at the bases of piñon pines or in the thick rushes near the creek?

This cabin on this ledge is my world right now, within the world of Disappointment. Reading the words of others helps take me beyond my selfish pout at isolation. The compilation, editing, publication, and distribution of *Orion*'s spring 2020 issue happened before our greater world changed during these last few weeks, yet each piece in the "How Earth Endures" issue feels absolutely apropos of our world now. As with "On the Lam" by David Treuer: "Dec. 6, 2019. We stand before petroglyphs. . . . Maybe four thousand years old? My daughter is fourteen. And there she is: an Indian girl . . . looking at Indian art 125 years after we were all supposed to have disappeared. But there we are. There she is. A world within a world." I'm in his world when Jessi barks and I streak outside and a coyote lopes into the trees.

⊂⊃-

We've moved the Criollos to the Nichols Wash pasture. Some calved at the mustang cabin; some have yet to calve. One evening after checking them I get back to the cabin early enough to eat dinner before dark while watching an episode of *The West Wing*, pretending that's our political world (I found the entire collection of DVDs at a pre-COVID yard sale, ten bucks). Suddenly above the banter of Martin Sheen and his staff I hear a cry that would crack any mother's heart, a sound I've heard before, felt before inside my skin, primal voice turning blood to ice as I run out the open door to see on the flat below a coyote on a fawn. I mean the coyote is *on top of* the fawn, pinning it down with the weight of instinct and hunger, and Jessi barks again as I yell like I would to turn a cow, *hyah, hyah.* When the coyote looks up the fawn pushes free and bounds through rushing water toward its mother, the coyote leaping through the creek after the fawn. The doe turns toward the coyote, chasing him back across the creek, where he runs into the thickets of willows and three-leaf sumac, weaving through tight stems and branches and out and across the creek and after the fawn again, who stops, confused, but not so the doe. She splashes through water and, mule deer fury inflating her chest, stomps her feet and charges the coyote, who leaps away from flashing hooves and angles up the cliff face on a trail invisible to me until this moment as the coyote uses it to disappear then comes out on top of the cliff. He pauses at the edge, watching the fawn below, who stands panting, lost, for as the coyote headed up the cliff the doe scrambled up to the rim—I could hear her hooves clattering on stone as she aimed at the same level as the coyote to chase him more. The coyote looks down from his ledge and shakes water from his thick winter coat like my dogs do after swimming—fur flapping and drops flying in a sunlit circle—then he vanishes into the piñon and juniper forest that ascends to ponderosas beyond the quarter-section and I don't see him again, nor do I see or hear the doe come back, and also I have lost sight of the fawn, who ran the wrong way up the canyon and what could I do.

That was the first time ever in my life I thought about shooting at a coyote. To scare him. I don't believe in shooting predators or scavengers; I believe in *not* shooting them. I believe they provide a tremendous service to the wild world. The world around me. But in that moment I felt an urge—what was it? No, *not* an urge to kill. An urge to protect. The fawn. As its own mother did in her challenge and pursuit of a hungry coyote.

That I believe in: protection, not vengeance. Not bloodthirst. But how do we protect our offspring in this climate of dis-ease? Whom do I call out for threatening my children, my grandchildren, my mother? Whom do I fight? Whom do I blame? What do I do? To withdraw is my only choice? Is that even in my nature?

No. It is not in this mother's nature to withdraw from that which will harm her children. I wish for a quick reunion of doe and fawn, and I wish to understand what the coyote knew as he watched and withdrew, what the fawn knew in her fleeting escape. Wild animals know when to do that—to withdraw for their own survival.

I pull up to the water troughs in the Nichols Wash pasture where Ken awaits my arrival, seven-year-old Lacey standing on the flatbed trailer that has the water-hauling equipment on its deck—an 1,100-gallon tank, pumps, and long, three-inch-wide hoses. She watches from above as cows come to water. I haven't seen her for days that spilled into weeks and my heart surges at the sight of her smiling in her purple hoodie and pink leggings, a pink ball cap pulled over her ears.

The jewel that is Lacey sparkles in my life like the stars above my bed at the ranch, placed there when it was her bedroom, she was corralled in a crib, and watching stars helped her to sleep. Ken stood on a ladder and stuck the glow-in-the-dark stars to the ceiling, and each night I'm at the ranch, as I fade into sleep with the stars, I think of Lacey.

She and Lucas sleep two hundred yards away, in the room that was my bedroom before we switched houses because in the "barn house" (interior walls sided with wood from the 1880s original barn) the cement floors were too hard and too cold for winter and toddlers, so I sleep in Lacey's star-studded bedroom in the barn house and she sleeps in my room in the old farmhouse.

Normally I'm with the cows in this remote valley, and usually I come into town about once a week, but *usual* and *normal* are losing their places in our language.

Nothing is normal anymore. I want to sweep Lacey off the trailer and squish her lithe, pink-and-purple joy to me. She stands near the edge, waiting for it.

"Remember," I say, "we're not supposed to be close right now."

"Because of the virus." She knows, and she doesn't know. In her body and in mine hums an instinct that we deny and that is just wrong. Hugging is instinct. This is when I want to cry.

Cows distract us. "Lightning had her baby," Lacey says. Lightning, the cow the kids can sit on. Her little roan-butted, day-old bull calf followed her across the pasture to water. "There's a problem," Lacey tells me, as Ken drives off to get the stock trailer into which we will load Lightning and her calf so he can take them to headquarters.

"Make sure she doesn't leave." Ken means Lightning, not Lacey, who wants down off the flatbed. Is there six feet between my extended hands, my torso and face, and hers? Not hardly. I lift her down but don't hug her. Instead I place a hand on her shoulder and tell her to stay behind me as we weave through other cows to stand between Lightning and escape.

The cows at water, some named by Lacey (Mango, Apple, Punkin Pie), are used to Ken and me talking to them and walking among them, but they get shy around children and watch carefully. Plus, those with calves on the ground get protective. My hand attaches to Lacey.

The cows start to mill. Ken seems to be taking a long time. Lightning wants to leave, and I step in front of her, breaking the umbilical connection between Lacey and me. I turn to see Lacey and swivel back to Lightning, who wants with growing intensity to follow the other cows.

"Stay close," I tell Lacey, reaching as I move to stop Lightning. My hand misses Lacey's shoulder. *She has to stay behind me.* Even a gentle cow could hurt her. I paw air. Then something soft and warm and tentative slips into my palm. I forget cow and calf and the trailer moving up the dirt road through this desert land that is our home within a world sick with illness and fear and feel only the soft punctuation of Lacey's hand in mine. I don't let go.

Differing from how the Bureau of Land Management works, the Forest Service requires that you purchase either the selling permittee's base property or 90 percent of his cattle. These were huge black Angus cows—not cows we wanted—but if we wanted the grass, we had to get the cows. In May we started gathering cow-calf pairs off Danny's winter-to-spring BLM grazing allotment near Hovenweep in Utah—thousands of acres of rock, stands of piñon and juniper, with willows and cottonwoods thick in the bottomlands.

Danny had different people helping in his absence—in addition to running a large number of cattle he had Forest Service, BLM, and private leases all over. One day Ken, Kathy's brother, Lane, and I pushed a bunch of cows and calves from the floor of Cross Canyon toward a steep, rocky road with a holding field on top. A friend of Danny's guided us. "Go that way," he would gesture, "toward the big rock by that juniper." I rode drag, driving the cattle from the dusty back, happy to let Ken figure out which rock by which tree. We made it to the steep, winding road, Tyler nearby on Ken's all-terrain vehicle, stepping off to manually push small calves around rocks and brush and over the berm back onto the road.

As we approached the top, the guy with scanty directions left to ride back to his rig. Cattle, horses, and humans hot and thirsty, confused calves trying to break and head back down to where they'd last seen their mothers, every

9. Ken, Kat, and Lane cowboying in Cross Canyon, Utah. Photo by Tyler Lausten.

one of us was tired and cranky. Savanna wanted to turn back like the calves, her legs trembling from the steep climb. I had to spur her up even steeper inclines. Or step off and lead her, which meant having to climb back on, my own legs shaking. Tyler had my water on the quad, and I drank when I could. No water for Savanna.

Finally out of the canyon and on level ground, the cows figured out where we were headed: to water. Cool water in a big pond surrounded by large Fremont cottonwoods. Cool shade. But the calves didn't know, and those not yet paired up kept trying to break back, which had Tyler, Savanna, and me on our toes, Ken and Lane riding point up ahead so they could turn the cattle through the gate and hold the cows at the pond until all the calves mothered up.

As we neared what I hoped was the end of the road, a large red heifer made a dive around a clump of sagebrush and took off at a run. I started

Savanna in a racing weave through the brush to circle ahead of the calf. A gust of wind came up and blew the biggest tumbleweed I had ever seen right into our path. It hit Savanna's shoulder. She shied, jumping sideways, while I stayed right where I was, landing on dirt where my saddle and horse had been one second before.

Rolling up to standing, I watched as Savanna ran off, then stopped, both heifer and tumbleweed having vanished. I caught my mare and led her through the brushy maze for a minute before remounting; heading toward the road, I heard the ATV. Tyler cut the engine.

"What are you doing?" he asked.

"Trying to turn that heifer back." I would *not* tell my sons what happened.

Tyler drove off and Savanna and I followed at a slow trot.

"What took you so long?" Ken said, as he and Lane rode toward me.

"I had to catch my horse," my resolve having apparently evaporated.

"What happened?"

I explained about the monster tumbleweed. "Savanna spooked and dumped me."

"You mean you fell off your horse," Ken said, implying that I had simply lost my seat and fallen. Which was maybe kind of true.

Savanna had actually dumped me a month earlier, when Ken told me to run to get ahead of some steers. Even as I knew the steers could only go so far before they hit a fence and turned, I spurred Savanna, who took one jump and started crow-hopping, Ken riding up from behind just as I was ejected. I stood up as he caught my horse so he would know I was okay, a strategy I practice often, getting quickly on my feet every time I fall so my sons know I didn't break.

This reminded me that falling from a horse isn't so bad, even for an older woman. I'd done it lots in my early years, often for fun, riding with the ranch girls at the summer camp, racing around bareback; jumping logs; swimming in the river—sliding off our horses' backs and grabbing their tails, letting them pull us through the water.

One morning when I was married to Keith, we were late to meet cowboys on the neighboring ranch to help gather steers, and we did the long trot for about a mile to make up time. I rode a gelding of Keith's, a young, dark bay horse named Lucas (for whom Ken would eventually name his own son). Coastal fog had drifted into the valley in the night, the morning cool and fresh, and even with the fast uphill trot I felt nervous about riding the big colt.

The cowboys greeted us and right away we started pushing steers across a flat toward the distant dry riverbed, which we would cross to end up at their shipping pens. The steers also felt fresh in the cool morning, and they took off at a trot, some at a run. When I leaned forward and squeezed with my legs to race ahead of the steers like the rest of the cowboys, Lucas broke in two, back humped and head down between his front legs like a true bronc. I rode him two jumps before he launched me, and as I flew toward the heavens I yelled, "I told you the sonofabitch was gonna buck me off!"

Keith had to catch my horse for me that time, and I had to get back on or face a long walk home. I would have gotten back on anyway. Later Keith and the other cowboys who had heard me chuckled about it, impressed—as I was, actually—that I'd managed to get that whole sentence out before hitting dirt. But falling isn't always funny.

The process of gathering Cross Canyon and shipping took a couple of weeks. Ken and I wove through southwestern Colorado and southeastern Utah, hauling horses to help gather and sort, hauling cattle as necessary. In a large set of shipping pens, Danny and his crew, which sometimes included Ken, would sort cattle—separating cows from calves so the cows wouldn't trample their babies in the hauling—and then load the cattle trucks and send them on their way, a two-hour one-way journey to what we call "the compound" in lower Disappointment Valley.

The compound is about three acres of dirt and gravel enclosed with chain link fencing topped with three strands of barbed wire, the seven-foot-tall perimeter fence a remnant of the former oil company owners' equipment and security—they wanted no unauthorized entry. Now clear of their unidentifiable objects, which looked Martian-like with big blocky metal shapes and wires and probes everywhere, we can't build anything permanent because of whatever might be underground. Instead we set up portable-panel corrals inside the formidable fence, and a lane and loading chute outside, where the trucks, forty feet or longer, could back up to unload cattle. The space inside the compound large enough for the pens and our pickups and trailers, the cows had plenty of room to move about in search of their calves. And we could hold them there with hay and water overnight or longer if we needed to.

After the last cattle truck finally unloaded, Ken left for home to see his family. When I felt sure the cows were paired up, I simply opened the big gate and let them drift, keeping the horses in the pen with apologies for the relentless wind and warmth of a Disappointment spring. The horses had water and hay, but they would have preferred the grass outside.

Ken and I would return early the next day. Other than cowboying, checking on the calving Criollos, and unloading trucks, I spent this stretch of COVID lockdown at the mustang cabin and so had a shorter drive to a bed—twenty-three miles one way, fifteen of them dirt and dust that matched the color of my Toyota, clothes, and face. After I fed the dogs and scrubbed the outer layer of soil from my skin I could drop into sleep despite a growling stomach.

Ken arrived before me and had already headed out ahorseback. As I brushed Savanna, whom he tied to the trailer to wait for me, he rode up on Kua, the big bay gelding. The dark contrast of three-day beard highlighting Ken's eyes—shades of green like the shirt and vest he wore in the still-cool morning—I saw in them something behind the exhaustion.

When he said, "I'm sorry, Mom," I knew he meant it before I knew what for. I watched his face as I buckled the breast collar and tightened my cinch. "A calf died," he said.

We rode out. A cow bawled loudly. She had cleaned her calf thoroughly, her large tongue, rough like a cat's, leaving marvelous, fruitless swirls in the black fur. Two months ago she had licked life into him this way; she didn't understand why now it didn't work. When another cow came near, the mother cow bowed her body toward the intruder, her neck curved and bulging in a clear message: I will protect him even in death. This was when I wanted to cry.

A mix-up occurred at the shipping end, this calf and his mother sent on different trucks, but I didn't see that he wasn't paired up when I turned his bunch out. His mother came on the next truck, her bag full. We kept her in the corral with three other big-bagged cows to see if their bawls would draw any wayward calves. If not, we would have to take the cows back to Utah, where their calves might still be running loose in the desert scrubland.

Ken off hauling something somewhere, I had watched a calf wander into the compound. At the panel fence that separated the calf from the cows, his tail twitched like a dog's tail wagging, his nose jutting between the rails. No cow rose, but I believed the calf, let him through a gate, and he went right to her, butting her to standing then nursing mightily—he had wandered the big pasture for a day without his mother and he was hungry.

That was likely what killed him. Enterotoxemia. Toxins from overeating.

I didn't know. I was just so happy to see him reunited with his mother.

Ken said, "I'm sorry, Mom," because he found the calf first. But we were both sorry. We were all sorry. The cow bawling, wailing, as I once did—we are mother and son who endured forced separation and we are working so hard to do right by our cattle and maybe for each other after twenty years, but we couldn't fix this.

The mustang cabin thirty-five minutes upvalley, I can get home at midnight or two in the morning and sleep in a bed and still be back as the sun rims the sandstone escarpments in the east. But prevailing exhaustion has me doing things like slipping into the edge of the bar ditch as my eyes close while I drive home or even in the dark of dawn as I head back to the cattle, but no one else drives this road at those hours so it's okay.

After a night of short sleep, I don't think to bring the one bottle of Gatorade in my refrigerator to my son who has slept in his truck and not seen his kids for three nights because that's a three-hour round trip and we have to check the cattle at first light, five thirty, looking for signs of enterotoxemia, the symptoms of which don't often show until it's too late, but Ken is determined. In this dry year, the cows don't pair up well. It's no one's fault, just a dry May after a dry April and dry months stacked back to January, when we started this deal and didn't know anything about COVID-19. We simply wanted green summer grass for our cows. And it's much more complicated than that. Ken is ahorseback at first light, hoping to simplify. To save.

Not thinking of the one bottle of Gatorade for Ken is not okay. When I realize I could have brought it, this is when I want to cry.

We had weeks to go before taking the cattle to the Forest Service lease on the mountain, and the whole lot of Angus and Criollo cattle became my job. Because of the dry year I had to haul water, watching in amazement as those huge cows stood beside our smaller—even petite—Criollos and guzzled three times the amount. I couldn't get them enough, and hauling water became more dawn-to-dark days, towing 1,100 gallons on the flatbed trailer, the 2005 three-quarter-ton GMC and me feeling the wear and tear. I found wrestling the stubborn hoses, lifting pumps on and off the flatbed, starting the pumps, and climbing on and off the trailer all day more frustrating than challenging, but the gnats in my ears, grit in my teeth, sand in my hair, and the constant push to get one more trough filled wore down what little fortitude I had. Like sandstone-silt water grinding down my callouses.

COVID continued to shut doors and kill people—I listened to NPR on the drives between mustang cabin and pasture and water source and water troughs. No rain fell. People in cities had to stay in lockdown. My grandchildren had a hard time with school, online and off. I still wasn't supposed to hug them. And, like billions of others, I couldn't see my friends or sisters or mother. Hard to feel excited about anything, even the tiny calves the Criollos dropped to the ground, their thin little legs trying to hold up their swaying bodies as they sought to nurse. Even the prospect of heading up to the mountain in a few weeks didn't excite me.

Tyler will bring me food and my mail because I can't get to town until something changes and the Angus calves are all okay. He texts that he's about to leave, but I'm ahorseback with the phone in my pickup because I don't want to lose it, so I don't know when he's coming. As the days lengthen toward summer solstice, it's still late and dark again when I drive home after hauling water and I'm wandering on the road to avoid the washboardy places, plus my eyes are closing, so I don't see the approaching vehicle until its headlights startle my hands on the wheel but not my brain and I swerve to miss him and keep driving, and a couple of miles later I think, *shit, was that Tyler?* I missed hitting him but also missed seeing him. I almost cry. The mail and meal he left for me go unopened.

After the back-and-forths to Utah with extra cows or calves until things are righted, the cattle get paired up except for one calf who doesn't find his mother because she isn't in Disappointment Valley or in Cross Canyon. A black whiteface with black circles all the way around his eyes, I call him Bandito. He robs milk by timing his exploits with other nursing calves: when they go in for a teat, so does he, usually from behind so if a cow kicks, she will miss him (they can't kick straight back like horses). Dogies, people call these orphan calves. This reference started among cattle people in the 1880s, its exact origin unknown—perhaps because the calves look bloated, or doughy, too young to digest grass exclusively. While Bandito may have a potbelly, he won't die of enterotoxemia. He will graze the dry grasses of Disappointment and then go up to the mountain with the pairs to graze those grasses and he will survive. I think of his strength, his resilience. I want some of it.

A day after Tyler left it for me, I go through the mail. Dirt caked on my clothes, face, and arms, I sift through envelopes and nibble at the Zia's salad made with sweet potatoes, brown rice, black beans, lettuce, tomatoes, and extra avocado, just how Tyler knows I like it. It's after ten at night, and this is the first meal I've attempted in days. Except that's not true. At the compound Ken set up a little barbecue to grill hotdogs, and I've eaten them right off the grill, hot in my fingers because I can't eat the wheat buns. Fortunately Ken can, but he's losing weight—I see it with my mother-eyes—while I am finding it. The weight.

Ken loses weight and I lose earrings. One of a pair of porcupine-claw earrings Tyler got me the last time he was in Alaska, the fall before quarantine. Alaska in September, rich red and rust mountains and sandhill cranes and bears and crowned mooses and the aurora and lover-of-night-sky Tyler with his camera—we were supposed to go back this fall.

Losing that earring from Tyler. And one from my grandkids. The Gatorade for Ken. The dead calf and the dogie calf and the drought and dust and wind and my little finger. Popped two years ago when it got caught in a rope, it didn't hurt until now when it's so swollen I think it might pop again. Swollen like a calf's belly when he's been off his mother too long and overeats upon reunion. *I didn't know. I was just so happy to see him reunited with his mother.*

The next week something happens in our world that's bigger than the loss of a calf and maybe even COVID. It sends fire through the people the way issues did in the sixties and seventies, and I watch it on my laptop, watch a man die on the computer screen on my lap, watch the cold eyes cold face of a white cop stare into the camera, no remorse, no feeling, just an unflinching hate-stare at the brave seventeen-year-old Black girl who films with her phone while the cop kneels and kneels on George Floyd's neck as George with his face in the pavement says *I can't breathe* again and again, *I can't breathe*, right up until he calls out *Mama!* And this is when I don't want to cry or not cry—I'm already doing it. I can't stop.

9

In the Rut

By retreating from that which we oppose, we render lifeless all opportunities for intimacy, and for community. To smile and step away is as fatal to possibility as is brandishing a finger of blame.

—Amy Irvine, "Spectral Light," *Orion*

Groundhog and Disappointment Valley, Colorado, Summer and Fall 2020

June 20. My last day of six weeks of hauling water. The next day: summer solstice. Our on-date. We gathered the cattle from the Nichols Wash pasture into the compound in the early morning, sorted them in the growing heat, and loaded them onto cattle trucks. The truckers started hauling the big Angus cows and small horned Criollos to a set of communal corrals at Groundhog, nine thousand feet above sea level in the San Juan Mountains. The Disappointment cowboys of old also summered cattle at Groundhog—only they drove them using horses.

In the high-country cool, the last truck unloaded and gone, we made an enclosure with our stock trailers and three of us ahorseback, Tyler, Kathy, and TJ filling holes on foot while the cattle paired up, a noisy business as cows and calves called to each other as if they were across a canyon and not just a few feet away. When we opened a hole, they flowed out. The three-mile drive up the steep road after a long day of gathering, sorting, hauling, and waiting felt like pushing water uphill. Ken ahead on Kua, leading, calling, showing the cows where to go, another cowboy and I drove them from behind, Tyler on a quad blocking holes while Kathy stepped afoot into the dense brush at the sides of the road to get wandering calves headed right, and TJ rode drag in Kathy's pickup with the kids.

Ken opened the gate at the summit end of the long climb and the cattle spilled into a green meadow fringed with aspens, the stock ponds full of snowmelt and water from the springs, and I watched as the colors of meadow and sky and aspens replaced the red dust through which I had peered for weeks. Forty-eight miles between this altitude and Nichols Wash, these pastures were as different as local politics.

We stayed with the cows another hour as they watered and mothered up again—some of the old Angus cows more interested in feed than in their calves, but the beautiful horned Criollos made sure their calves were nearby. Noticing a sick Angus heifer, head hanging, ears down, ear-tag number 108, I trotted over to tell Ken, but the day had gone long and the veil of darkness was lowering even in that high country on summer solstice, and we would have to wait until the next day to doctor her. Cows quietly chewing their cud, calves nursing or napping, we rode away, the sky flaring up in a final rosy orange before turning dark and starlit, our horses heading toward their new summer home: from a hot, dry lot to a six-acre pasture of fresh, succulent grasses.

We set out ahorseback early, Tyler in his side-by-side, to check the cattle and find 108. Ken's horse seemed to float like a cloud over the meadow, while Savanna has a rough, jarring lope so we do the long trot, me posting in time with her reaching front legs, or standing in the stirrups, thighs and calves like the suspension in a truck, absorbing the impact.

Nearing the cattle, we slowed to a walk. My rope down and loop built, Ken spotted the sick heifer first, moved in close, and swung, his loop settling over her head. I stepped off Savanna, Tyler ran over, we grabbed Ken's rope, and Tyler flanked the heifer, laying her down on her side. As I settled upon her, placing a knee on her chest and one on her neck, holding her foreleg bent and back so she couldn't use it to get up, I removed the rope, and Tyler held her hind legs so she couldn't kick. My troubled knee in the wrong position, I shifted my weight slightly, and in that split second of release the heifer swung her head in a great lunge for freedom and met my face with her skull.

Tyler held on as I flopped back and Ken jumped down and Savanna, her mecate looped into my belt, pulled out of the way. I grabbed the front leg again, my face throbbing.

"Are you okay?" Tyler said, and I could see that they didn't know what to do—doctor the calf or help their mother.

I nodded—I was conscious—so Ken hurriedly loaded the syringe, Tyler and I held the heifer, and Ken gave her the shot and boluses. When we let her up, my sons turned to me. Though I didn't taste or smell blood, I said, "Are my teeth still there?" and pulled up my lip.

"Yes," Tyler said, reaching out to help me stand. That he could look at me confirmed it—if blood had pooled and spilled, he would have looked away.

"You shouldn't ride back," Ken said, so I walked to the side-by-side between my two tall, handsome sons, my arms around their waists, theirs around my shoulders. Tyler helped me in and drove me back to cow camp, carefully avoiding bumps, while Ken rode, leading Savanna.

As I reposed in Ken's camper with ice on my face, everything around my eye colored and swelled. Lacey and Lucas came in to look at me. Outside, Ken adjusted the stirrups on my saddle, Kathy swung up onto Savanna, and they rode off to push the pairs to the Dressel Pasture, the first of four in a rotation determined by the Forest Service (each summer we will start in a different pasture, the grasses thus grazed in different months). That afternoon we switched—Kathy with the kids, me on Savanna, Tyler wherever we needed him.

Cow camp sits near the crown of a rounded mountain with meadows spilling down all sides, patchworked with aspen groves and a few stands of Colorado blue spruce. The Forest Service permit reaches nearly ten thousand feet at its highest point, the lowest point at about eight thousand feet, where Groundhog Creek runs along and a few ponderosa pines grace the steep hillsides amid firs and spruces. Groundhog Creek joins Fish Creek in a meadow we lease for a few weeks in the spring and fall. Fish Creek empties into the West Dolores (the intestine linked to the dancing pig's stomach).

I moved up to cow camp and into the "cow cabin" from those hellish weeks of hauling water, and even when it's still chilly at eight in the morning after a cold night at this elevation, or when I feel the air pulling oxygen from my lungs—like walking with Tyler yesterday to cut a path through aspen windfall—I'm glad to be here. At 9,220 feet, we're close to alpenglow and clouds, the sunsets circular—the colors not just aglow in the west but swirling above and around laccolithic Lone Cone to the north, dropping down in the east to fill the drainage divide between Lone Cone and 13,296-foot Dolores Peak, the clouds almost touchable at this altitude.

Ken, Kathy, Lacey, and Lucas sleep in their camper, and Tyler in his van. In the shell of log cabin, my cot and bedroll occupy a corner, and my clothes fill mouse-proof containers beneath the cot and spill over an old metal chair.

By "shell" I mean that the cabin is unfinished: particle-board floor splintering underfoot, the log walls poorly chinked, no insulation in the steep ceiling. No running water. No kitchen, though Tyler built a stick-frame counter for a found sink and rigged up a water jug and drainage bucket. Cold storage is the ice and coolers we bring, and a propane refrigerator Tyler found and installed. The bathroom is an outhouse shared by all.

When a friend asked me about that, saying, "Isn't using an outhouse kind of, like, gross?" I said, "Look at it this way: either we have an outhouse, or we don't."

After each day's work we sit outside in a horseshoe of camp chairs by Ken's barbecue, eating smoked and grilled Cachuma Ranch beef and Kathy's potato salad and coleslaw. The kids and I drink water as my sons drink beer and Kathy sips her mixed beverage, six of us in our mountain bubble in the clouds.

A couple of weeks after I bumped heads with 108, Ken said, "You've been acting weird ever since that heifer hit you."

I called my doctor. "I feel fuzzy and tired, and I can't remember things."

"You probably got another concussion," she said. "You need to rest and stay off the computer—no more than an hour a day of computer work."

That's when I received my under-contract book manuscript from the editor with a list of revisions to make. Printing out a hard copy, I conducted research the old-fashioned way—using real books—and because the head-butt affected only my brain, head, and teeth (sore but there), I could still ride and did so nearly every day. When the prescribed two months off the computer passed, I went to the mustang cabin and worked 101 hours in one week, making all the changes on the computer version and missing my deadline by a day.

10. Ken and Lucas after checking cattle at Groundhog. Photo by Tyler Lausten.

Meanwhile, COVID raged on. So did the drought. Without any rain, my heart sagged. Upper-body muscles sagged too—hard and taut from all the tugging and lifting and carrying I'd done hauling water, now they held reins and ropes as my legs developed summer muscles.

Cowboying in the high country, I felt like the Disappointment cowboys of old, checking cattle and fences, feed and water. Checking for strays. Sometimes Ken joined me, riding Rita, his sorrel mare, or Kua. Trespassing cattle seemed constant—apparently people think that because it's public land, it's okay for their cattle to graze grass we paid for. Aside from that, I found it lovely up where grass grows green, purple and yellow columbine grace the shadows of aspens, Rocky Mountain elk ghost through the trees, and black bears sniff at us as we ride along.

That's what we were doing one day when a man revved up a steep hill on a four-wheeler, going cross-country, which, like cattle trespassing, is against Forest Service rules—other than on designated roads, we're only allowed to use a motorized vehicle for fence work. Clearly the man meant to fly right past us. I stepped Savanna in front of him.

Forced to a stop, he said, "We're short about twenty-five cows. Have you seen 'em?"

"Every day," I said.

The man cut his engine. He looked older than me. Old enough to know better.

Ken rode closer.

"I've been pushing them back onto your side of the fence," I said.

"I wish you'd just push them across the neighbor's pasture and onto the road. We can't gather them if you head them back through the trees."

"Get a horse," said Ken.

"I have a horse. It's just too old to ride."

I didn't say *maybe you're too old to ride* because in five years I might be his age and reduced to straddling a quad. I sat Savanna comfortably, looking for better words.

"Your cattle have been grazing this pasture for weeks," Ken said.

"Oh, it's no big deal. They do it every year."

It was our first year on the Forest Service permit. We were learning. I found my words. "You'd better fucking get them off of here."

His face reddened. He wore no hat. Not a real rancher, I thought. Like me.

"It won't matter," he said. "They'll be back the next day."

"Because your place is fed off," Ken said. Meaning overgrazed.

The guy was fuming now. "You have to fix your fences."

Ken and Tyler had gone around miles of perimeter fence before we turned our cows out, when I was still hauling water in the lower country. And while Colorado is a fence-out state, that law doesn't apply to Forest Service or Bureau of Land Management land. When it comes to federal land, the cattle owner is responsible for keeping his cows home.

"They'll just do it again next year," he insisted.

"No, they won't," Ken said.

The man's red glow faded. He started his ATV and sped off, trampling our grass, breaking federal law all the way to the county road. Tired of wanting to do right in the face of a culture that insists on making its own rules, and tired of COVID though it had only been a few months, as Ken and I rode on through aspen groves and open country I wondered at my hard heart. On a far hillside, the man's cows grazed freely. We trotted our horses at them, startling them into the trees and onto the trail home they had made.

Ken opened the gate. "He's right," he said, "they'll be back tomorrow."

I have thought that what I missed most in these long weeks of pandemic were hugs, visiting with girlfriends on a deck in the sunshine, a lover, but that's not it. Social distancing isn't new to me—not physical distancing, which *six feet apart* really means. To me, social distancing is a valley nearly forty miles long in which only seven people live—two couples and three single women: one recently widowed, one working on a mustang sanctuary, and one me.

I don't live out here full-time, though I want to; instead I now spread myself between this valley, cow camp, and the ranch headquarters near Dolores—I live where the cows live. Which has me in Disappointment Valley from October into June, with trips to headquarters and town every week to ten days or so to pay bills—I don't get mail out here, though I could; it gets delivered on Tuesdays and Fridays. And to do laundry—I don't have a washing machine, though I could, but I'm on catchment water and solar power, and in times of drought I don't have enough water to wash clothes, and in times of storms I have to conserve power for more important things, like refrigeration and my computer. (I do have a flush toilet!) I go to town for groceries and fuel. And to see my grandkids and family.

I plan these trips around what work needs doing. Ken and Kathy will go to the farmers' market on Saturday, taking our grass-fed-and-finished beef and, masked and physically distanced, sell our product while I stay at headquarters with the kids, washing machine at work.

At sixty-five, I'm at the beginning of the at-risk category of older people. But even before COVID restructured our lives, I was happy to stay with the grandkids and let Ken and Kathy talk to strangers, though many of our customers aren't strangers anymore. They've bought our beef for years, and I actually enjoyed the social fixes in the seasons when farmers' markets were open, before we were all shut down. Now reopened, Ken and Kathy the only essential workers allowed, I spend the time with my grandchildren—my nonessential but ever-important task.

After a third summer of no monsoonal rains (which adds to COVID depression), the parched hillsides and dry arroyos of drought convince us

11. Disappointment country: Kat leading Criollo pairs up the road, Ken trailing them. Photo by Tyler Lausten.

not to put any more stress on our Disappointment country. Even though BLM says we can still run cattle on the allotment, we haul all the Criollos and Angus to the ranch headquarters, where we will sell some Angus cows (the open—not pregnant—and oldest go first) and feed the rest. Which puts me in Disappointment Valley only for hunting season, when I patrol for human trespassers—every year someone crosses the line and shoots at a buck on land I wish to be a sanctuary for wildlife as well as for me. I have yet to catch anyone in the actual act of killing, though I have chased armed men off my property with threats of calling the game warden and pressing trespassing charges. Which I have done. Armed with cell phone and voice, I don't even consider fear, only the violation. That right there is a glaring depiction of white privilege.

At the mustang cabin for a few days to watch for trespassers and write without too much interruption, I'm doing just about my favorite thing—working while still in bed at eight in the morning—when I hear two shots, not exactly close together but close enough that I can guess it's one man, one rifle, one deer.

In the pre-winter chill, I look out the window through binoculars. This is the third rifle season in southwestern Colorado, the only remotely busy time in Disappointment Valley. Road traffic increases tenfold—I might see as many as twenty moving vehicles on a given day, pickups or Honda and Kawasaki side-by-sides peopled by men, and a few women, dressed in camouflage and hunter orange. Foot traffic also increases, though not as much. The bowhunters of the earlier season were all afoot, needing to get close to their prey, but third-rifle-season hunters stick closer to the road. Thirty miles of that road is the dirt-and-gravel county road that goes mostly through public lands but also bisects the few private holdings, which keeps residents like me on the alert for people hunting without permission.

I know a hunter fired the shots; I don't know if he (I assume he's a man) is trespassing. When the sun clears the rimrocks, lighting needlepoints of piñon pine, I see a white pickup parked half a mile away, reflecting morning light that bounces off something hunter-orange above the cab. I've seen this truck before.

Hurrying to get dressed and investigate, I don't bother to braid my hair, instead wrapping it into a sloppy bundle at the nape of my neck, strands tucked beneath a knitted cap. I grab my gloves but don't even think about a mask—my neighbors miles to the east and west, we rarely get within six feet of each other.

The white pickup is parked near my fence. In my thick down jacket I hope I look as puffed up as I feel as I step out of the safety of my old Toyota to open the gate.

A man in camouflage down to his boots walks along the BLM side of the fence. He has blaze orange trimmings here and there, a knife in a sheath hanging from his belt and strapped to his thigh, and a rifle in a sling over his shoulder. He's not doing anything wrong, far as I can tell, so I drive west, watching in my side-view mirrors as he climbs into his newish, slightly lifted, white Toyota Tacoma with Utah plates, details I will remember. The man himself is slender, young (late thirties?), with straight, shoulder-length, Norse-blond hair. Dropping over a hill, I continue west on the part of my property through which the county road runs, looking for signs of trespassing, this without any consciousness about my own trespassing onto Sister and Ed's land years back. Another sign of white privilege—I felt entitlement to that land because my family once owned it. What of the people before white people, the millions across this continent, and their descendants, for whom this was once their home ground? It seems only white people act as if entitled, when we are so not.

I drive farther, because this is not only deer and elk habitat but also mustang country, and I might as well look for wild horses while I'm out. Finding no trespassing hunters, no mustangs, I turn around and head back east. The blond man in his white Tacoma and I drive by each other in opposite directions. The road, although bisecting my property, is public domain. In my mirrors I see the flash of his brake lights and reverse lights. Clearly he's looking for deer. I puff up again and stop, my field glasses trained on his Toyota.

When the white truck disappears, I turn around and creep after it, thinking I might see the camouflaged man before he sees me. But it's hard to put the sneak on someone driving the county road when we're both in pickups and the only ones out so far today. And he's already coming back. I slow, pull to the side. He stops abreast of my open window. Blond, but older than I first thought, with gray in his beard, his hair matted in places from a week of hunting, eyes blue, a round, kind face. I deflate a notch.

"We wounded a deer," he starts.

And restarts. "My friend wounded a deer. I think it might be on your place."

"Not good," I say, re-puffed. Crippling game is the worst thing a hunter can do.

"No," he says, "not good." He looks at me, waits. I wait too. "My friend's tracking him," he says. "I'm wondering if we can see if the buck is on you. He's packing a back leg."

Injured. Three-legged, or almost. "What can I say?" I say.

"My friend's following his blood trail. It leads to your fence." The buck must have crossed onto my property through or over the wildlife-friendly fence—strands of smooth wire on the top and bottom making it easier for elk and deer, and for me, to go over or under, but cattle and horses still respect it.

Now I know what to say. "Fuck. You have to find him. The buck. You can't leave him."

The hunter in the white Tacoma knows this—he seems genuinely upset. I turn my dirty Tacoma around in the road again and park behind him. While he radios his friend to tell him they have permission, I write down the information I've memorized plus the Utah license plate number. Just in case.

As the hunter and I step out of our pickups, his friend pops up behind a rise. He's also tall and white and wears a brown beanie, jeans, camo jacket, and hunter orange. He beckons.

"May I go with you?" I ask the first hunter, though it's my property we're about to cross and I don't need permission.

"Of course." He mutters as we walk up a sloping gray hill of Mancos Shale, "I wish he was a better shot."

"So do I," I say.

We slip under the fence to the BLM side. The friend shows us a pool of congealed blood. "Blood from the lungs," the first hunter says. I don't ask how he knows.

"This isn't my first rodeo," the second hunter tells me. Clearly he's also upset. As I think that the metaphor doesn't quite work in this situation, he adds, "It's often a rodeo when I hunt. This isn't the first time I've wounded a buck."

"Then you'd better get better," I say.

A slight grin crinkles the first hunter's sunburned cheeks. His blue eyes shine.

Hunter 1 and I track the buck, and the doe the buck was pursuing, to my fence. No blood. "You can see where the buck jumped," Hunter 1 says.

I point out where he landed on the still-frozen earth on my side, and this hunter and I slip again under the smooth wire. Hunter 2 steps over with his backpack and rifle.

Hunter 1 and I move slowly, carefully, across the frozen ground, my gloved hands out before me, palms down, scanning as if I'm water witching, hoping for a vibration, a sign.

“Here’s the doe,” Hunter 1 says, indicating a faint imprint on the hard dirt, narrow, toes close. “And here’s the buck.” A wider track, the animal bigger, heavier, dewclaws pressing the ground behind the hoof.

We continue to follow the sparse tracks closely, sometimes me pointing, more often him. We reach a second fence, there to keep my cattle and horses off the road. Hunter 1 and I go under near where the buck and doe jumped it.

The tracks keep heading downhill, showing between clumps of warm- and cool-season grasses and gray shale. We move around greasewood and big sagebrush toward the creek and coyote willows, their leaves crisp and falling, the rabbitbrush mostly beyond bloom, the spent stalks of cattails yellow and waving. Though drought has kept the creek dry much of the spring and summer, we had snow last week, so trickles connect the puddles. In the riparian area, rich with growth despite drought, the Fremont cottonwoods with their big, round leaves pull enough moisture through their taproots to shelter riparian oases thick enough to hide deer.

Hunter 1 stops, looking over the terrain. “He’s fully in the rut,” he says. “His neck was swelled out like this,” his hands spread apart, showing a thick, bulging neck, “and he smelled like a buck in the rut. They piss all over themselves.”

And a doe finds that attractive? I think, when I see that Hunter 2 has worked his way ahead of us, following his own path, while Hunter 1 bends and stoops. “Blood,” he says, and I see it on the crinkled coyote-willow leaves. “Keep looking,” he says, “about two feet high.”

I do, missing much of the blood but pointing out tracks.

Hunter 1 nods. “He’s still with the doe. I’m surprised he’s not down yet, losing that much blood. We’d smell him if he was down. With this wind, we’d smell him.”

I sniff. My nose runs. It’s still cold but the ground softens with the morning. I find a track of the doe, then of the buck.

“He’s sticking with her,” Hunter 1 says. He returns to the last place he saw blood on a willow shoot. “See,” he says, “it’s from here to here.”

“The stalk bent with him as he passed.”

“You’re right.” He pushes the willow over and we see the way it swept across the open wound. “I can’t believe he’s still going.”

“What we do for sex,” I say.

He looks at me. I shrug.

"You're right," he says again, and slowly, carefully, follows the blood path on leaves.

Social distancing comes to me naturally. I haven't gone to a bar since getting clean nearly thirty years ago. Parties are family birthday parties. Before COVID, "going out" meant restaurant meals with family or friends. Readings. Bookstores.

Running the ranch with Ken, some days together, many days apart, in summer I ride the mountain meadows and aspen groves looking at cattle, looking for cattle. Now it's fall and we've finished gathering the high country, but because the drought is severe, "exceptional" the official term—the worst drought category, meaning there's just not enough feed or water anywhere—we're in a quandary about how many head to sell. Selfishly I lament because I won't have the winter work the cattle give me out here: breaking ice in the creek in the mornings; hiking deep into the backcountry to search for a missing cow; noticing how elk and Criollos eat the same bunchgrasses, down to the same length, and how they leave the plant alone once they take that bite; watching cattle browse the salt-desert shrubs, the elk not so much. Following mountain lion tracks across the snow, just because, or watching a bobcat stalking a rabbit, the eye-patterns at the backs of the bobcat's tufted ears staring at me. Already I feel untethered without that work to look forward to. Perhaps that's why I've thought about missing hugs.

Others out here have lived way more isolated than I do. Cliff told me about Coyote Don, how he occupied a hunting shack behind an old barn upvalley, not leaving the area in the winter or seeing anyone for months. Cliff said come spring Coyote Don would have to learn to talk all over again. He had no kin, no possessions of any value other than hunting knives and guns, and he hunted whatever, whenever, wherever he wanted. I might have had the sense not to confront him if he trespassed, but he died in a fire in that old shack long before I moved to the valley.

Hunter 1 reaches down to examine a yellow stem of cattail. His left leg trembles when we pause, and he moves stiffly at the hips. I've reassessed his age to maybe fifty—too young for stiff joints earned with the years. But I think that's why he goes under the fences despite being tall enough to maneuver easily over the tops the way my similarly tall sons do. Under is also easier for me, despite my own compromised leg—no barbs snagging my jeans as I stretch to clear wire.

I hear a thud, hooves on dull earth. Cocking my head to help my ears pick up sound, "Shhh," I say. Ears—Jessi's, Savanna's, mine—help a lot when looking for cattle and wildlife, telling me location and size, Savanna and Jessi often finding calves or bears before I see them. The thud doesn't come again. Only Hunter 2 in the willows, not tracking, really, probably just hoping, as I am, that the buck will jump up okay or has already died without too much suffering.

Again Hunter 1 returns to the place he last saw a distinctive mark, the brush of blood already turned the color of rust in the dry air. I curve around to the largest Fremont cottonwood. Toward the sound. Paralleling the steep bank and trickling creek from above.

Hunter 1 comes up behind me. "Too steep," he says.

I nod but keep looking. "There." Tracks where the earth clumps soft and moist at the base of the bank, which slopes more gradually following a cattle trail.

"I wouldn't think he'd go down that," he says.

"I have a three-legged dog in the truck," indicating my own Toyota Tacoma, more than a decade older than his, the exact color of the Disappointment Valley dust that covers it like paint. "He's missing his back left leg and can go down much easier than up."

The hunter nods, maybe thinking about his own range of motion. He offers no information. And why should he? We are two strangers thrown oddly together in an intimate search for traces of blood on autumn willows, our heads bent so close together at times that I'm glad I brushed my teeth if not my hair in my rush to leave the cabin earlier in the morning. And wonder about not wearing a mask.

Hunter 2 interrupts the moment. "I'm sorry but I have to go."

I don't know how to respond. This time I keep quiet.

"He has a five-hour drive," Hunter 1 tells me. To his friend, he says, "I'll make a sweep around these willows and then give you a ride back to camp."

Hunter 2 turns to me. "Thank you for letting us do this. What's your name?"

I tell him. "And yours?"

"We're both Todds."

So instead of thinking of them as Hunters 1 and 2, I could have been thinking Todd 1 and Todd 2. It doesn't matter now—Todd 2 needs to go. We turn toward the road. As he tells me about knowing the other Todd since high school, Todd 1 appears behind us. I didn't hear his approach. He and I go under the fence. Todd 2 still has his pack on and wants to step over. He hands Todd 1 his rifle.

"Is it loaded?" Todd 1 asks, and then checks for himself. The first hunting accident I knew about happened like this when I was six—two boys from my sister's third-grade class going over a fence with a loaded .22. We could hear the sirens from streets away as the ambulance passed through the neighborhood, but Billy Cook was already dead.

At the two Tacomas—one white, newer, cleaner, with Utah plates, the other smaller, older, Colorado plates and the color of dirt—we part. I drive to the cabin with my dogs and reassurances from Todd 1 that he will return to search the rest of the quarter-section until he finds the buck. I eat a quick snack and brush and braid my own matted hair and step back outside. Because the day has warmed enough to allow it, I sit on the porch in my puffy jacket and start to write this down. Bow stretches out in the sunshine, Jessi sits at the edge of the porch, and we listen for the rumble of a truck crossing the cattle guard—the hunter returning to finish the hunt—but the three vehicles that bump across go on up the road.

I write, and wait, and write. Jessi joins Bow in slumber. Todd 1 doesn't return.

Finally, I think I'm finished, or ready to give up. Hopefully the buck has died or will bleed out soon. If he crosses the fence back onto public land he might aid hunters as bear bait—bear hunters are also prowling around—but if he ends here, on me, he will be safe eating for scavenging coyotes, ravens, and eagles. And maybe a bear or two readying for winter. Like me, in a normal year—building up the woodpile, fixing weather stripping, caching a supply of canned goods and dry dogfood, and fixing lots of fence before the cattle come—but I won't live at the cabin this winter.

At headquarters we will still have to break ice each morning, and feeding will take hours; I will stay close to family, my grandkids, with my dogs and my horses nearby. In this time of COVID I could rejoice at being in the proximity of people as well as animals. But the longing goes deeper. It's more than hugs I want. This cabin, with my dogs and sightings of birds and bears and mountain lion tracks and mustangs, rarely a truck on the road once hunting season is over, quiet returning to my life the way it has to this day. Still . . .

He said he would come back and find that buck.

I give up on waiting. On hope. I have to pee. And eat a real meal. I stand and stretch and turn to head inside to warmth and food, to comfort. In one last glance at the road, I see tucked in near my gate the white Toyota with blaze orange on its roof. Jessi at the porch edge knew about the pickup all along. I scan the flat below the cabin, the sagebrush that grows tall with age on the far side of the puddled creek, the deer trail that angles past chunks of sandstone fallen from the cliff above, and up through junipers and piñon pines toward another sagebrush flat.

I don't see the hunter. But he's out there. Todd is there.

10

The Truth I Cannot Tell

Sometimes pain is the call of a wound that needs tending, and sometimes it is the sting of its healing.
—Melissa Febos, "On Loving and Leaving New York: Home"

San Juan River, Utah, and Ranch Headquarters, Dolores, Colorado, Fall to Winter 2020–21

Exceptional drought and COVID continuing, we mourn death losses and the missing monsoons. I think of loneliness and season and the triggers I find in the turn of light on leaves preparing to let go. I have my own autumn sadness when in my mind I see the Sierra Nevada black-oak leaves changing from bright yellow to orange to falling. While I love the season, that sadness creeps in. And then, along with the natural shortening of days, comes the enforced time change. I have to be careful, caring for my psyche as I would a puppy, fondly, firmly.

This year drought has exacerbated it all as I've watched the grasses and the creek and the wildlife struggle for simple survival. The world suffers on so many levels, yet for me drought seems the hardest to bear. Is that selfish? I don't know. I do know the ache as I watch a puddle in the creek recede, the tracks in the mud around it holding the tales of the critters searching for a sip. Where will they go when the puddles dry, the surfaces cracked and hard?

In the driest Flagstaff years, when Smith and I lived in the cabin in the ponderosas, pronghorn moved up from the surrounding sagebrush steppe to the forest in search of water. I watched them pace our fenceline and didn't place a trough on their side and fill it from our precious water supply. I wish I had. There's that thing about not feeding wildlife so it doesn't become dependent on us, but water? In drought years—in any year—what makes

12. The section in Disappointment Valley. Photo by Tyler Lausten.

me deserve water more for my toilet-flushing than pronghorn do for their survival? How will it get figured out in the future, who gets water and who doesn't? Is a bee's need for water less important than mine? No, and not because we need the bees to pollinate the plants so we can continue to have food but because bees are beings just as we are. So, what, we water the bees? Yes. We do. Terry keeps water in shallow dishes with rocks on the bottom so the bees can land, drink, and lift off without threat of drowning.

Some snow has come to the valley. Deer, elk, and mustangs can turn ice crystals into water, but it's too late and too cold for the moisture to benefit the plants that tried so hard this summer to grow.

Knowing I wouldn't winter in Disappointment, I said yes when my friend Amber invited me on a San Juan River trip with her nine-year-old son, Orrin, and two couples—water in a time of drought a luxury, same with time away from the ranch. I chose not to take my own boat—rigging after too long off the river, finding leaks and straps and gear—instead floating on Amber's blue, thirteen-foot Hyside, sharing the bow space with Orrin, each of us on our designated sides as we honored COVID precautions despite the trip being outdoors.

In Flagstaff I was invited on my first river trip. Unlike the fancy, high-dollar commercial trips, on a private trip we did all the work ourselves—hauling gear up and down the riverbanks to make camp, cooking the meals and cleaning up, washing dishes, rigging the boats after breakfast. I went on as many private trips as possible through the spring-summer-fall seasons. Eventually I worked some on the river. Now my hands mostly held the reins, but on the San Juan I held the oars again. Palms wrapping around padded grips, without thought my arms, torso, legs, and feet knew what to do and I felt a chill, not from splashing through a riffle but the chill of body memories, in this case good ones, the whisper and sunshine of an autumn river reminding me of a previous self.

Amber switched places with me, and Orrin and I lounged on the cooler that doubled as our seat. Feet resting on the bow to thaw, we leaned back and soon our shoulders touched. This was a hard year for him, for my grandkids, for every child worldwide. Orrin held the fear that his mother would get sick. I shared that fear for my own mother, who at eighty-seven lived in a senior residence that took every precaution. Her daughters not allowed to see her, I wouldn't have risked an airport or plane even if we were. This river trip was a stretch. But we had three rafts—three bubbles if you will—and Orrin and I grew more comfortable as bubble-mates with each passing river mile.

We entered part of the canyon where the steady push of water through time had undercut the sandstone formation. Sunlight shining on water reflected up onto the rock in circles and waves and currents of light. "Glimpses!" Orrin said. The reflections moved as we did and vanished as the riverbank changed to a sandy beach where cottonwoods thrived despite invasive tamarisks and Russian olive trees.

"He was six when he started calling them that," Amber said. "I couldn't correct him."

We entered another stone corridor, circular smiles of sunlight gleaming off water onto rock. That's what a river trip is, I thought. Glimpses of color and light; of desert bighorn sheep high on the side of a canyon; of a mule deer doe dipping her lips to the river until we drew near. Glimpses into other people's lives as we floated, evening glimpses the talk around campfires.

Fires restricted in this year of drought, Angela made a circle of tiny, solar-powered lights. Cold descending under the moonlit sky, water heating on a stove for dishwashing and tea, we sat around our solar-powered fire as Angela sang us a lullaby in her lovely, Gaelic-sounding voice. Orrin asked her to sing the song again, and we joined in as if we had voices to match hers, because on the river shyness erodes like sandstone as we squat to pee at river's edge or change clothes beside rafts that don't actually reach our waists.

As others retreated to their tents—Amber and Orrin sharing, the couples sharing—I set mine up in the kitchen where it filled the space between stove tables and serving tables, the wall of the canyon beyond, the river below. Loneliness is but a thought, I thought, and in wool socks, knit cap, and every layer of fleece I had, I found sleep in the cold night.

In the morning, wisps of clouds rose in the west as light rose in the east and a shade of rose entered the canyon from the sky, coloring walls and floor and the ceiling of this Earth in blush, in rouge, my heart flushing with a color that felt like love.

After breakfast Amber, Angela, and I jumped into the river, me the middle in height and weight and the oldest by far, and so self-conscious after a long time of no one seeing me, yet as the frigid river awakened my senses, I realized I didn't care.

Election Day found me at the mustang cabin packing some things to take back to the ranch for a winter built on summer drought, surprised at how despondent I felt after the days of river and people and laughter. But the whole world—at least the western world—balanced on pins and needles, knowing that our sanity was at stake, if not our lives. Nothing to do in this valley strung between not knowing and knowing but wait, though I could have cleaned or walked or written. But I was stalled out with a dead battery—fear? Dread? What is despondency, anyway?

I looked for glimpses. The sky clouded over. I wondered if life-giving rain lingered on the horizon—rain a most positive sign. Finally I headed to the ranch, where Tyler and I sat side by side on the couch, watching the returns on our computers, shifting for news between NPR, Stephen Colbert, Trevor Noah, and Rachel Maddow.

General malaise persisted even after Joe and Kamala won. Tyler left for California and winter swells and to build river surfboards in a warmer shop. I settled into the cold with my dogs; Ken, Kathy, and the kids were in their house two hundred yards away. Sometime in December a package arrived in the mail: a box of See's chocolates and a thank-you note from Todd 2 for letting them look for his buck on my property. I wrote and thanked him back. I didn't know he was sick. The galleys for my book arrived and between morning and afternoon chores I spent the time proofreading. More waiting—for calving season to start, for the book to appear in print, for COVID to be over. I knew I should work on a new writing project, but I couldn't find it inside me: creativity, energy, a new impulse or idea.

The world turned white. Chores took even longer in the snow.

After parking the tractor and feed wagon under the cover of the big equipment barn, Ken and I walk down to our houses on the road that parts stands of piñon pine, juniper, and Gambel oak, Ken with his long strides and quicker pace increasing the distance between us with each step. I see Solstice in the house pasture next to an old juniper, one of my Criollo first-calf heifers, her markings like white clouds in a dark sky. Slowing but not stopping, I note that she just stands, still, under the shelter of the tree's branches, away from the other Criollo heifers who wait near a gate for breakfast.

Snow crunches to ice beneath my insulated, knee-high Neoprene boots. Where it's uncrunched, the snow measures a foot deep on top of a baselayer of packed ice on the dirt road. I would follow in Ken's footsteps in the fresh snow, but they are too far apart. He doesn't pause as he passes Solstice.

Earlier, when we fed the Angus cows in the lower pasture—the remainder of the cows we got with the Forest Service allotment—two new calves bawled forlornly, wet-shivering, clumps of ice hanging from their ears. I drove the tractor pulling the wagon, Ken balancing back there as he forked off large flakes of hay and the cornstalks he buys from the Ute farm so the calves have dry places to lie. No cab or roof over either of us to protect us from the elements, I shiver like the calves, the snow having melted through my knit hat and heavy jacket and insulated overalls into my flannel shirt and silk baselayer and tank top and sports bra, clear to my flesh, where snowmelt meets sweat as I hurry to catch up with Ken. At first I don't notice his tracks veering off to his house, and when I do I keep hustling toward the hay to get the heifers fed so we can return to the lower pasture where we left the two calves cold and bawling miserably.

I love the small, sweet cows like Solstice. But it doesn't matter what I love when snow falls and cows are hungry and calves are getting born. No time for preference—this is a time of doing the next thing, whatever it is, however you feel.

When feeding, one of the suspect mothers of the two new calves—206, a tall black whiteface cow—kicked at a little bull calf. Black markings like hands coming together in prayer across his white face, the calf tried and failed to get a teat in his hungry mouth before the cow wandered off. Another cow, a large black Angus, meandered through the feeding cattle, looking, sniffing, searching for her newborn. But the second bawling calf, a solid-black heifer, hovered at the lower end of the field and the second cow seemed not to hear her.

I shove pitchfork-loads of grass hay over the fence to the heifers. The snow keeps coming. Winter surprises me every year—the cold and the snow—because I grew up coastal and tropical and didn't know until first moving to the desert years ago that deserts are so much more than hot. The summers suit me, when this desert country *is* hot, and dry, and so striking with its monsoon storms, warm-season grasses springing up, prickly pear blossoms blooming. The snow, too, is stunning on the mountains, but we're heading toward spring today and the snow is wet and cold and I'm cold and wet and I see Ken coming down with a bottle, this for a twin born two weeks ago. The mother took the smaller twin, abandoning Chloe (so named by Lacey) to a future as a bottle calf, comfort coming from my grandkids, their mother, and me as we feed Chloe and pet her, but we don't lick and low as a mother cow would and Chloe is lonely. She butts Ken as he feeds her the bottle of warm milk. The snow does not cease falling.

"Solstice is standing off by herself," I tell Ken.

"She's fine," he says, finishing with Chloe. "Get the old towels," and he hurries past me, back up to his house. I go to mine, not bothering to remove anything wet, chunks of snow tracking me across the cement floor. The stack of towels stands ready on the couch, laundered and stiff from air-drying by fireplace-insert heat. The dryer doesn't work. Something about the 220-power source. We will have to dig down to the power line with the backhoe when the earth thaws. This winter my life hangs by the fire.

Ken has my Toyota running, exhaust fuming behind it, the heater turned up high. I put the towels on the backseat, set the fresh bottle between my feet, and say, "Solstice."

Ken gasses through the ruts left by the morning feeding, snowdrifts already filling the furrows. "I saw her with another heifer. She's fine. We have to see what's going on down here."

I jump out to open the gate, snow slapping my face, and leave the gate open, as the cows won't venture out while there's still hay on the ground. On the snow. Ken maneuvers across the snowfield through humps of calves mouthing hay or lying on the cornstalk beds. Cows munch with their heads down, or up as they eye us, wondering if we're here to feed them again already. There's the small prayer-faced bull calf, his voice loud and mournful. And the little heifer, farther away, her cry wrenching through the hush of snow. As the tall cow, 206, heads off toward shielding trees, we follow her. She stands in the snow-shadow of a large, thick-branched, one-seed juniper, looking around, confused. She half-circles the tree, sniffing the snow and the branches and the detritus near the trunk, and walks back toward the hay.

"She's too old to be stupid," Ken says, which means that first-calf heifers can be like me when I had Ken, learning how to nurse and care for a baby, while to seasoned mothers those acts come easily, and cows can usually find their calves. But in this cold, wet-snow morning something has happened that throws the cow—and us—off.

In the blizzard of snow and cows feeding we don't see the second cow, but there's the prayer calf bawling to the sky. Ken drives close, stops, throws open the door and grabs the calf, and when I get the back door open he sets the calf on the backseat. Twisting awkwardly, I start rubbing the calf with a towel. "Not too much," Ken says. "Leave some mother's scent on him."

Ken has the bottle. Inside the Toyota's heat I start to sweat, but the calf trembles with cold as I rub him and break ice cubes off his ears. Ken inserts the nipple and pulls it when the calf's lips find it and soon the calf latches on, drinking with deep gulps, and Ken takes the bottle away. As I keep the calf from climbing onto the console between us Ken drives the small pickup toward 206, who looks across the white landscape, the air so thick with white

I can't see the promontories and ridges of the Mesa Verde skyline, or even the piñon-juniper rim of this pasture.

Ken pulls close, steps out, grabs the calf from the backseat, and sets it near 206, who we hope really is his mother. Invigorated but not full from the warm milk fresh in his belly, the prayer calf reaches for the teat, the cow turns away, and he follows; she stops, he butts her, she lets him suck, and we head toward the next calf. The second possible new-mother cow still searching, she stops at a white lump on the ground, sniffs through the cold cloak of snow, and a calf jumps up and goes right to nursing, still humpbacked, legs curved from the womb.

"Also born today," I say, noting the cow's ear-tag number to record later. Storms bring on the calves. Six will be born this day. Ken and I won't stop working until well after dark.

The little all-black heifer has increased her piteous wailing. Ken plows through the snow toward her and we repeat the abduction-and-warming process. When we plop her back in the snow no one pays attention. Then through the blurring white we see 206, her head up, looking, sniffing the cold air even as the prayer calf nurses.

"Shit," Ken says.

"Twins?"

"We don't need more twins," he says. But he steps out and grabs the black heifer again, thrusting her onto my lap, and steers to 206. I push out of the passenger seat with the calf in my arms. Because she's a twin she's smaller than normal but still forty-five pounds of wiggle, and I run three steps toward the cow, set the calf down, and jump back into the Toyota before the cow can give chase, which they're wont to do. Ken backs up twenty feet and we watch. The prayer calf still latched on, the tall cow sniffs this new being; she sniffs through towel and people smells to her own scent and starts licking the cold away.

"Yep, twins." I take off my sopped hat, my hair also wet. Hats and gloves on the dash near the heater vents, we leave the pasture, close the gate, and park near the barn.

"Let's get dry before checking them again," Ken says.

I'm already through the gate into the house pasture where the Criollo heifers eat hay in the snow. Solstice is with them. I walk among them, looking at bags and vulvas, which tell me how close they are to calving. "Solstice's bag is huge," I say to Ken's back.

He's heading toward his house. "I saw her earlier. She's fine."

I look. Some blood on her tail. Her vulva smaller than yesterday. Her bag tight. "She's calved. I'm going to look for her calf." I walk north through the snow toward where Solstice stood alone under the juniper, not noticing that Ken has climbed the fence and headed west. I see lumps of cow shit covered in snow—any one of them could be a tiny calf—and I trip toward one then another then to the spot by the juniper and it's lying there stone still, red fur wet from snow and birth-slick and I fall to my knees, shed my gloves, and feel it for heat for breath for life and with none of that present I pick up its head and try to make it breathe as I cry out like the twins in the lower pasture bawling to the sky.

I shake it. Cold. Nose mouth ears cold. Ken walking toward me along the fenceline. "Is it alive?" he asks. I thought he'd gone inside.

I shake my head. Shake my heart. I shake the calf—truly there's no life in there. The afterbirth pooled nearby. When I saw Solstice earlier, alone beside the tree, I walked past on the snow-road without stopping to look more closely. Without climbing the fence into the pasture to check on my first-calf heifer, who was born on winter solstice high on a plateau in a stand of piñon pines in an eleven-thousand-acre pasture to a Criollo cow we had bought from the ranch in southern New Mexico not knowing she would calve out of season, and I hadn't watched closely, only noticed that the cow went missing in a storm. I looked for her for two days in all the roadless areas—climbing the steep, snow-covered hillsides to the mesa tops, combing through piñon-juniper stands, scouring arroyos—until I found not only the pair but the birthplace. I named the cow Walkabout, the calf Solstice, and today I walked past Solstice without stopping to check her and I can tell you I hated myself right then.

Ken says to go get warm, and he heads to his house. He feels terrible too, I know.

I stay kneeling in the snow before the calf, both of us wet to the skin. Solstice had not finished cleaning her off. Yes, her. A tiny red heifer. Full Criollo. For what reason did she die? All I can think as I bend and touch my forehead to her cold fur and bleed tears onto her still body is *I was not there.*

I've only done it once, though I have wanted to many times. When I got clean—went through detox and five weeks of inpatient treatment and no longer had drugs to use when the white lightning of pain or anger seared through me—my mind went to cutting, to hurting myself bigger than whatever caused the hurt. It felt good, this truth I have not told, my sharp hunting knife slicing through the skin of my arm—that part where other people get banded tattoos—slicing again and again until the outer skin split like when you skin an animal and the elastic of the hide separates to reveal flesh and the blood slowly seeps to the surface and beads. I walk away from the tiny calf to check on her mother, thinking about where to cut. How deep. I'm burning.

Solstice is eating. Which of my knives is sharp enough, I wonder. Inside beside the fire I pull layers of clothing like skin off my body. Jacket heavy with snowmelt, draped over a chair, dripping, the straps of the insulated overalls pulled off my shoulders, hanging from my waist. The calf lying dead in the snow. The wrists? Flannel shirt shed. Another log on the fire, sparks flaring. My hair dripping down my back through black silk baselayer and cotton tank and my bra. Calf dead. *Dead!* Because I didn't stop, instead hurrying after someone else's agenda. My skin red with cold as I peel off silk. Heat reaching me finally from outside me, fire still burning within—in my stomach, my arms. White lightning I called it when rage burned down my arms and I wanted to strike out, but now I want to strike in again and again, and I look at the crinkled skin of my past on arms where sun has burned and points have punctured, there, I look for the tracks of old pain. From before. Before I got clean. The before and after of me. Young and old, the same and different, unidentical twins, both me, all me; Ken at the door. Entering.

"We better go check on them." He steps back outside.

Still in my boots, having not pulled them or overalls off, I find dry silk and flannel and hat and cover my skin and scars, pulling the overalls up, straps over my shoulders, the jacket back on.

The Toyota already running and warm, "I looked at Solstice's calf," Ken says. "Its hooves are clean. No mud or dirt from trying to stand. It never got up."

"It's snowing. The hooves wouldn't show dirt."

"It was either stillborn or it suffocated from the sac over its nose."

"I didn't stop. *I didn't stop.* I was following you. *You* didn't stop."

"I didn't see her." He hadn't looked sideways. The big hood of his jacket like blinders. He didn't see her.

"I told you she was standing, alone."

He drives through more drifting snow.

"I *told* you. You didn't listen." The fight is in me, and I want it out.

"*You* didn't listen," he says, "to your own intuition. *My* intuition told me to get to these two calves. Yours was telling you to stop, go look. But if she was standing still, the calf was already dead. She'd already had it and it was dead."

He stops at the gate. I get out, want to slam the door, prop the gate open on snow, get back in, and Ken drives down toward the cattle. We scan the cows—there's 206, foraging through what's left of the hay. She hasn't slipped her afterbirth; the string of it hangs beneath her tail. Most of the calves huddle on piles of hay or cornstalks. I see the small curl of the prayer calf like a dog sleeping, but the black heifer stands, bawling.

I look at Ken. "Would Solstice take it?"

"You mean graft it on her?"

"We could try."

Number 206, an older cow, appears worn and on the thinner side. Tired. Confused by the twins but trying to make it right. Afterbirth hanging, which happens—they don't always pass it cleanly like Solstice did—but sometimes it presents problems.

Ken maneuvers toward the bawling black heifer. "We better do it now before the cow gets attached," and he's out the door and the calf's in the back and we slip and slide away before 206 knows what's missing, stopping for the gate and again at the barn, where Ken puts the new calf with bottle-calf Chloe temporarily, and I trudge through the snow to get the little dead heifer, holding her snugly to my chest like my own newborns. She weighs no more than thirty-five pounds, these full-Criollo calves from first-calf heifers so small.

Ken has a large box cut open and flattened on the cement floor of the barn. I lay the heifer down on the cardboard bed, my hand resting on her forehead for only a moment. Ken looks at her. His hunting knife sharp, ready, he rolls the calf onto her back, exposing the belly. Knife near the throat, he slices into the skin, following the line down to her navel, sometimes going over a spot again and again until the outer skin splits and the inner flesh is revealed, red as the little heifer's coat, which the black heifer will soon wear.

I watch my son on his knees on the cold floor, both of us cold and tired though it's still morning—tired of the year, the drought despite snow, death; he concentrates, careful with the sharp knife, following a pattern his father taught him, a pattern hunters know, but he deviates, the calf not gutted like a deer, stripped only, the hide sliced cleanly around the wrists, but they're ankles, really, so the black heifer's legs will go through like arms into sleeves.

I step back out into snowflakes and bring Solstice to a pen. Ken has finished skinning. The naked carcass stays on cardboard, and he dresses the black heifer, pushing her front hooves through the sleeves of the dead calf's hide, which stretches over her back, then pushing the hind feet through. It must be cold to the live heifer at first, certainly strange. We have to hurry to get her warm. As Ken readies the squeeze chute, I move Solstice from one pen to another, pressing her forward with my voice, my body near her ribs, her hip. She enters the chute and Ken closes the gate behind her and squeezes her slightly with a lever above his head. She's caught and stands quietly, but he puts a cow halter on her anyway, dallies the lead rope around a bar, hands me the end of the rope, and I hold her head so she can't fight as he maneuvers the black heifer in her new red coat toward a teat. Solstice kicks at first but Ken's persistence helps the calf find the teat and warm milk dribbles down her throat and it's good and she suckles for more.

11

Headwaters

> In those days of crispness I want to linger long enough to hear every sound and look far enough to see into forever.
>
> —J. Drew Lanham, *The Home Place*

Lone Cone, Groundhog, and Disappointment Valley, Colorado, Summer 2021

We climb higher, the Tacoma grunting along the scree-and-dirt track at 10,600 feet, aiming toward Lone Cone's timberline and the end of the road. Tyler has traveled all over this mountain, hiking and camping above the limits of trees, and he wants to show me something. He wanted to show me last summer, too, but work at cow camp across the divide kept me too busy for adventures beyond the daily thrills of checking cattle and fences ahorseback in bear country.

COVID restrictions modified somewhat, my younger sister has spent three weeks with us as we prepared to move the cows upcountry: shopping and stocking refrigerators and freezers at the ranch, readying the cow cabin for summer occupation, putting up the lay-down fencing. Peg will leave in a few days, which gives me a reason to go with Tyler that is more important than my own marveling. Tyler drives, and Peg, quiet with awe, sits in the backseat with Jessi.

Tyler stops for birds. Any kind of bird. Anywhere on this road that holds only us this early summer afternoon. His long camera lens finds birds where my eyes cannot, and he clicks away then looks at the screen, telling us names for which I don't have my own internal images. Gray jays I know, but we don't see any as we ascend above aspens into alpine firs and spruces.

Gray jays first thrilled me in Alaska with Tyler at Denali National Park and Preserve. And on Tyler's birthday in mid-November last year, as we hiked along a snow road on another part of this southern thrust of Colorado's Rocky Mountains, a pair of gray jays followed us for an hour, watching, circling, bouncing from tree limb to tree limb to better see us, Tyler's lens rating their movements as my binoculars struggled to catch up. Why their soft grays stir me the way the faded denims of piñon jays do, I don't know. Some things I leave to my heart.

"Here," Tyler says, pulling onto the shoulder. "It's a short walk."

Peg, Jessi, and I empty from the Tacoma as Tyler unbends and stretches. Peg has come to Colorado from sea-level Central Coast California, and she has come from a bout with COVID. The elevation is hard on her, and my lungs aren't yet acclimated to higher altitude after wintering at seven thousand feet. As we walk slowly, I stoop to phone-camera photograph each unfamiliar high-mountain wildflower. There are many.

"Come on," Tyler says, and I remember that he is showing me something special.

In the months when the lockdown first occurred, Tyler got stuck at the ranch. Rather than flounder in malaise like his mother, he became a more avid birder. Fascinated since boyhood with anything sky, as he socially distanced he took to the backcountry with camera, lenses, and tripod to better learn the birds, bringing home hundreds then thousands of photographs to study until he could identify myriad birds on the fly.

Observing him, I realized that I pushed blindly through the days, wishing them over, hoping to outpace depression rather than looking for beauty and wonder. Sometimes glimpses would come in flashes like the click of Tyler's shutter, and I would stop and notice the magic of snow, ice crystals on water, my granddaughter's large blue irises encircled with a darker color of blue, the eyes of a sage.

But. My writing had stalled out with my heart.

My book launched and Peg came to visit after she recovered sufficiently from COVID, and on summer solstice we moved the cows to the high country, including full-Criollo Solstice and her Angus calf (neither she nor the calf know they are not blood relatives). Finally I have accompanied Tyler to this spot near timberline that he's waited a year to show me.

If I paid attention with wide-angle eyes rather than zooming in on tiny blossoms, I would have noticed an openness in the forest. As Peg wanders off to see the area for herself, I trip over a log, releasing the aromas of sun-baked and moist decay. Walking more carefully, I watch my feet, then look up . . . and it's there before me: clear, shallow water reflecting sunlight and spruce boughs and delicate grass stems, a natural, spring-fed pond amid the trees, the scent of fresh water mixing with recycling forest and new growth. As I walk around the pond from the still-water end with its skim of lichen-colored green toward a point where the trees pull together again, scat of elk and deer appears in the bog moss that squishes beneath my boots. I look for tracks—this is a lynx reintroduction area, maybe a mountain lion's home—and refocus on water.

A spring and winter's frozen moisture feed this place in which water gathers and pauses and moves so slowly toward the tiniest stream that I find the movement imperceptible, though a rill of water escapes, its voice the sound of a baby learning to laugh as water finds its way between and beneath and around mossy roots and fallen branches and trunks of trees turning into forest floor. Blossoms of splitleaf paintbrush erupt beside the delicate stream, outer leaves of flaming pink opening, and as I stand and absorb pond and petal, spruce and sky, I feel something loosen inside me.

Tyler appears. "That's the source," he says.

I look at him, at his blue eyes and blond curls and big smile. Because of the lengthy custody dispute early on, Tyler is the son I mostly raised, and in the ways of sons and single mothers, he knows me.

"The source of Disappointment Creek," he says.

He has waited a year to show me the source of the creek that runs through miles of our lower country and runs past the mustang cabin, this mountain pond the beginning of the water that flows through my life.

I wish I could say I hug Tyler, but the year of not touching doesn't escape me so instead I get as still and quiet as the water in the pond. Here, in the good years, melt from the snowpack on Lone Cone (which Lacey calls "Snow Cone") drips down the mountain, joins the hidden spring, fills the pond, and releases into the trickling stream, which, joined by other small tributaries, becomes a creek and curls behind a ponderosa-clad hill to begin its meander down Disappointment Valley, more drainages adding snowmelt and rainfall, the terrain dropping through montane ecosystem to high desert, where salt-desert shrubs mark the land: winterfat, fourwing saltbush, rabbitbrush, greasewood, shadscale, broom snakeweed.

The lower country is so different from this high, clearwater pond in the shade of Douglas fir and blue spruce, bright pink wildflowers rippling outward. I want to strip and wade into the water to my waist and hold my arms out wide like CMarie Fuhrman in those exquisite O Idaho photos on Facebook and thank the water gods and sky gods and Earth gods and Creator and All That Is for the wonder of water, of life. But Tyler is the only photographer present to capture the moment, and he is my son, and I realize he has disappeared to give me these fresh breaths of water alone—and no doubt to look for birds—and I kneel in the soft, moist moss and cup my hands to the stream again and again, drinking all I can from the source. Then I sit on a log that crosses the delicate headwaters of Disappointment Creek. And I write.

Amy M. Hale, who cowboys and writes for a living, says, "Cowboy is a verb. It is something that you *do*, not something that you are. It isn't about your outfit. It is about a skill set."

On many ranches, cowboys don't actually cowboy every day—they don't ride among cattle every single day. Sometimes that work happens in seasonal bursts (the seasons themselves may differ, based on the location of the ranch. In Central Coast California we calved in the fall, because the growing season started then and ended in May or June, depending on rainfall, opposite of what we do in Colorado). During branding season, we gather cattle from pasture to corral, where the work takes place with the help of neighbors (or not). On a big spread this could take days, or weeks. Summers, we ride to check cattle and move them from one pasture to another until mid-October when we gather and ship them off the mountain, this rhythm maintained by most ranches around here. Fall works include weaning and shipping—cattle again gathered to a set of pens where they get sorted (cows from calves) and hauled to fall or winter range, the sale barn, a feedlot for some (*not* my Criollo calves).

When I cowboy, I hope some skills come with me to speak through my hands on the reins and legs along my horse's sides. I hope my mind stays

13. Kat and Savanna with Little Red (Criollo). Photo by Tyler Lausten.

open so I can hear where the cattle might be—with my ears, with Savanna's help, and with my intuition: *If I were a mama cow, where would I hide that calf? If I were a steer, where would I linger? If I wanted to escape, which way would I go?* Cowboying can amount to solving puzzles: finding the critters, deciding how best to move them, watching their ears to know which way they're thinking of going and when they're about to break. Even in the corral, it's important to read cattle and to time moves right. If I urge my horse one second too soon, the cow may turn back instead of going through the gate.

Or late—in that one-second pause the calf hits the hole instead of turning back. Ken can see the moves I should make, and when, but he can't control me, and this frustrates him no end. Of course, he makes the same mistakes (though not as often)—I think everyone on a horse does, because you've got cattle, horses, and people present, independent beings with their own minds, muscles, and intuition.

Sometimes we dance, and that's the beauty of it, Savanna's body and mine turning in time with the cattle's moves. The rest of the time we rectify mistakes.

Cowboying may include any number of activities and responsibilities, as other work on a ranch abounds. Fence projects, always—maintaining fences, which means walking or riding long stretches, fence pliers and tie wire in hand or saddlebag. Some spreads, so big they have different employees or even crews for different jobs—cowboys, fence crew, mechanics, haying crew—may have several projects going at the same time. Someone else would take care of all the fencing while Ken and I gathered, for instance, and I will say that Tyler has done a lot of fence work without us. But he's not a full-time ranch hand; he's my son. Does he want to be a ranch hand? No! Even so, he helps with sorting and hauling cattle, and with fencing.

On the national forest we have the lay-down fencing, which we put up before taking the cows up, and take down when the cows leave, before the first big snow. These fences have treated posts set in the ground every hundred feet or so, with metal T-posts set in between at sixteen-foot intervals. Wire runs the length of the fence but isn't clipped to the T-posts; with tie wire we attach it to aspen staves, and weave it: bottom (smooth) wire on one side, for the duration; the next two wires (barbed) on the opposite side of the T-posts; top wire (smooth) on the same side as the bottom wire (the smooth wire makes it wildlife friendly). To take the fence down we lift the top wire over the T-posts, which puts three wires on one side so the staves fall over; hence the fence lies flat on the ground and the weight of snow won't tweak or break the wires. It's a great, pain-in-the-ass idea, befitting snow country.

Over time the snow pushes the set posts deeper into the ground—when we got the Forest Service piece we inherited a bunch of short fences. Plus the permanent fences built long ago have lots of broken wires, and shorter T-posts each summer.

Danny had taken down a long stretch of a bad fence, pulling up T-posts, rolling up the wire, leaving big piles of each. Our Forest Service contract obliged us to build a mile of new fence to replace the old. First, with Ken's bulldozer, chainsaws, and muscle, Ken and Tyler would have to clear dozens of downed and leaning aspens, Ken on the dozer pushing litter into huge mounds off to the side to make way for the new fence. Next they would build pipe H-braces at strategic places—where the fence makes a turn or a gate needs to go. But drought and fire bans restricted the bulldozer and welding our first summer, so the cattle walked freely over the line where a fence should have separated Saddle and Groundhog Creek Pastures (all pasture names courtesy of the Forest Service). At headquarters, Ken and Tyler cut thirty-two-foot lengths of oil-field pipe (provided by the Forest Service) into nine-foot lengths, and this summer, after making the "dozer trail," they started the hard work of welding pipe and stretching wire. Next summer, with even the grandchildren helping, we will tie the wire and complete the fence, the division of pastures a surprise to the cows.

Fixing fence possibly my least favorite task, I do it, often alone when in Disappointment Valley, the fences as old and rundown as those on the mountain but not as short (less snow). The Criollos don't bother the Disappointment fences. Maybe because they simply prefer the desert, or maybe because they know the grass isn't any greener on the other side.

One day on the mountain, checking a boundary fence on Savanna, I encountered a man stopped at his gate. He introduced himself. "Just call me one of the Georgia Boys," he said, "though I'm the dad." I'd heard of the Georgia Boys, who had private land adjacent to our Forest Service lease. We talked for a while, enjoying the cool breeze of mountain country. He asked me about myself, the first person (man) to do so other than Cliff in the valley. "People say, what's that author-woman doing running a bunch of cows? I thought I'd ask you."

"Thank you." I meant this and told him some of my ranching past. "My great-grandfather's in the Cowboy Hall of Fame," I said, hoping he'd share that tidbit the next time someone wanted to gossip *about* me instead of talking *to* me.

When I met his wife, she asked, "Are you the author?"

I nodded and smiled. Not a bad reputation to have, I realized.

C ⊃-

If we're working on a fence, we don't say we're cowboying. Maybe that's the difference between rancher and cowboy, as far as jobs go. The rancher (or ranch owner) might do a little of everything, including a lot of paperwork (which is worse than working on fences). The ranch manager, in this case Ken, looks at the bigger picture, consults with me, and together we make decisions, though I sometimes defer to him when it comes to the cattle—especially the Angus cows, which I now think of as his—so basically Ken works for me, and I work for him.

But I don't have to weld. Or drive the bulldozer. When Ken's father wanted to teach me to drive the Caterpillar D-8 he bought with money from the sale of the last cows, I said no.

In between seasonal and project work, or when we've finished with horseback work early in a day, we might sit in camp chairs in the shade of the aspens at cow camp, the kids balancing on the rough-hewn teeter-totter or roping the dummy steer. Sometimes friends visit and even camp with us. Sometimes cowboying means drinking beer or whiskey around a campfire into an evening (though not for me).

C ⊃-

Up on the mountain, some days just seem like days—often I don't know which day of the week it is, because it doesn't matter to the cattle, the horses, or us until the kids go back to school. But days are not just days. They are birthdays and wedding days and anniversaries and death days. And anniversaries of those. These days happen all over the world, in all time zones, all the time.

Today in our little world within the world, Walt turned three. His father brought him up to cow camp to join us for lunch, followed by fishing in Groundhog Reservoir. We sat beside a large rock that serves as a table, watching some new Corriente cows (not Criollos, but a good deal Ken found) circle a pasture, checking the parameters of their new world.

Walt's father made him a sandwich. After a few minutes we noticed that Walt happily munched on bread alone.

"What's this?" his father asked, picking ham and cheese up off the grass.

"For the cows," Walt said. He's three. Today.

Today in my small world, inside one of the minutes in which we ate and conversed and enjoyed a three-year-old's company, Robin died. A text came through later as I sat in the GMC in the midst of thunder and distant lightning and rain sprinkles, watching the new cows continue to mill as I contemplated saddling up and checking cattle in a pasture a couple of miles away.

Robin had cancer. She'd been fighting it and living with it and in remission and it returned while her partner, my cousin Nancy, got cancer and fought it and lived with it and did not remiss but died. For the last four years of their many years together, they both had cancer and chemo and radiation and pain and sickness and love.

I was writing a book while they had cancer. Nancy read several drafts. She didn't line edit; she gave me feedback in a big way—what worked and what didn't and why—and I would change things in a big way. She helped give the book a course I couldn't find alone.

When four galley copies arrived, Nancy was very sick. I wanted to send her one, because suddenly it appeared that she might not make it until the May publication date. In her copy I handwrote the dedication that would be in the published book. It was to her. At the post office I debated over $48 to overnight it or going priority for $7.95.

Her son told me that in her last few days she wanted *Desert Chrome* close, on her nightstand, and that he read parts of it to her in her last hours, he and Robin and Nancy's sister Mary in the last circle of her world.

That $48 was the best money I've ever spent.

In May, I sent Robin, Jason, and Mary copies of the published book, the dedication to Nancy there in black and white.

In June, Robin sent me a card. I showed it to Peg. In it, Robin mentioned that she found the "calming truth" of page 265 especially poignant. Peg turned to the page. Read it aloud. A description of mustangs, of Raven and of Kootenai, "Raven's lifetime friend. The next year, Kootenai disappears. She is just . . . gone. A memory floating above the trees."

In July, Nancy would have turned eighty. With TJ I was doing an in-person reading and presentation on Nancy's birthday and intended to dedicate the event to her, but in the excitement and mayhem of in-the-flesh people, a stage and chairs and a microphone with loud feedback, I forgot. I hadn't written it down. It was in my mind only. In my heart. Not in words. Except in the book. For Nancy.

Two days later Walt turned three and Robin died. I sat in my pickup with the news as tears fell from the sky and cows milled and finally bedded down in green grass surrounded by aspens and wild rose and snowberry bushes, and I decided not to ride, instead driving slowly on slick roads down to the ranch where the roads turned dry and the sun shone and together Robin and Nancy floated above the trees.

July 24, when the temperature should climb into the high eighties, I am not cowboying. Instead, in jeans and Tyler's big flannel shirt, I drink hot chocolate on the porch of the mustang cabin. The wind-downed thermometer reads sixty-two degrees straight up—and I'm cold. A heavy mist settled in the night after a light rain and now clouds cover the entire sky, though the mist has risen, and with it smells of wet earth waft toward my nose like the rich steam of cacao. Landforms rimming the valley have returned—great Dakota Sandstone buttes and fins and cliffs to the north and east, Lone Cone and Groundhog Peaks, the Glade stretching across the south, La Sal Mountains far to the west, over there in Utah.

From across the canyon a rock squirrel emits a high-pitched warning. Small, white-rumped and -winged birds fly nearby. An orange hummingbird less than two inches tall rests on a piñon branch, leaving before my eyes can focus. A Woodhouse's scrub-jay bears the colors of the absent piñon jays. No swallows this morning. The other evening two common nighthawks dive-bombed bugs with the cliff swallows, angular wings making sharp dips and turns.

Though some human sky traffic has returned, but for birdsong and water it's still mostly quiet out here, just the hum of silence and occasionally the refrigerator. I relish whatever quiet-woman moments I can gather up inside me—fortitude, for later.

The other morning I saw a big black bear ambling along the mostly dry streambed, and I snuck to the edge of the cliff upon which the cabin sits to watch him as he bent toward a puddle. Peeking over the rim, I could see his muzzle and tongue, the ripples made by the kiss of a bear's lips on the face of a desert pool. It was so quiet I could *hear* the bear drinking, lapping at a puddle like a dog, the sound rising like the mist and steam of this morning and settling around me, the small-miracle massage my heart needed.

Now soft raindrops touch juniper and piñon, fourwing saltbush, bottle-brush squirreltail. Ricegrass that pushed through the dry spring and still has green shoots coming. The galleta surely has grown taller since yesterday—we got fifteen hundredths of an inch overnight in a slow, steady female rain, as Diné refer to moisture falling as gently as a bear's lips to water.

I listen for the diesel motor of Ken's Dodge. He and Tyler will arrive soon with a flatbed trailer to haul Ken's bulldozer to the mountain where the huge fencing project awaits. Another kind of strength: male.

This gives me a day off—a day on the porch, observing. Writing. Piñon jays! I haven't heard their raucous caws for a dry month's worth of days and feared what their absence might mean. Like the rain, they are back, at least right here right now.

We desperately need more rain—the tiny trickle eking from the headwaters pond on Lone Cone can't alone carry water far—and with open arms I will welcome monsoons when they arrive: thunder, flashes of lightning, flood, hard male rain returning life to the creek like piñon jays crying the sky alive. The way bears and my boys nudge my spirit awake.

Following the flock of piñon jays with my ears, I hear a diesel pickup—a mile away, closer. I know the turns, the gaps in the piñon and juniper forest where sound grows, the quieting down where the road rounds behind the hill. Like the crunch in the three-leaf sumac that marks the bear feeding, or the bawl in the aspens that marks the calf for its mother, and for me as, on Savanna, I make a final sweep of the thousand-acre pasture of trees. But that was yesterday. And tomorrow. Now it's young men and birdcalls that mark the morning.

12
Ode to Rain

The virga is struggling to make landfall.
—TJ Holmes

Disappointment Valley, Colorado, Summer 2021

At the mustang cabin on Sunday, as now nine-year-old Lacey and seven-year-old Lucas scrambled down the bank to play in the creek bottom, I said wait, look at the debris trapped behind the willows, at the mud, the puddles, the gouges in the bank near your shoulders from the last time the creek flashed, the mud not yet dry. I said look at the sky. It's monsoon season and we're actually getting monsoons. The creek is not a safe place to play when clouds grow in the sky. Even without rain right here, the creek could flash.

They pouted. They like creeks and ponds and mud.

But they climbed up the bank and looked for special rocks until we all had to leave to head back to ranch headquarters.

The creek did flash. I saw the evidence the next day. High water, rocks, logs, and debris had flown down the trail of creekbed, eroding culverts, stretching water gaps, the new scars in the banks higher than the kids' heads.

Two days later, after riding through cattle in the meadows between aspen groves, I drove on dry roads from cow camp back toward the cabin. Rounding a bend, I saw water running in Alkali Wash, an arroyo I had only seen dry. The water itself wasn't high, but the high-water mark showed several feet up the side of the arroyo. Rain clouds lingered on the far abutments that stand watch over the eastern end of the valley, but the road remained dry, the sky above blue.

14. Lacey and Lucas in pj's and pond mud at ranch headquarters. Photo by Tyler Lausten.

After stopping to take a video of Alkali Wash, I drove on, eager to see Salt Arroyo. And film there. I left the road to watch the water at what we call Little Cojo, a beach by a corner of creek at the section where the kids and I swim and inner-tube-float the late spring and early summer snowmelt from Lone Cone. But this runoff came from *rain*. After four summers of drought, Disappointment Creek caught and carried water that flooded the banks at Little Cojo.

Back to the road. Dead Dog and McDermott Arroyos running. Each ditch, gully, ravine, arroyo, some unnamed or with names I don't know, running.

Realizing I might beat the flash flood home, I raced water to the cabin. At the gate I had a twenty-minute lead. With journal, cell phone, and dogs I perched above a big bend in the creek, listening. Sound grew and faded as the creek's curves amplified and moderated it. Above the high mountains to the east, the sky darkened and lightning arced through it, thunder echoing. Still dry in my desert. Both dogs distraught from the booming, I put them in the safety of the Toyota. At the bend where the largest Fremont cottonwood grows—where two days before the kids had scrambled up the bank at my grandmotherly command—a change of sound.

Rushing and roaring, the debris flow rounded the bend and came straight at me as I stood on a solid ledge of Dakota Sandstone fifteen feet above the mass of water carrying logs and branches and *trees* churning in the tumultuous wall of water, the trenchant scent of unearthed debris and oil shale slicing the air.

Running back to the Toyota, I drove the rest of the way up the hill to the cabin, parked, and stepped out, followed by Jessi. After lifting Bow out, we three perched on the cliff high above the creek, listening to sound accelerate as around an elbow the flood came—a wave of detritus pushed over muddy puddles by crashing water frothy with pine needles and pine cones and sticks and the trees and the hollow sound of boulders banging into other boulders. A few raindrops dimpled the earth at my feet. Dark sky. Lightning closer. The muscle of flash and flood grew. A whisper of rain. A flock of maybe forty nighthawks followed the leading wave of floodwater, their white-marked wings flitting above the creek-river and then gone, replaced by an acrid smell as the creek, filled with Mancos Shale silt, roared and roiled and raced on past.

Now, again, I'm driving back to the mustang cabin from cow camp, twenty-five miles gate-to-gate, driving down the switchbacks that reveal Lone Cone in its talus-sloped wonder. I stop to photograph the mountain enshrouded first with virga, then in a sheet of rain, lightning striking all around the peak. It's late afternoon but the day has darkened into spotty showers as I pass through ponderosa pines, those meadows greened up from recent rains, lightning still alive, the road now dry, now wet again but not muddy. I put the Toyota in four-wheel-drive anyway. As I move under a canopy of ponderosa pines, quaking aspens, and narrowleaf cottonwoods, something light like mist rises up ahead of me on this road home . . .

And I think it *is* a curtain of mist, from rain on warm gravel, and I head toward the canopy opening and drive through the curtain and immediately enter a rainstorm like none I have ever seen . . . *rain* bouncing off the road with such intensity that it's raining *up* from the ground as a solid mass of water floods down from the sky, then hail falls so hard I fear my windshield might break and I can barely see the road, windshield wipers on high not fast enough, the rain faster and I switch on the defrost as rain and panic-breath fog the windows, and I can only hope it's just started, this cloudburst, that I am at the beginning of the rain. I glimpse through the Toyota's mud-streaked windows the oozing black runoff filling the bar ditch to my right while on the other side the shoulder cuts steeply down to the creek, and I think *keep fucking driving fast as you can*, and I can't see ahead enough through the massive wall of water I'm inside, but *do not stop*. Lightning flashes beside the Toyota, thunder cracking simultaneously. *Fuck.* Cannot stop, *keep your tires on the road*, the bar ditch running alongside, creek on the other side but down below as adrenaline chokes me and my heart skips I'm sure and I know people drown this way, but not me, not now, drive through it *drive* and I do, I am . . .

Driving on the other side of a nightmare in daylight, hands cramped on the steering wheel, lungs gasping for air, the rain stopped like a faucet turned off, and I slow but keep going for the monster rain might follow me and I want to cry but there is enough water here already.

The next day, because I have to return to cow camp, catch Savanna, and ride through the cattle again, the dogs and I head back upvalley and I see all the places where the slick mud of the bar ditch crossed the road, including the place where I could see outside the window that churning chocolate slurry rising. After I passed in my dash of terror, water carried logs down from higher ground and they high-centered on the road, logs with a girth larger than my two grandchildren and me wrapped in a hug. Logs carried by water like fear, flooding.

Shy of monsoons for the past three years, now, in the fourth year, the ground is so dry and parched and hard that it can't absorb the moisture—even in parts of the valley where no cattle or wild horses run. Have ever run. You can be in drought and still have flash floods: typical of this desert, this soil, this season, rain can crash down in sporadic cellular rushes too hard to saturate the ground so that even if it rained two days ago the water will run off. These quick, potentially dangerous floods are the nature of desert country where monsoon season is normal, and desired—we depend on summer rain. The lack contributes to continued drought and, as with weather everywhere, also speaks of climate crisis.

In Disappointment Valley we measure drought by the hundredths of an inch. We measure it in the tracks of elk, mule deer, and pronghorn at the dried edges of puddles. We measure by types and colors of grass: yellow in midsummer tells us drought is severe—our language—or "extreme" to "exceptional" in the official language of the National Oceanic and Atmospheric Administration.

In Disappointment Valley's Spring Creek Basin—the 21,932-acre Bureau of Land Management herd management area where wild horses live—we measure drought by the condition of the grasses, by water in the catchment tanks and troughs, by water in the dirt tanks or ponds. We measure drought by dusty prints on gray soil or the big, round, dried-mud mustang tracks sculpted into the dry creekbed, and we measure it by where the horses graze, by the shine of their coats and fat of their flanks. We measure drought constantly.

I text TJ: ".03 in the gauge this morning." Three hundredths of an inch in the rain gauge. Measurable but not enough moisture to cure dust.

She responds: "I got 0.12." Or none. Or more. Rarely do we get the same amount, despite only seven miles between us.

While five other people live in the valley, only four live in the three houses on this stretch of county road, though I can't claim full-time residency. Another way I measure drought.

Disappointment Valley also holds one of Colorado's wild horse herds managed by BLM. Spring Creek Basin Herd Management Area, which on a map is at the heart of Disappointment Valley, has had wild horses within its perimeters of ridgelines and badlands and fencelines for decades. Before that—prior to the Wild Free-Roaming Horses and Burros Act of 1971 (Public

Law 92-195)—wild horses existed within the contours of Disappointment Valley and beyond. Place names within and outside the valley suggest that free-roaming actually occurred: Horse Park, Filly Peak, Sorrel Flats, Wild Horse Mesa, Pony Draw.

On December 15, 1971, Congress unanimously passed the Wild Free-Roaming Horses and Burros Act into law (seems like the last time Congress unanimously did anything). The law gave federal departments governorship of designated public lands on which wild horses and burros lived at the time. It "mandates that these horses and burros are managed in a thriving ecological balance with the land and as part of the natural landscape." With responsibilities of stewardship came a commitment to protect wild horses from harassment, capture, and slaughter.

Much controversy exists across the West about how to manage mustangs. Native to North America, horses evolved here over the course of fifty-five million years, then they supposedly vanished in the Late Pleistocene extinctions eleven thousand years ago. Yet horses had already spread to other continents, where they thrived, and some were brought back to the Americas on Columbus's second voyage (along with ancestor Criollos). In 1519 Hernán Cortés reintroduced them to the North American continent, where they may have mingled with horses that survived the die-off, as Native tribes attest.

As more horses arrived with more colonizers, Native horse cultures flourished, and many horses lived wild and free—some having escaped, some turned loose to breed among themselves, and some simply never encountering people. Mid-twentieth century, wild horses were ruthlessly gathered and sold for slaughter under the most inhumane conditions, and when a young woman followed a truck dripping with blood and saw injured and bleeding horses sold to kill buyers, she launched a campaign to stop this practice. It worked. Velma Johnston, aka Wild Horse Annie, can be credited with the mind, passion, and footwork behind the passing of the act, joined today by other quiet heroes: the women and men who document, dart, and work in partnership with government agencies to better the lives of mustangs in the wild.

Documenter of Spring Creek Basin mustangs since 2007, TJ knows who foaled, who died, who changed bands, who stole whose mares, who got injured and then disappeared. Important data for multiple reasons, not the least of which is that it supports a successful fertility-control program in Spring Creek Basin using native PZP.

Porcine zona pellucida, or PZP, is a vaccine that makes a mare's eggs reject a stallion's sperm. Injected annually through darts fired across distance into the rumps of select mares, it doesn't harm mares, fetuses, or nursing foals, and doesn't disrupt herd dynamics: mares enter estrus, stallions breed them, everyone's happy, with no foals born of the union. Because of TJ's documentation and working relationship with our BLM herd manager, Mike Jensen (with whom Ken and I work on anything to do with our BLM grazing allotment), we have avoided a roundup in Spring Creek Basin for more than ten years—a record.

TJ lives with mustangs every day. Drought or no drought, she goes into Spring Creek Basin almost daily and checks on the horses at Disappointment Valley Mustang Sanctuary, a nonprofit effort to help mustangs removed from Spring Creek Basin have a home near their birthland. The sanctuary is also desert. Another way to measure drought: thinking about how much supplemental hay to feed, and when, and do we need to haul water because Disappointment Creek has gone dry again?

Summer of 2021 we had rain—downpours like the one I drove through and others I witnessed. Ponds filled throughout the basin; the catchment systems filled; the creek ran; springs and seeps held water. Warm-season grasses flourished—we had *green grass* in Disappointment Valley. And in the high country. With green on the ground, we moved from "exceptional" drought down to "moderate," according to NOAA. The mustangs of Spring Creek Basin grew fat and sleek (they're always beautiful) and roamed into parts of the basin they had avoided due to lack of water, which meant I was apt to see them from Disappointment Road and the cabin.

In the high desert of northwestern Colorado, however, a different saga unfolded: their ongoing exceptional drought continued, monsoons keeping company with the Four Corners region without entertaining the northwestern corner of Colorado at all. Another measure of drought: mustang removal.

In some areas, both environmentalists and cattle ranchers want mustangs off the range, and environmentalists also want cattle removed. Both are such complicated political issues that I shy away from public debates and arguments. Sometimes, though, I get caught; sometimes being pro-mustang opens the gates for anti-cattle people to rant. At an event in Telluride, with TJ's phenomenal wild horse photographs a rolling backdrop to her stories of living with mustangs in the valley, and for me, reading, I was struck by words from the audience. A woman asked why we have fences in Spring Creek Basin. When we explained that wild horses have tens of thousands to hundreds of thousands of acres in which to run, but they still need to stay off highways and away from towns, she challenged us. I said that in Spring Creek Basin the fences also keep cattle out of the herd management area, and that was it.

She said that fences as well as cattle throughout the West need to be removed, and I wanted to ask her if she'd ever removed a mile—even a few feet—of barbed-wire fence (when Ken and Tyler loaded the rusty, tangled piles of wire and T-posts from the fence Danny had taken down, and hauled it to Belt Salvage for recycling, the load weighed *1,500 pounds*, earning them $41.25). Instead I spoke loudly over the mic to stop the argument and refocus people on the joys of mustangs and the effectiveness of fertility control: we advocate for something that *does work* and is within our reach, not something that will take years to unravel like the 660,000 miles of barbed-wire fences across the West.

In Sand Wash Basin Herd Management Area near Craig, Colorado, they entered a fourth drought year and grasses withered to dust even as our hillsides turned green. While BLM can reduce livestock numbers and allotted time on the range, mustangs can't get pastured elsewhere temporarily to return at a later date. So the horrible happened: BLM decided to remove wild horses from the Sand Wash Basin area via helicopter roundup, starting "next month."

Sister advocate and longtime Sand Wash Basin herd documenter and darter Stella Trueblood sat at the table when the wild horse and burro specialist told the advocates the news. Nonnegotiable, he said. The measure of drought.

Her stomach leaden, Stella took it in. Hundreds of horses she'd known for years, many from birth, were destined for removal, but the alternative they faced was worse. Starvation. The range was toast. "I won't be there to decide which horses go and which stay," Stella told me. She'd done this too many times. TJ did it once. In 2011, in the last Spring Creek Basin roundup, TJ stood at the chute as each captured horse was run through, aged, and vetted, TJ's soft voice deciding the fates of fifty mustangs: freedom, or loss of it. She cried for days.

BLM caught 684 Sand Wash Basin mustangs in an aggressive helicopter roundup that lasted eleven days. Because they switched to helicopters from a gentler bait-trapping operation, BLM conceded the return of fifty mustangs to the range. Despite her earlier decision, Stella was there, looking at a list of who would stay: twenty-five stallions (although it ended up twenty-four as the onsite vet discovered that the pinto stallion PJ, son of the famous pinto stallion Picasso, had eye cancer and had to be euthanized) and twenty-five mares. Each mare, darted in the chute with PZP, got released with the stallions back to the wild, while hundreds went by truck to Cañon City. We can also measure drought by degrees of pain.

In the fall of the previous year, when Ken and I gathered the cows from the high country, we took them south to the ranch headquarters instead of to the BLM allotment—no summer monsoons meant no water and no feed. Even some of the desert shrubs, which Criollos love, dried up and withered away. I had begun to spend summers on a tripod of place: cow camp, mustang cabin, headquarters. Because even though the cows are up high, I have to check the cabin in Disappointment—remove dead mice, inspect solar batteries, check my water catchment system and the creek and the grasses, look for mustangs, write.

Another way I measure drought: how often I stay in Disappointment Valley. How much writing I get done without the seemingly constant interruptions of phone calls and fences down and cattle out. If no rain falls, trips and words become infrequent at best.

Summer of 2020, Savanna and I stayed mostly at cow camp in the high country.

We also measure drought by how many cows we have to sell, and the price of hay, the lack of hay. Hay prices quickly elevated due to no summer rains, while cattle prices plummeted as people sold to avoid the high feed prices.

TJ has to procure winter hay for the horses at the mustang sanctuary regardless of drought—there's just not enough feed on the tough soil to carry the horses through winter. At the ranch headquarters, we have to feed our horses and whatever cattle winter there. That year, after we gathered everything off the mountain, we sold more than one hundred Angus cows. All the calves. Paid off a note—a thin silver lining of a drought that gutted so much of the Four Corners region, where other ranchers sold whole herds.

TJ secured hay for her sanctuary mustangs. Not allowed to feed the wild horses in Spring Creek Basin (or anywhere on public lands), another measure of drought: what happens to mustangs if feed runs short, which it had for four summers in northwestern Colorado.

We know what happens.

TJ and I had an event scheduled at the Dolores Public Library in which I would read from my newly released book and TJ would talk about the mustangs of Spring Creek Basin and PZP, and we would both respond to questions and tear up at some of the answers. She came to Cachuma to get me. "Whatever you have to do tomorrow," she said as she entered the house like a dancing wind, "cancel it."

"Huh?" I said.

"Just, cancel it. We have to go to Sand Wash Basin. Mike called earlier. He said, 'What are you doing tomorrow?' He's leaving for a family vacation. He said I have to go. Tomorrow."

"To get horses?"

For several years, Mike Jensen had promised that he would bring in some outside mares to support genetic diversity. While the mustangs themselves are pretty good at avoiding inbreeding, it helps to introduce new blood every once in a while. Of the 684 captured Sand Wash Basin mustangs, we would welcome three fillies to a new, verdant and wild, high-desert home in Disappointment Valley.

"You have to come with me," TJ said.

TJ and I have ridden shotgun for each other on numerous mustang adventures. "I can't," I said. "I have a root canal." Two weeks of toothache, the remedy scheduled. "See if Tif can go."

Fellow mustang advocate Tif Rodriguez came to the library that evening and stood with her husband and TJ making plans. I promised to meet them when they returned with the horses Stella had selected for Spring Creek Basin.

A soft shawl of late-afternoon light fell across the basin as TJ drove over the cattle guard and up the rutted dirt road. I had already located several bands when I met the trailer, but TJ wanted to turn the three fillies—two long yearlings (not yet two) and a two-year-old—loose within sight of water, more important to their immediate comfort after a seven-hour drive than mingling with new horses. In the last several days they had been chased by helicopters, captured in pens, assessed in a metal squeeze chute, and loaded into this terrifying contraption, and as I stepped slowly onto the running board for a look, they crowded into a corner, seeking safety in the nearness of each other.

Daylight ebbing, TJ backed the trailer so it pointed at a full pond a quarter of a mile away. Tif stood to one side, her cell phone ready; TJ stepped far enough away with her camera that she wouldn't spook the horses; and, as quietly as I could, I unlatched the trailer door, pulled it open wide, and hid behind it.

And we waited, the door propped heavily against my bent knee as I tried to get my own phone camera working to film the release. The horses' movements echoed loudly within the aluminum trailer. I couldn't peek—seeing me could send them into a fear we wanted them never to feel again. So I listened. Felt their movements through the heavy door. One wild girl stepped closer to the opening and suddenly she leapt free, her head high, feet high as she trotted quickly away from the cage that had held her. She ran, snorted, looked back, circled, and dropped her head to the green, native, warm-season grasses of our desert.

No movement or sound from the remaining two. I did peek. They hugged the depths, leaning against the trailer wall away from the lingering light. We waited. The first freed filly, a dun, fed and trotted and circled back and grazed more. Minutes passed. My thigh cramped. Worried about darkness and three mustangs new to the terrain, we whispered that Tif should move to the far corner of the trailer, step up on the running board. Slowly, quietly, she did.

And the next two wild ponies, a dun pinto and a palomino, burst forth like racehorses from a starting gate, heading toward the bolder, older filly and fresh green grass and freedom.

In the low light I might have seen the glisten of tears. TJ and Tif had delivered these mustangs to a wild life with other mustangs and grass and water, and the horses trotted and circled and grazed and looked about. TJ's camera clicked away and Tif and I watched as the summer evening light grew as soft and golden as the coats of the three new fillies.

15. Dun-pinto mustang mare with her day-old filly, Stella. Photo by TJ Holmes.

Early the next morning, I sent Stella the cell phone footage I'd managed to take. "It makes my heart happy," she said, "to see them free and in such a beautiful place."

In two years, TJ will ask me to name the dun pinto's newborn filly and will wholeheartedly agree with the choice: *Stella.*

Despite the harsh measurements of drought, we still find joys small and large in the dry, dry desert.

13

Abandoned Meander

That open country is so huge you can feel lost and abandoned in it or you can work to feel a part of it, like ya belong to it and it belongs to you. Like a part of you is rock and stone and stream and all the open sky. Ya get past lonesome then.

—Richard Wagamese, *Starlight*

Groundhog, the West, and Disappointment Valley, Fall to Winter 2021–22

Ken went to the Groundhog store for dinner supplies (hot dogs). We didn't get the cows moved from one pasture to another because of fence work and the other things that can go wrong, or that take longer than planned, which happens more often than not when working with livestock, so we'll stay at cow camp another night and get an early start in the morning.

Ken rode the Cowboy Trail both Friday (root-canal day) and Saturday, and I've been ahorseback for a week (since the day after my root canal). Savanna and Rita graze around us and the dogs sleep deeply as Ken barbecues Cachuma Ranch beef and store-bought hot dogs. No greens to go with it, but the meal will carry us into sleep. Tomorrow we'll have a protein-bar breakfast. After moving cattle we'll head back to the ranch where we can shop in a real small-town grocery store.

Ken and Kathy held Lucas's birthday party at cow camp. Twenty-four people. I went off to fill the horses' water trough and find a private bush, then sat on the water trailer for a moment, relishing the peace. Barbecue smoking, kids running around, yelling, laughing, parents talking and drinking, and I escaped to the quiet with my dogs.

Today I have the quiet and the dogs, but the sense of escape eludes me.

Ken and I went back up to Groundhog this morning and rode out to find cows in the wrong pasture—the same cattle we had just moved. We pushed them back into the Dressel Pasture and up toward a stock pond. Marshmallow led a bunch into the aspens while the main group moved up the road as we intended. "Let 'em drift," Ken said. Better than us bumping and jumping through downed trees to turn them, and we *want* the cattle grazing in the forest, where feed covers the floor. If Marshmallow led them deeper into the trees, good.

The cattle in the wrong pasture all had horns. Some Criollo, some Corriente; some we've had for years, some for a couple of months. During our first summer at Groundhog, I decided the horned cows learned from the experienced Angus cows how easy it is to work through the lay-down fencing, the big cows leaning over fences to graze on the other side, or reaching under, either way pushing the fences lower to the ground, the smooth wires on the top and bottom not much of a deterrent. The horned cattle, light and lithe, saw the lowered fences and learned to hop over. And heavy snow has pounded the permanent T-posts and cedar posts deeper into the ground, making for short fences in the places without lay-down fencing. But why do the Criollos feel the need to hop fences like teenagers of the last century hopping freight trains—simply because they can?

This morning we saw not a single Angus cow, because they're deep in the Dressel where they're supposed to be. The pasture that's mostly aspens. No open hillsides. What the horned cows have in common, in addition to horns and many admirable traits, is that they don't like trees. Or rather, they don't like aspens. Neither does my horse and, truth be told, I don't like them that much anymore either.

Criollos and their descendants are known for their desert adaptability, their willingness to travel long distances to water, their desire for browsing and not just grazing. And our cows have done all that. Their first year on the BLM Salt Arroyo Allotment they traveled as deeply inland as they could, right up to the base of the rimrocks cliffed above them. I had to hike miles to find them. Some I couldn't get close to, just binocular-distance away. I would locate them and lose them and find them again.

Mango's Mom, one of the Texas cows, went into the piñon-juniper forest in the hills to calve ahead of schedule. Searching, I went up and down steep arroyos and slippery embankments until I spied tracks beside a small stream of snowmelt and followed them toward a shape under a juniper, which turned into a cow, then a cow-calf pair. I glassed enough to tell that the calf had nursed and was healthy before I trudged back down to the road through mid-shin-deep snow. After several days Mango's Mom came down to water at the troughs we set up near the road that year, her calf following closely, but by that time I had driven the rest of the cattle to the mustang cabin. Without the safety of the herd, Mango's Mom retreated to the safety of trees.

Now, despite the succulent grasses that grow tall among the aspens, she will not stay in a thousand-acre pasture of grass and shade and water aplenty, because of the trees.

When people in the West think of quaking aspens, they likely think of beauty: fall leaves turning green-gold, then pure gold, then russet, and plastering the forest floor; white bark in winter; the shiny, trembling, silver-green growth of spring. Of course it's the autumn leaves that compel people along miles of wash-boarded county roads to see hillsides of color. To easterners our trees may pale in comparison to the riotous colors they know, but in the West, aspens dazzle us year after year.

I too get swept into a rapturous state by the colors, chest opening to a kind of glory—until I have to enter the forest on a horse in pursuit of cattle. Tall trees crowd out sunlight, high branches sway or jerk overhead in the wind, trunks rub against each other, windfall everywhere so that going off-trail means getting trapped in corral-like dead ends, Savanna having to back up and trip her way out while the cows go around in places we don't fit. In times like these I'm glad only some of the cattle (the Angus) want the trees, the Criollos, out in the open, much easier to handle, until it's time to go in—and stay in—the pasture of aspens.

This morning when we saw all those beautiful horned cattle *out*, Ken threatened to sell the offenders. The Criollos. *My* cows. And not for the first time. "Next year," he said, "we're selling anyone who crosses a fence."

I nodded, silently praying that my favorite cows don't make the mistake. Problem is, I have about forty favorites. Some may have to go.

16. Ken and Mango (full Criollo) in aspens. Photo by Tyler Lausten.

When I worried to Danny about the Criollos' reluctance to stay in the trees and how they take advantage of short fences, he said, "You can train 'em; might take three or four years."

Ken, grandkids, Kathy, and her family in their house, Tyler down in his shop, people surround me, yet I am alone with my thoughts. My fears. It's more than losing the cows, it's losing the lifestyle. Whether cowboying or ranching, working with animals and weather fills at least part of every single day. In Ken's threat to sell, I hear something bigger: the threat of endings. Sadness weighs heavy.

I bake brownies, gluten free but not sugar or fat free, the warm aroma a comfort. Too impatient to let them cool, I burn my mouth on melted chocolate chips.

On the phone, my mother asks if I know what catastrophizing means.

"Is that a thing?" I say.

"Yes, it's a 'thing.' It means that you go beyond reasonable worry to the worst ending possible and stay there."

"Is that what Ken does?"

"I was thinking of you."

C ⊃-

This past week I have been everywhere, it seems. Sisters, Oregon, to get a 2003 Chevy pickup and a gooseneck trailer a friend had for sale; Ashland to pick up my sister Terry; Greenville—*O Greenville!*—in the Sierra Nevada; to Winnemucca, Nevada, where Craig worked the summer before the fall that killed him. I wondered in Winnemucca what life would have looked like if he didn't die. Probably we both would have kept drinking, for a while, but it's likely I wouldn't have sought hard drugs. Because he wouldn't have died. And we would have lived much of our time outside. Even though I know the pointlessness of these thoughts, the memories hover.

Like the fear of death that got dropped upon us all. Not just COVID. Fire.

I think of how I learned of Greenville burning.

At headquarters, I let the dogs out and followed them into the cool, the sun almost up. They wandered toward green growth—grasses and weeds—resulting from July rains. While the Northwest cooked like it hadn't before in recorded history, the Southwest finally got a monsoon season that drenched us out of "exceptional" drought. (Still, we need more rain.)

My feet on the wooden deck, my arms bared to the chill, dogs meandering, a slight shiver ran through me. The sky bore the dusting of dawn. But it was past dawn. Past rain. No longer did the recent cleansing filter the air, and I wondered whose smoke filled the valley from the west, muting the Mesa Verde skyline. The Pack Creek Fire in nearby Utah? The Bootleg Fire in Oregon? Which of the dozens of wildfires currently burning bled smoke this far east?

An hour later, as Ken and I headed out in the side-by-side to feed steers and horses, he said, "I just talked to Dad." They talk often. Often about fires as Keith has bulldozers and lowboys and is on a list to fight wildfires in California. I waited. Ken looked at me. Kathy had just cut his hair, and it startled me how much Ken resembled his father. Especially his eyes, hazel-green with a veneer of, what? Moisture?

"Dad said Greenville burned last night."

I guess he kept driving but all motion around me stopped. "Greenville?"

"Yes. Last night. It burned down. The whole town."

The town where I graduated from high school. A town that held memories of dances and parties and prom night, of the ring Craig gave me while we sat in his pickup outside the gym. He couldn't find one he liked with my birthstone in it, so he gave me one with his. Ruby. Then he died in the forest that, years later, burned in the Dixie Fire.

The arguments now, the blame—tree-hugging, spotted-owl-loving environmentalists protesting rampant logging, which led to too much overgrowth and undergrowth—old high school friends hating those who really only wanted the clearcutting to stop. People like me, Bay Area girl living with the family of loggers while I finished high school in Greenville.

I have a pair of socks I bought at Ayoob's Department Store in 1971. Craig was with me. I used to have two pairs—one red, one blue—but I threw the threadbare red ones away years ago, regretting the action as soon as I took it. I still have the blue ones. First love gone, the store gone, the town now gone, and in my drawer, fifty-year-old socks.

California continued burning, the Dixie Fire eventually consuming nearly a million acres, the largest single-source wildfire in California's recorded history.

Time to bring the cattle down off the mountain, Terry and I had to make 1,100 miles in a hurry—from southern Oregon into California, then east through Nevada and Utah to southwestern Colorado. We passed snowless Mount Shasta—no one remembered seeing it that way, ever—then the road into Lassen Volcanic National Park: closed. And suddenly we found ourselves in the northernmost burn scar of the Dixie Fire.

I didn't know we would pass through it—maps on flat screens don't show the dips and turns of a road flanked by lava and blackened ponderosas. Ash-touched lava beds rose and fell between seared pine trunks, needles gone or singed dark orange. Burnt orange. On the highway toward Susanville, with a twenty-foot stock-combo gooseneck trailer and a tight timeline, I said, "It's hard to be so close and not go."

"We could drive south to Chester," Terry said.

"Then to Greenville?"

She nodded. And she's my big sister, so I made the turns to Chester. Streets and front yards scarred, the fire entered yet spared much of this small Sierra town. An Ayoob's Department Store—I didn't know they had other branches. So much can change in fifty years.

We drove near the shoreline of Lake Almanor, the water alarmingly low, and crossed over the dam, the tiny community of Canyondam a melted heap. As we moved along charred curves, patches of green ponderosas alternated randomly with gray-brown earth until the highway squeezed into a single lane and traffic stopped. The ashen forest rose steeply to our left, dropped steeply to our right, ponderosa skeletons the only trees left standing. Or lying in cold decks perpendicular to the road, huge Caterpillar earthmovers with their grapples like monster claws grasping death and death and death and piling it roadside. No sound rose beyond the earthmovers a mile away. No birdsong or movement. The land itself silent.

After thirty minutes, the flagger allowed us to creep forward. A fine mist of ash covered the pickup. As we approached the edge of human ruin, the smell hit my stomach. I knew that smell from my mother's house burning down long ago, my fingers digging into waterlogged soot for days looking for evidence of our lives for the insurance company. In Greenville I pulled over as soon as I could and Terry and I gawked like tourists in Yosemite, only in Greenville it wasn't at wild *life* but at a fatal, visceral wound filled with gangrene rubble and the maggots of death.

At my mother's house my fingers smelled of ash and death for days.

The Dixie Fire burned 963,309 acres. It started on July 13 and ended on October 25, burning for three months and twelve days.

Terry and I sat in the pickup in the middle of a town at the center of a million-acre burn scar. To our right, a café—no roof, partial walls, the large front window melted to nothing, the metal frames of chairs standing uniformly around tables that no longer existed. Everywhere walls folded in on themselves, warped metal roofing on the ground. Light poles melted, drooping. Only stone and brick chimneys upright, and tree skeletons. Chunks of cement everywhere, pipes sticking out at odd angles, everywhere.

Generations of rubble. Memories burned to the ground.

We continued through town along the main street. The destruction of Greenville a mirror of the destruction by COVID. The pandemic a mirror of the Earth's own suffering. The forest clean, ready for rain and regrowth, but the town's guts thick and heavy and not biodegradable like the carcasses of deer and bunnies and bears. Where would the rubble go? Where was there a landfill large enough to hold a whole town?

And all the burned memories. No container for all that.

Road crews stopped us again near the Y, where Indian Creek joins Spanish Creek and becomes the East Branch of the North Fork of the Feather River. Motor shut off, I stepped from the pickup to look. Some California black oaks still stood. They had turned fall colors, the change caused by scorching heat, not season. Far below, the river ran clearly, banked by green grasses, not mirroring the fire at all. Nor did it show the high-water marks of the 1996–97 New Year's Flood that happened the last time I lived in the Feather River watershed twenty-five years before. It took a full lane of this highway near Dog Rock. Traffic stopped for a month, with a "window" open for an hour mornings and evenings so people could get to town for work or school, and home.

Terry and I looked at the canyon's steep sides, devoid of brush, and spoke of rain.

It would come a month later, record rainfall in drought-ridden California. Flash floods everywhere. The rockslide that would happen downriver of where we stopped that afternoon would hold whole trees. The rocks crashing down from canyon walls bigger than my 2004 Toyota. Mud and debris the width and depth of three semi tractor-trailers overriding the highway. Debris the size of a small town's rubble.

The next year, my fifty-year high school reunion would take place but not in Greenville, even though our high school managed to stand stoically upright through the fire. Pieces of the demolished town would get hauled off, one gas station would pump gas, some new buildings would sprout, and a sheen of green would spread outward from the small creeks and bigger

17. Tyler, nine, and high-water sign beside the Feather River. Photo by the author.

rivers and color the forest floor. Humans and the Earth have renewal in their makeup, which may be instinct. Like fortitude. Like love.

And, though I can hardly bear to say this out loud when so many people have lost homes and pets, family and belongings, fire has been part of that renewal. Sometimes at the mustang cabin, as I ponder the deaths of drought-singed and beetle-rotten trees, I think that if fire blew through my part of the valley it would take out those trees and those beetles and nurture the soil. Even if it burned the logs that make my home. Which it would.

Then again, when I walk from my house at headquarters one morning to see *mist? dust? smoke!* spewing from the barn, near panic strikes and I have no thoughts of renewal as I call Ken and look for flames and check the propane tank, empty, and the electric cords to Tyler's shop, unplugged, and look for the horses and calves, eating far enough away, as I say into the phone, "Come down right away, smoke's coming from the barn!"

"From where?" Ken asks. "What's burning?"

"I don't know just get here!"

Less than two minutes later Ken runs from his pickup with two fire extinguishers in hand. I have brought two from my house. He pulls the clip on one and disappears as I call 9-1-1. "Make sure nobody goes inside," the dispatcher says, collecting information while I yell at Ken to get out, which he already has, and I jump in the Toyota and race to the top of the property to meet the firefighters and show them where to go.

From outside the barn Ken has found an ice defroster the weaned calves pulled from the water trough, the wires gummed up, chewed. Heat worked under a stall door, creeping up the door and adjacent wall, where short flames started. Ken has all power shut off and a hose soaking the door, hay, the wall. The volunteer firefighters shoot fire retardant at everything, and then Ken and another young man remove charred paneling and soak the smoldering insulation and more wall.

During the commotion my mind rests on nothing enlightened. Only on the safety of Ken and the animals and firefighters. Our potential barn fire gets stopped before it takes hold, unlike the one at my mother's house and millions of acres and thousands of homes; adrenaline surges through me nonetheless.

⊂⊃-

Terry and I get back to the ranch in time, the new-used trailer put right to use. My mare not an "in-your-pocket" horse (so gentle they're practically a nuisance, apparently a desirable characteristic if you go by Craigslist ads), Savanna tolerates some petting and then she's done. But this morning as I groom her before saddling, she rolls her head and neck around me in an affectionate gesture, like a sideways kind of hug.

Snow fell in the night, the footing slick for the horses and cattle but the work has to happen. Today. Ken, Kathy's brother, Lane, and I started in twenty-three degrees Fahrenheit. Hours later, it's still twenty-three degrees. It won't warm up. Yet there's so much beauty: the snow-tinged peaks, Lone Cone completely covered, some aspens still turning, clomping hooves on the dirt road releasing the scent of wet, brown leaves, the air a mixture of fall crispness and a little of winter's early decay.

Savanna's hug stays with me as we make a big sweep of the Dressel Pasture and push the cattle into the Holding Pasture. I trot Savanna across the snow to get ahead of some Angus pairs. The movement warms my legs. Holding the cattle up while Ken and Lane bring more, lead cow Bobbi sees me up ahead and turns left toward the pond—the right way. The other Criollos follow her. I love Bobbi.

The Criollo pairs will go to Cliff's in Disappointment Valley, happy to return to their desert—Cliff has a few hundred acres of feed we can graze while we fence-wean the calves, fence-weaning easier on both calves and cows as they gradually get used to being apart. We'll watch for sickness, and then we'll haul the calves to headquarters, where Ken will continue his parental watch. Over the next few months, I will stairstep the cows from Cliff's to the section, the BLM allotment, the mustang cabin, to TJ's by spring, the way the old-timers did, though they didn't have all these fences to contend with—they had meadows for grazing and water stops along the way that they didn't have to ask permission to use. Times have changed a lot since then, and in part that's good. While some men and women out here still pack pistols on their hips, they're less apt to use them on each other.

Savanna, Jessi, and I move the cows from Cliff's to the section for a couple of weeks, and when the calendar says it's time, I open the gates to the adjoining Salt Arroyo Allotment so the cows can drift out. The next day, after hours at my desk writing, I have to break and get outside, my ever-ready excuse that of checking cattle. I load Bow, Jessi loads herself, and soon Jessi and I kick a bull of Danny's out (he jumps the cattle guard instead of finding the gate I've opened). Driving east I see Curlie, Lightning, Roanie, Pretty, and some steers, walking in the direction of the water trap. They will go to the creek and drink and linger but won't stay long.

I drive into Little Cojo, where I sit on the flood-hardened bank in the chill of a pre-winter day. Bow bites ice and chases bubbles. Jessi does her border collie laps, then digs a bed and lies in it. Bow will keep chasing water as long as it runs for him, making him a happy old dog. Later he will have to pee and pee and pee, and standing will be hard for him, but Bow doesn't complain or feel sorry for himself. A model of joy all his life, three-legged and one-eared and grinning, his stump tail wagging his back end so hard sometimes that he falls over, he tries to help when I lift him in and out of a vehicle. Sometimes he can't stand, the nerves to his one back leg asleep, and I support him by his stump until he can right his leg. He looks over his shoulder and says *thank you* with his eyes. Gratitude and love.

Why does this seem hard to come by in the cattle business? Why are the challenges followed by fear that the Criollos will have to go, followed by a feeling of defeat? And then that fear, of a life without cows. Without Bow, whose days are numbered.

Ken's Catahoula has puppies, and I keep a beautiful brindle. I love that pup yet find him a challenge to train. I've only trained border collies and border-collie crosses before, no hound dogs. He doesn't listen well, and he runs off as if the cattle are always a mile ahead of us. For some reason as we approach the third rifle season in Disappointment Valley, I have the thought that if I see the Todds, Todd 1 will fall for my pup. In my vision, I give the pup to Todd 1.

Two days later, a pickup I don't know has parked on BLM near my gate. On my way out, I see two camouflaged hunters returning to the truck: the Todds! We all hug and I let the pup out of my two-years-older Tacoma, and Todd 1 does fall immediately in love. We can't visit long as I have to meet Ken at the section, and when I tell Ken the story—including the vision I'd had—he says, "Do it." We find the hunters at the BLM corrals, and I ask Todd 1 if he would like to have my pup. His face lights up. Driving away I feel a huge sadness, which amplifies when Jessi doesn't understand where the pup has gone—for some reason I didn't have her in the Toyota with me, so she didn't see the leaving. Sometimes even right decisions hurt.

We decide to sell Money, who, despite her size—at the top end of the horned cows—has proven an agile fence-jumper (due to the longhorn influence, Ken says). Her steers get huge, her heifers produce, but up on the forest Money pays the fences no mind. We have given her every opportunity to change her ways, but now her offspring copies her, and she has to go.

Selling Money breaks the dam. We eliminate the calves she's raised, finishing her steers for beef and selling the cows. We sell Curlie too, as she also came with bad habits. And Rabbit's mother. Ken says we should have done it sooner. Finally I can see that he's right, as bad habits like bad apples can ruin the bunch.

At this point of Disappointment Creek, the watercourse forks, water parting and running on both sides of an island. Our first year here, a flash flood wrapped a cow around a large Fremont cottonwood that grew right in the fork. A whole cow, her belly against the trunk and her legs hugging the tree, a pair on each side, her head alongside her forelegs, neck twisted, face up. A red whiteface cow, Hereford, we didn't know whose. Couldn't find a brand. First she was dead, then bloated, then a carcass, then bones draped with hide. For a long time—I mean years—skeletal bones clung to the cottonwood, until last summer when old-fashioned monsoons returned and sent floods that loosened and carried debris and trees and bushes and bones downstream. Now just the spine and ribs remain at the fork in the river, so embedded in the exposed roots of the cottonwood that a person could walk by a dozen times and not notice, bones, roots, trunk, and earth all the same shade of Disappointment.

Right now the low water takes the right fork, moving at a slow, steady pace that offers no sound despite all the rocks over which it riffles. What is it running—two cubic feet per second? Less? I don't think of creek-water going silent, but it has; even when the breeze and Bow still for a moment, and the blue jay quits scolding, this water has no sound.

I have heard it run loudly enough to scare me into my own silence, have seen this whole riparian corridor covered in a flood of churning pewter, have witnessed the ferocity that killed a 1,300-pound Hereford cow and wrapped her around a tree. When flooding happens, the creek-river chooses neither right nor left, it just runs, carving out the right bank's meandering bends, junipers tilting sideways toward the river as their soil base disappears, while on the left side the river cuts the new channel deeper. Eventually the water will choose the more direct channel over the meander, which will become abandoned. Abandoned meander.

Not necessarily a good thing, as meanders slow the flow, slow erosion, and help detritus turn to soil. Other places in this creek-river the newer, straighter channel already runs first, but in high water the meanders still fill and flow. If rivers are a metaphor for life, what is this one telling me? Like the straighter channel, I have cut and run, from drugs, from a marriage gone bad, from death, even from love. What now?

The creek runs sleepily today, the drama and mayhem of the monsoonal summer having passed. Still, it runs.

⊂⊃-

We pulled the horses' shoes and turned them out at headquarters, Savanna too. After a big December snowstorm in Disappointment, tracks at the cattle guard stopped me. At first I thought our cows had drifted with the storm and walked across the snowed-over grid. Looking more closely: elk tracks. Most of them the size of the steers' tracks but narrower. The storm brought them down from the mountain.

At every stopping place along the road—cattle guards, gates, fences—a maze of tracks accumulated in the snow where elk stopped and merged and milled until one leapt and the rest followed. Dozens of elk, yet I had seen but one—an early arrival loping across a flat, perhaps looking for company. Like Huston's two-year-old steer, standing all morning near the protein blocks waiting for someone to join him.

After Tyler left for California and winter surf, I stayed at the mustang cabin full-time. On a warm(ish), breezy day, snow melting, the dogs and I walked again to the beach at Little Cojo. The creek iced over, I went downstream looking for thin ice. This time I could hear water singing as it slipped between the rocky creekbed and the ice cap. Many elk had crossed the ice, and I wondered if they were able to drink. Hearing a louder gurgle where a juniper had slid into the creek and formed an eddy, I saw that the circulating water kept a throat open. Elk found the opening and made it bigger with their many hooves. I jumped on the ice, making the hole bigger still in hopes it wouldn't freeze over in case the elk headed back this way.

⊂⊃-

My friend Amber, single and gorgeous and intelligent and tall, just turned forty-two. I said to her, "I never expected to be sixty-seven and single, but you have time." Time I thought I had when I was forty-two. Yet here I am again in holey and patched jeans, black silk long underwear showing through, my flannel shirt snagged and torn, hair brushed and braided, teeth brushed, face washed, and that's all, for who will see me today other than Jessi and Bow and some cows?

Earlier from the porch I watched Danny's cowhand trailing eight cows down Black Snag Road half a mile away, through a gate, and out of sight. I'm guessing he pushed them to the BLM corrals four miles away. I'm guessing he's as close as I'll get to a person today, though I did see the postman drive by—it's Friday, one of his two weekly delivery days. Actually, I only saw his dog, an Australian shepherd who loves hanging her head out the passenger window. Walking to the creek to check ice and flow, I waved as they passed. Later I saw the red mail truck heading back downvalley, the second of the two vehicles I'll see all day.

Ravens call in the distance, and wind speaks through branches of piñon pine. Voices of birds and the creek drift up the cliff face to this shelf of land. Human sound is my own breath, pages shuffling, ballpoint pen rolling out words, and a flight path of infrequent planes. The refrigerator kicks on now and again, and if I stood near the box that holds the solar-panel batteries I could hear that faint hum, all other sounds produced outside the human realm.

Some days I do feel longing, yet even at sixty-seven and single it's not possible for me to linger long in lonely amid birdsong and windsong and creeksong, and soil slurping up melting snow, with herds of elk and deer on the move somewhere and wild horses grazing or napping in spots of sunlight beyond the ridge. Coyotes may yip and howl in the night, and maybe the great-horned owl who shelters sometimes across the canyon will hoot for company. I won't hear the mountain lion, bobcat, or raccoon whose tracks may show tomorrow in the soft soil near puddles of melted ice, but they also live here.

Piñon jays! Their cries enter the quiet. I don't see them but knowing they're out there somewhere, like the rest of the creatures who inhabit this valley, fills the space where lonely could live, like the creek's sweet voice, leaking through sheets of ice, reminding me of love.

I still have my fifty-year-old blue socks. But I wonder if this—the mustang cabin, Disappointment Valley, cow camp, the ranch—is another meander I will someday abandon, by choice or by force; if my lovely Criollo cows will in fact be my last cows.

And yet. The barn didn't burn down. And while changing the course of what could have been a calamity, I thought only of the present and immediate future: what *now*, not what *if*.

Today I have my cows.

14
Eddies

That's truly a boat-sucking eddy over there.

—Rebecca Lawton, *What I Never Told You*

Disappointment Valley, Colorado; Salmon River, Idaho, Spring to Summer 2022

Today I'm supposed to meet someone from The Nature Conservancy at the section, an annual event. I sometimes feel as if I'm in grammar school getting graded as TNC assesses the forage and riparian areas and evaluates our management practices, the protocol outlined in the contract we inherited when we bought land with a conservation easement already in place.

On the road I just saw a woman in a dark SUV with a straw hat on the dash. I waved, but she didn't slow. Ken had asked her to call with an ETA; probably she thought she could do that out here but once you drop into Disappointment it's AT&T or nothing. I wait by the creek at Little Cojo for an hour, and just as I'm about to give up, she pulls in.

I guess by her first glance at the opposite bank that she thinks cattle have denuded it.

"That's Disappointment Creek," I tell her. "With each flash flood the water cuts more into the bank on this side and deposits more silt on that side. But the floods also uproot the willows that hold the soil in place. Monsoons and flash floods and highwater and drought are what happen out here."

What rivers does she know, I wonder—clear Sierra streams of snowmelt running through granite, water filtered by stone, close to the source, no Mancos Shale?

I talk about our Criollo cows.

The creek runs at a good clip—the kids could get a pretty long inner-tube float out of it. "We can cross if you like," I offer.

She frowns under her sun hat. She must be at least thirty years younger than me.

"We might get wet to our knees but if we cross, we can go up that steep trail," hard to locate through leafy cottonwood branches. "From there you can see the inner basin. The grasses. The winterfat. Or you can drive up Ryman Creek Road and hike up a different steep trail without crossing the creek."

"I think I'll do that," she says.

"Good choice." I smile and return to the benefits of Criollos.

"My family raises black Angus in northern Colorado," she tells me.

We walk through the riparian area. The understory, thick with the tangle of wild prairie rose, willow, and serviceberry, scratches and snags. I point out where the elk and cattle congregate—the elk in winter, the cows not since last fall—areas where greasewood, basin big sagebrush, ricegrass, and galleta cover much of the soil. Maybe she doesn't know this desert, I think, and doesn't see this as lush. Or maybe I am ruined by love and don't see it as barren.

She does know of the family ranch in California, which The Nature Conservancy now owns. "Jimmy Poet got the lease," she says, and my heart plummets. Had we known it was up for lease, would Ken have wanted to apply? He loved that place so. And what would happen to our cows, to me, if he were to go? But that is wasted imagining, as Jimmy Poet has the lease. He must be about my age, maybe older. Keith and I roped at brandings at his place on the San Julian. Keith stayed in Santa Barbara County. Poet stayed. Sometimes staying gives you opportunities, while I chase dreams away.

Needing a bump to get out of an eddy and back into the mainstream of my life as a writer with cows, with my sons, and alone among gray ribbed hills, I leave for a writing workshop on the Salmon River in Idaho. It begins right after we take the cows to the mountain—only for the writer David James Duncan would I take off at that time, but my kids don't understand. I have read and admired DJD for thirty years, he rarely does workshops, and this one, on the river . . . well. I go.

While other writers focus on salmon—the fish and the river—and the four dams on the Snake River, and how those four dams have endangered multiple species and Native peoples for whom salmon are a way of life, and how those dams need removal, my story starts with a heifer named Ruby.

She was my first cow, and if I write about the last cows I want to start with Ruby. Brahma-cross, hybrid vigor, Ruby cleared those pasture fences and crossed a highway to get to her calf, and she found him, my first-cow Ruby did, and I felt so proud. Now when my cows do something similar, they get yelled at and I feel scolded. What has shifted here? My sons young when Keith sold Ruby, they didn't know her and maybe they don't know the story, yet Ken's voice echoes his father's when he gets frustrated with the horned cows and threatens to sell them. We go round and round without landing on an answer beyond anger. A solution.

The truth I cannot tell is how hard it is. Working with animals and weather and the drought and financial drought and fear. I am afraid our best intentions as stewards of the land may not be good enough. People say our beef is the best they've ever tasted—and we know how healthy it is—is that enough?

Ken wonders this too. And sees the money the Angus calves bring. He doubts himself, doubts his wisdom in us developing our herd of Criollos.

I don't doubt that decision. Not at all. I doubt *me*. Perhaps this is the eddy that holds me in its grip, self-doubt the obstacle that causes my thoughts to spiral, my brain to spin like water circulating behind a big rock, highlighting my fading strength and abilities. My eroding confidence. I see that my efforts to please are unpleasing. That I am losing my son's respect, both my sons' respect, rectifying the past an impossible task at which I'm doomed to fail.

I am afraid of not having my cows. Of losing the parameters of my life that hold me together the way riverbanks used to—without my cows I am a river let loose of canyon walls, and where will I flow? *Down* is all I know. It used to be I had an idea, a picture, of what I wanted next, or where (or whom), but I have no pictures. I have no idea. Maybe another life awaits. Maybe I like this one. Unable to break through the eddy line to my own dream world of reality the way I used to—currents of daydreams and night dreams merging and guiding—for years now I've had no dreams on the other side of this.

By the time I was fifty-six years old, I'd moved thirty-five times, an average of once every nineteen months. For the last dozen years I have lived in the same place, longer than anywhere else, even Hawai'i. I still move often. Have lived in different houses at headquarters. The mustang cabin. Cow camp. Stationary doesn't suit me any more than it does the Criollos. We need room to wander. These days I wander afoot and ahorseback and alone and away. But not away from my kids.

I think about life without Ken again, which guts me like the death of 345's calf who drowned in an irrigation ditch last week, the calf somehow falling in and dead before Ken found him, 345 the first Angus cow to greet the tractor on winter mornings, clouds of breath blowing from the tractor, from the cows bawling for hay, from us, me holding back tears on a cool spring day when Ken tells me about 345's calf because I can see that the loss cuts to the deep parts of him despite the hard veneer he wants to make of his face, and I want to cry for the cow as she bawls for a calf, forever silent, as I cried for my own children, alive yet gone, and I think of Ruby jumping fences and crossing a highway to get to her calf, and I struggle with Ken not really over cattle but will I lose him again if the cows go? And maybe he thinks I will leave him again too. Which I probably will.

I think about my grandmother and Sister. About how those two women shaped their lives once cowboying was over for them. My grandmother on Benedito at Mount Diablo, riding through oak trees and wildflowers and green grass and serenity until she couldn't anymore. Sister surrounding herself with animals and birds and land, her cows and horses an anchor to her past. She accepted her age and limitations, walking out to talk to Ruby and the other cows on the opposite side of the fence until she couldn't anymore. She didn't accept Alzheimer's.

I think of my friend Pam Ewing. For many years she and her husband ran their own cattle, or worked on ranches for others, until things changed. As they do. Ranchers don't necessarily want to hire a seventy-year-old cowboy. And the ground does get harder with the years. Pam got bucked off, hurt. Now she and her husband have acreage, horses, dogs, chickens, each other. A beautiful home remodeled by Pam. And three cows.

Heidi Redd—fifty-five years on her ranch—how did she reach the decision to retire?

I don't understand what's happening inside me as my outside keeps getting older.

Am I the very definition of catastrophizing?

As soon as I hear anger in a son's voice, my adrenaline kicks in and my thinking stops. The frustration of the other party intensifies. Finally I move past fear and freeze to anger. *Then sell the fucking cows*, I might yell at Ken. On a physical, visceral, animal level, my fear-freeze-fight pattern is heightened by PTSD. I might go to an almost-panic state of thought, about age, loss, endings, death.

When I was a child my mother often said that I would make mountains out of molehills. Smith said I could make mountains out of gopher holes. Funny, I have thought of myself as an optimist, my beliefs built on faith that things do get better, and that positive attitudes help that happen. Can optimism be an antonym for catastrophizing: instead of thinking of the worst outcome, think of the best?

C⊃-

On the Salmon River we move, floating, running rapids, making and breaking camp each day. Morning, noon, and evening we gather in a big circle, talk, write. The guides do all the cooking and cleaning up—they won't even let me wash dishes. Each afternoon we make camp in a different place of beauty. Ponderosas and Douglas fir on the canyon sides, rocky beaches and sandy ones, pine needles beneath my Paco pad, chill and stars in the air, then morning sunshine. Some rapids have washed out with the high water—the guides, all women but one, talk about how different the river is at this level.

Everything about this river differs from what I know, from color to texture to canyon walls. I don't even *want* to row. Watching the canyon pass, the river splash, and people laugh is enough. But. I have this thought: Had I not gone back to cowboying, would I have gone back to the river? To rowing my own raft? If not that, what? Like the banks of a river, Rebecca and my fathers were my guides (my bio-father twenty-eight years sober when he died), mustangs and cattle and Ken taking it from there, and the power of *what-ifs* lessened. Now it's back.

I used to tell my students that fiction is made of *what-ifs*, nonfiction *what-is* or *what-was*.

I am on the river *now*.

C⊃-

Miles downriver, the Salmon a gentle swooshing between rocky shores while Sheep Creek pounds out of a steep side canyon, I think this is the way of this river: the place beneath my feet, the water and walls that wrap around us, infiltrated by thoughts thrumming in from outside, my heart the confluence where currents stir and sometimes battle before they blend, but blend they will, turning smooth as the fine grains of sand that pillow my toes, as the green water gliding past. This is what we are, isn't it? A confluence of now and before and hope or excitement or fear about what's to come.

Today we will leave this camp for the last leg of the trip, the river taking us for a final ride: the largest rapids. And then the take-out and bus ride and town, motel, shower, the latter of which I don't even feel I need (though others might disagree), the clean, green water so different from my cloudy, silty home rivers.

I haven't seen my cell phone for a week. On the bus I pull it from the depths of a dry bag and turn it on. No service. Good. I'm not ready for the outer world just yet. I put the phone away but don't turn it off, and on a straight stretch of road it starts pinging with texts.

At an evening river circle I had told the group that my book was a Colorado Book Awards finalist, that in a couple of nights at an event in Denver the winners would be announced, that I wouldn't know the results until we got off the river. In the days following, people asked if I was anxious. "It's a done deal," I said. "I've either won, or I haven't." But on the bus, I dig my phone out again and start scrolling through texts, knowing my family will have reached out to let me know either way. My reading glasses also stashed, I can't read anything until I see TJ's text, all caps: DESERT CHROME WON!!!!!

Jumping up, I turn to face the busload of Freeflow Institute writers, teachers, and river guides with whom I've lived for a week, and I give them a big smile and a thumbs-up.

From his seat behind me, David James Duncan understands. "You won!" he says, rising and giving me the biggest hug ever as people cheer. I walk down the swaying aisle then and hug every single one of them.

Hours later, when we get to the motel, I do shower, but I don't wash my hair. I want to keep wearing the river, and everything it carried, in my hair.

18. Ken and Lacey with horned Criollo cows and huge Angus cows (notice the difference?). Photo by Tyler Lausten.

Ken, Lacey, Tyler, and I stayed at cow camp last night; we played five-card draw until after eleven, when we called it because Lacey had had enough despite the fact that she kept winning. Such an awesome little girl, so smart and funny and cute and spunky and moody and not wanting to go outside until she does, and then she's just *happy*. She rode her mom's gelding yesterday, Ken on his sorrel mare, and together they loped through the green grass up the hill and away.

Today Ken and Tyler will go to the far southwest corner of the Dressel Pasture to put up the lay-down fence and do the predictable repairs, the quad and side-by-side stationed for shuttle purposes; chainsaws sharpened; T-posts, wire, and belts holding fence pliers, clips, and staples ready for the patch jobs where fallen aspens have broken wire or hold the fence to the ground.

Today I get Lacey, who has brushed her hair and pulled it back and put on special owl earrings for Unk Ty. She wears her shirt and leggings from yesterday, but up here we don't care. I'm still in my flannel pajama bottoms, waiting for the day to decide its temperature.

On the river we have hand signals for when we get separated, a kayak rounding a bend first and then we see the kayaker, too far away for a yell. Or someone falls in and hauls out on a rock. We pat our heads in exaggerated movement, our hands up and down on the tops of our heads asking if the swimmer is okay. The person downstream will pat her head or helmet if she is okay. The other signal is a circle above our heads, like swinging a lariat. If that person wants us to eddy out, because eddies can be places of safety, she will do that, and we will motion to the rafts upstream, all of us eddying out.

This morning I pat my head, and Lacey's: I am okay. We are okay.

Wanting to move some cows to another part of the Groundhog Creek Pasture—the part that's actually along the creek—Ken, his young cousin, Hunter, who is visiting, and I gather a bunch of cow-calf pairs to push down the Cowboy Trail (so named by previous cowboys because of its steep, rugged, aspen-clogged, mile-long descent to Groundhog Creek). Some additional cattle start heading our way. We don't want the two groups to mix—our bunch already paired up—but a bull we need lumbers among the newcomers.

"See if you can sort him off," Ken says.

I trot Savanna across the open meadow and turn her toward the edge of a copse of aspens rimmed with round-leaf snowberry bushes, intending to cut through the trees to get to the bull without spooking the rest of the cattle. But Savanna trips, her right front leg tangling in viny, trailing snowberry; she tries to recover but keeps tripping and I have time only to kick my feet free of the stirrups before she falls all the way down, my shoulder slamming into the ground, her gray back and my saddle rolling slowly up my right leg, and then slowly back the other way.

Savanna lunges onto all fours and spooks at me in the grass. I can feel and hear Ken and Hunter racing toward me, their horses pounding the earth like bison. I try to push myself up—so that Ken can see me, know I'm not hurt—but my arm doesn't work right, and in an ungraceful ass-in-the-air move I lunge to standing the way Savanna did as Ken leaps from his horse, grabs Savanna's mecate, and says, "What did you *do*?" all in one motion.

"*I* didn't do it. Savanna fell down."

He checks to see if I'm okay. If Savanna is okay.

My foot in the stirrup, left hand gripping the saddle horn, I say, "You may have to help me back on my horse," because I can't grab the cantle with my right hand. As I step up, Ken does indeed have to push his mother's seat into the saddle.

We start the cattle down. Each step jars my shoulder. As I hook my thumb into my belt I remember the cowboy on Santa Cruz Island who dislocated his shoulder when his horse fell with him, yet he refused to abandon the job. Now, Ken ahead calling the cattle, the cows resisting the steep downhill trek and worrying over lagging calves, Hunter and I ride hard, working our horses back and forth, pushing cows, steers, and bull as the dogs weave through the understory to bite heels or noses, our horses sweating and stumbling over downed aspens, Hunter's small gelding jumping logs that nearly touch his belly. We reach the bottom an hour later. And that's the end of the trail for the day . . . except for the going-back-up part.

We watch the cattle mother up again, making sure each calf finds its mama in the bottom of the canyon, where green grass grows thickly alongside the rushing creek. I ride over to Ken. He studies me. Helps me off my horse. I look toward the Cowboy Trail, so steep I usually lead Savanna partway, either up or down. I can't see the trail for the trees.

"You don't have to go back up," Ken says. He has already devised an alternate plan. He makes a sling of my sweatshirt, finds a spot where he can get cell phone service, and calls Kathy. We ride along the creek, then through it and across an open meadow rimmed with ponderosas and redrock and arrive at a dwelling. It has a chair outside in the shade. I sit and wait while the horses rest and Ken visits with the chair's owner until Kathy shows up with a horse trailer.

But hell, nothing's broke, as X-rays later confirm, and I chastise myself for not following Ken and Hunter back up the Cowboy Trail. The next day, when I can't lift my right arm to braid my own hair, I think it possible that maturity and wisdom have finally set in.

Kathy has surgery scheduled, and I'm supposed to watch the kids. Instead, Tyler and Hunter take turns as Ken drives Kathy to Durango and waits at the hospital, comes home late, and goes back in the morning. Peg flies from Cali to Colorado to help. She stays two weeks, cooking and cleaning for everybody while my arm hangs in a sling and Kathy recovers. Hunter, only eighteen with a small herd of cattle in California, cowboys alongside Ken for the duration. I am not supposed to ride for at least three weeks—a long time eddying out of my job. I figure once I can braid my own hair I can get back on a horse.

The day after Peg leaves, Lacey and Lucas at the river with Tyler, Ken and Hunter up at Groundhog, Kathy resting, I head to the mustang cabin. Rain fell near the Groundhog turnoff minutes before I get there. I'm driving one-handed, my arm still in a sling, but when I hit mud I have to grip the wheel with both hands until the Toyota slows to creeping. Pain sears through my shoulder but more than that my face hurts. Or tooth. Or the hole where the tooth used to be. Peg took me to the dentist and waited like Ken for Kathy, though not as long, as the dentist pulled a tooth. Each day the place of extraction gets more painful, while the shoulder improves until I do something sudden like grab the wheel and the SLAP tear retears.

The road wet and muddy down the switchbacks, the creek runs surprisingly low under the bridge. The road east of Cliff's is dry, but Alkali Wash and Salt Arroyo have trickles. I drive past the cabin to look for mustangs and see a lone gray stallion in the distance, probably Kwana, whose band was recently stolen. At the cabin, the rain gauge reads .43, what has accumulated during my absence, and the soft green of warm-season grasses calms the glaring gray soil.

The creek runs higher at the cabin than it did at the bridge ten miles upvalley, which means rain hit the country around the abutments and promontories near Cliff's, filling the arroyos and side canyons that empty into Disappointment Creek. Which might mean another flash flood is on its way.

At four in the morning I awaken. Listen. Jaw throbbing. Pain or sound woke me. Then I know. I leave my bed, grab the flashlight, step into flipflops, step onto the porch, onto the earth, into the dark, angling the flashlight toward the creek, where I see the white of flood splashing off rocks. I feel the pounding water in the earth beneath my feet.

⊂⊃-

The COVID pandemic apparently passes, though people keep getting sick. Antibiotics relieve my jaw of pain, and my shoulder gets better enough for me to braid my hair and ride. The cliff swallows have returned to the colony built onto a sandstone cliff opposite the cabin, flying in from somewhere in South America. Colonies can contain as many as two thousand nests. Here we have maybe seventy-five. Each nest, shaped like a gourd with a hole in the belly, is constructed of about a thousand mud pellets made by the swallows. Some nests crumble or fall between breeding seasons, when freeze-and-thaw loosens them from stone, and the returning swallows went right to work repairing nests or starting anew.

The cliff swallows, a migratory species, will leave as suddenly as they arrived, which was on a day when my sons and grandchildren came for a sleepover, when TJ experienced the biggest flash flood ever and seven miles upvalley we didn't get a drop.

Naught but a lonely dark cloud to the west, Ken and Tyler decided to take the kids rockhounding at Nichols Wash. They hit light rain near the BLM corrals and kept going, with rain so spotty out here. A thin sheet of water crossed the road near TJ's east cattle guard, and they kept on, reaching the flood as it poured out of Dawson Draw, over the road and berm, to enter TJ's driveway and yard. Thick, red-gray water parted around her cabin. She stood on the porch waving as Ken hollered to see if she was okay (they don't know the river signals). The water reconnected at the back of her house, forming an eddy that rose high enough to spill into her basement and fill it with water. And mud.

TJ has a sump pump, which sucked up the water but not the mud that settled to the basement's bottom. The old outbuilding on the other side of the fence that encircles TJ's yard flooded as well. Surely these buildings have flooded before. What did they do century before last to deal with flooded houses? Or was climate and life so different then that monsoons didn't hold all this moisture, all this intensity?

⊂⊃-

A turkey vulture just buzzed the swallow cliff. For the first few years here, neither TJ nor I saw any turkey vultures. Like, ever. Slowly they have shown up in summer, as many as three per season. They don't mark the carrion for us. Mostly golden eagles, ravens, and magpies feast on animals hit on the road. In winter we see bald eagles and more goldens. Once I saw eight juvenile and adult golden and bald eagles together in a cottonwood tree. Someone had hit a deer, and TJ dragged it far off the road so the raptors wouldn't also get hit.

The raven fledgling must have fledged. The pair had only one this year, and hopefully it survived the red-tailed hawk that shows up around fledging time. I don't know if it's the same hawk, but for a couple of years one with feathers missing from the left wing hovered in the hood.

The cliff swallows seem so busy, but they do sleep, in trees in the non-breeding season and in their nests as soon as they're partially finished. In completed nests I can see through binoculars the sweet swallow faces at the holes as the birds look out; later the open beaks of babies will show as the parents bring food. I wonder if the ancestors watched swallows building their cliff colonies and copied, knowing to leave when things dried up.

No piñon jays. Although permanent residents of the high desert, they move constantly from one piñon-juniper stand to the next, feasting primarily on the seeds within piñon pinecones, then burying seeds for later. A single bird can carry as many as forty seeds in its mouth as it flies to a cache site—and then remember where it put them. Any forgotten seeds will sprout and help replenish the piñon part of declining piñon-juniper forests. "The trees can't regenerate without the birds and the birds can't survive without the trees," writes Audrey Kruse of the Grand Canyon Trust.

Almost time to go, says my gut. I don't stay put either.

15
Wild Life

What does "wild" mean, anyway? . . . A wild place isn't one unchanged by humans. It's a place that changes us.

—Melissa Sevigny, *Brave the Wild River*

Disappointment Valley, Colorado, Summer to Winter 2022

At the mustang cabin I walk around to the porch and hear a most distinctive sound—*after* I've stepped over it in my flipflops—a sound like no other except a bull snake, but I know this is the real thing and look down to see it slithering over a rock. Still rattling. Small, young. As I step away to grab a nearby shovel, Jessi goes in for a look and I yell *get back* and she does—she knows this command well, as I use it daily in cattle work. The threat has coiled itself against my stepping stone, ready to strike, and it does strike, fangs to metal as I scoop it up in the shovel and carry it away from the cabin.

The next day in the 102-degree heat we walk to the creek looking for a place for Bow to get wet. Thick slippery clinging mud everywhere, my flipflops quickly get heavy with deep slime, of which Bow wants no part. We step across on rocks, and in the mud beside a puddle I see perfect bear tracks, already crusty around the edges—from yesterday, not today. My tracks have wet mud all around, the difference between fresh and older. She must have toured the creek in yesterday's heat, looking for a drink. It was so hot I didn't do anything other than read and write, sweat and drink water, grumble and feel bad. The rattlesnake not helping—first one I've seen near the cabin.

The bear tracks have a different effect. Though I would prefer to see the bear, seeing the tracks ignites a visceral buzzing like a rattlesnake's tail. Going up to cow camp the other day I did see a bear lumbering in the open. I stopped the Toyota and grabbed my field glasses as he stole through the grass to the edge of the aspens, where he stopped and watched me as I glassed him, but I could see only his huge head and large ears and snout.

A dozen coyote voices erupt as the day turns toward evening, though it's probably only two or three animals. The air has cooled to ninety and the dogs race in big circles around the cabin as if ten degrees means everything. I too feel better as sunlight slants across the valley and reaches for the far rimrocks. Swallows gurgle and flit.

The mysterious sound I hear each summer is the male nighthawk's booming. I thought it was a sick elk, even a sick man, but now I know that the deep whirring-buzzing-throat-clearing sound is made by the air rushing through the displaying nighthawk's feathers as he dives suddenly, steeply, toward earth. The sound thrills me, as does the fact that I figured it out all by myself.

In Disappointment Valley I live at the edge of wildness, and I realize that through different means I have sought this for years. Paddling offshore in Hawaiʻi when a humpback whale breached so close to the outrigger canoe that we rode the swells its body made. Snorkeling above a white-tipped reef shark as the shark whipped its tale, stirred up sand, and vanished. Seeing the same kōlea (Pacific golden-plover) arrive on my mother's Maui lawn each August (some return to the same place year after year), tired, hungry, and drab after a three-thousand-mile nonstop flight from the western Alaskan tundra. His stature and colors would change over the months until elegant stripes of dazzling white started at his forehead and trimmed his black cheeks, throat, and neck, glitter of black, gold, and white on his back, which meant the handsome kōlea would soon launch toward breeding and nesting grounds in Alaska.

Cowboying has an element of wildness—because I'm out. There. The hours I spend in the saddle with cattle give me a sense of freedom, adventure, perhaps a hint of danger. Does wildness mean being outdoors, alone, far from a town, the possibility of danger present? Not necessarily—even drugs in a cityscape pushed me to the wild side. J. Drew Lanham says in *The Home Place* that wildness means living in the unknown. I think about this.

As Savanna walks through the trees or trots across the meadows, I look for cows, signs of sickness in calves and steers, and wildlife. Rocky Mountain elk, mule deer, black bears. Marmots and chipmunks, and once I saw the disappearing flank of a snowshoe hare. Beaver and muskrat, and Tyler has seen a weasel. Twice. I've not witnessed a mountain lion, bobcat, or lynx at Groundhog. Yet. No groundhogs either.

Groundhogs are one species of marmot, yellow-bellied marmots another. Yellow-bellied marmots inhabit the rocky and talus slopes of alpine Colorado (and elsewhere), while groundhogs don't live in Colorado; therefore, I presume that Groundhog Peak and the surrounding area were named for the marmots.

I bet those early cowboys felt wildness in an even more fundamental way. Except, for them, it was just life.

Despite hot days, at the mustang cabin a cool wind brushes the morning. My head, eyes, and nose have allergies. TJ says she gets allergies from kochia—immigrants in the mid-1800s brought kochia, native to Eurasia, to North America as an ornamental plant. It happens that cattle eat it, and apparently someone planted it in the pastures near TJ's house. It breaks at the base when mature and rolls along like a tumbling tumbleweed, spreading unwanted seed. I don't have any at the cabin, yet.

Broom snakeweed blooms autumn's bright yellow (pretty, but poisonous to cattle), common sunflowers along the road too, and soon the rabbitbrush will follow. The fairy-wing leaves of fourwing saltbush will dry to pale yellow then a bland tan, then they will drop. Cottonwoods along the creek still hold their summer greens, while the willows have begun to change.

The horizon of bulging cumulus clouds also changes color, turning darker near Lone Cone and Groundhog Peaks. This could mean another wash of rain—the ground at Groundhog so wet on Wednesday that Savanna and I slipped and slid down the slope from the red gate to the pond following sliding cattle tracks—or it could mean nothing.

Another plane. At the beginning of COVID, the days here were truly quiet, no sky or road traffic, just bears and bees and dogs and creek. And birds. Now jets randomly blast the sky, leaving their contrail clouds behind them. "Jet tracks fucking up my sky," wrote a poetry student in the graduate program at Northern Arizona University.

A canyon wren sings, and piñon jays sweep from the sky to light on nearby piñon-pine branches, float to the forest floor, peck through remnants of an early snow at the bases of tree trunks, and lift and call and swoop away. Piñon jay populations have fallen by 85 percent in the last fifty years, according to Grand Canyon Trust and Defenders of Wildlife, the latter of which petitioned for endangered species consideration for this favorite western bird.

The days shorten. Tyler takes me back to Lone Cone's high slopes. A chill wind updrafts from the steep drop of canyons below. The colors! Rust, yellow, coniferous green, blue-spruce green, and the yellow-green of aspens turning. Brittle gray spires amid the living green—so many trees dying. Gray talus. Gray ribbon of road. Gray jay whistling. Snow white. Terracotta slopes to the east. A red squirrel. Dark-eyed junco, the white flash of its tail; Townsend's solitaire. Nuthatches chirp, a sweet little bark; the scee of chickadees. Ravens circle and call.

Turning to face the sun in the lee of Tyler's van, the crisp, clean, frigid air still chills my cheeks and brow and the fingers of my left hand while sunshine without wind warms my knees. I can smell Jessi's sun-warmed fur as she passes me to check on Tyler. I wish she would sit on my feet. The maroon down jacket I found with Tyler in Alaska, pulled out of the closet for the first time this year, gratefully worn. These amazing mountains: swells and crags and crests and peaks and sky. Bow drinks from a tire-track puddle, then wanders off to sleep . . . in the shade.

I can smell the cold in the wind. Taste the season changing. Hear the whisper of winter in the high country. Soon we will bring the cattle down off the mountain.

Driving to the mustang cabin on one of my last trips over the mountain before snow would close the road, I hadn't yet seen the neighbor's dead cow so was unprepared as I rounded a bend. The cow lay beside a cross fence in the middle of the ponderosa-rimmed meadow, and something lifted from her and seemed to fly along the fence toward the shelter of pines as I reached too slowly for my field glasses, but I know it was a mountain lion. That long bounding gait, not a lope or run or trot like a dog or coyote, and that tail.

The next time I drove in that way I had binoculars in hand as I slowed at the bend that would reveal the dead cow. Movement parallel to me but on the far side of the pasture made my foot hit the brakes; more movement followed, also parallel to me but nearer the fence separating the road from the pasture. Three beautiful, lush-coated, winter-ready coyotes loped up the valley, one rimming toward the trees, the two closer to me exposed and watching as they moved fluidly around a low hill and out of sight.

A little farther down the road, a fourth coyote, lying between the road and the fence, bloody and dead. I stopped to look at her. Touched her soft fur. She could have been hit by a vehicle not a bullet, but I doubted it, so I checked. Gut shot, and one through the lungs.

The road over the mountain now closed, I have settled into Disappointment. After a fresh, deep snowfall I drove a couple of miles upvalley to see where my cows had wandered—easy to track in the snow, except that in deep snow I find it harder to discern cow-elk tracks from cow-cow tracks. At a fence marking private land, a flurry of tracks showed in the corner near a closed gate—this year's elk pushed out of the high country by snow.

I could see where they mingled before finding a place to jump, and where they parted, some going through an open gate and up the fenceline, some on the road side of the fence. Moving east, I saw where more had jumped the fence, continuing northward across the road and toward another sagebrush, greasewood, native-grass flat, and BLM badlands.

One set of tracks singled itself out and I followed it, wondering if perhaps those were cow-cow tracks after all. The prints stayed parallel to the fence and then made an oval in the snow and disappeared—a moment of indecision followed by decision. I looked closely and found the launch site where the solo elk had lifted off, cleared the fence, landed, crossed the road, made the same oval of indecision on the other side, then cleared that fence and joined the expanding herd. I didn't find any cow-cows.

The next day, elk tracks crisscrossed every open, snow-filled field, and about seventy-eight lay in a bunch watching an intruder—me—warily, with another thirty not far away. These elk could hardly stay still, and I think it's because they have gotten hunted so heavily in these parts for so many years. When I encounter them in the depths of the backcountry, where no roads exist and no vehicles of any kind can go, the elk don't spook and flee but watch me as I skirt them and then we all go about our business. They aren't harassed back there the way they are near a road, and they know this.

One day when Lacey was four and Lucas two, I received a particularly disheartening rejection, so I did what any other rejected writer might do under the circumstances: not chocolate, laundry. Bending to the machine to lift out spun Wranglers, I saw through the window a large brown clumping in the farthest field south of the house. The circling of many large animals. Not cattle—no, this was a herd of cow elk and yearlings and three still-antlered bulls lumped tightly together on the lower side of an electric fence. They stood, milled, looked west, circled.

I forgot about laundry and went outside with my field glasses. Soon more elk joined the original thirty-three, flowing out of the junipers and across the field with the grace of water pouring and reaching and pooling with other water. Eventually a few younger cows stepped away from the herd, creating a gap instantly filled by the main body, and in this way the elk herd leaked slowly west. I went back inside to finish putting clothes in the dryer, glancing out different south-facing windows, pretending to clean but really just milling and circling, myself.

For two hours those now one hundred elk moved yards west then retreated east, and it occurred to me finally that this was their first spring migration since new neighbors purchased acreage adjoining the ranch and built a house. And dog pens, which housed two large Rottweilers. The structure and those big barking dogs kept the elk pooled in our lower pasture.

Outside the glass in my front door, my grandkids appeared. Lacey wanted to play a storytelling game, so she, Lucas, and I scrunched together on the living-room rug and they pulled painted blocks from a pile, pairing an image from one with another, connecting them with words.

Their dad called to say the elk had moved up to the pasture just east of our houses, so the kids and I put on our boots and snuck around onto the deck to watch the elk. The herd must have retreated to the junipers earlier, then followed the fenceline north in the cover of trees, but now they had to cross a different open field and confront another damned damming fence.

My despair might have escaped in a sound because Lacey said, "Shhh." And then she took my hand and said, "I feel sad." Now we three scrunched together on the bench on the deck and watched the flow of elk as their dark ruffs blurred with their winter-tan sides and the few antlers and one blond elk in the middle, and the herd moved up across the pasture to a corner fence and back to the trees and up again and finally one, two, three, seven at a time jumped the fence—*our* fence—and moved into the next stand of trees, mountain-bound.

Did Lacey understand that the elk just wanted to go where they wanted to go and they couldn't, because of us? Because of our continuing human encroachment into their backyards? Maybe she didn't get that part; maybe I didn't say it aloud. Maybe I just said it was sad because they wanted to get to the high country and had a hard time figuring out how, or maybe I didn't say that and she's four and smart and warm sitting next to me for those long moments of watching wildlife try to figure out how to be wild and follow instinct despite fences, and Lacey seemed to understand what she saw even if I didn't give her the words. Which I hope I didn't.

Or maybe I hope I did. The way my mother and aunt gave me names of trees and wildflowers; the way Sally Carrighar gave me grouse and a weasel in *One Day on Beetle Rock*.

After finishing laundry, I stopped in at Ken's, where Lacey and Lucas sat on the couch with their dad. Lacey could see the refrigerator through the kitchen door. "Oh," she said, pushing off the couch, "I forgot to give this to you." She disappeared for a moment, reappearing with a yellow sheet of the same kind of construction paper with which my mother raised my sisters and me. "I made this for you."

On the yellow paper, painted Popsicle sticks arced over a field of green. In the sky above the rainbow, green, purple, and orange Popsicle sticks flew randomly, and I could see that the outlying sticks were Lacey's version of Ken's deliberate, schematically colored rainbow.

Ken pointed to the sharp green blades and rounded bumps in the field drawn at the bottom of the page. "What's this?" he asked.

"It looks like grass," I said.

"Animals," Lacey said.

Ken: "What kind of animals?"

With the *duh* intonation of a four-year-old, Lacey said, "Elk."

Though Lacey and her father had made the Popsicle picture days before, Lacey saw in the grass of her imagination the moving herd of elk under a rainbow sky. And so did I.

A cow elk had struggled to free her right hind leg from the death trap of a "wildlife-friendly," high-tensile-wire fence in Disappointment Valley. Somehow she'd stepped between the bottom two wires and they twisted and tightened around the thick, solid bone of her leg midway to her hock and she had already died when I first saw the hump of her lying in the snow, her neck stretched out and her pretty face caught in a tangle of sagebrush, her legs spread as if still running, an eye and a patch of meat from her rump already gone.

The next day, her rump mostly eaten, her red ribs showed, and some stomach contents had spilled out. Her neck still reaching, her head still caught, like her leg, the snow around her was muddied and packed down. A young golden eagle soared high above. Ravens perched on big sagebrush nearby. And magpies.

As I moved away, something else moved too. Not a bird into flight—no, this was a land being, though it lifted up out of an arroyo as if it had wings, pausing to look back before moving in a quick slink into the thick brush of greasewood and sage. I reached for my phone not my field glasses—to take a picture? Instead of just watching with my own eyes?

Bigger than a border collie but less than half grown, it had red-tinged, fluffy winter fur clear down to the black tip of its long, fluffed-out tail. It had speed and stealth and sage on its side while I had stupidity on mine—because I didn't want a picture, damn it, I wanted to see the cat as clearly and for as long as I could, but some dim habit of technology thwarted me, though I still have an image of movement up and out and behind and away, this wild thing able to escape the existing manmade efforts at control.

Beside the elk, juvenile cat tracks, and just there, the nearly four-inch-by-four-inch round tracks of the juvenile mountain lion's mother.

Soon the ribs made the cage for which they're named, and I could see through them to the ground beneath. Skin gone from her stretching, now bony neck, patches of fur lay about on both sides of the elk and both sides of the fence and up and down and all around. With some of her facial hide removed, her teeth showed in a grimace, her eye even more socket than before.

Despite her tortured death, fighting to free herself then yielding after the struggle, the cow elk gave of herself to the wild community. I can only hope that the lion hunters patrolling this valley so they can chase and control and kill wildness don't find the little lion or its mother. At dawn on the mornings after a fresh snow, lion hunters patrol the road, their rigs easy to spot by the large custom dog boxes in the beds, the heads of hounds sticking out the rows of holes. The hunters send their hounds on any trails the keen-nosed dogs find. Sometimes I hear baying in the distance. Sometimes closer. Sometimes I hear shots.

One morning after chopping through a thick layer of ice covering the creek so the cattle could access water, I sat in the Toyota on the road searching for cell service, and a pair of lion hunters stopped alongside me to see if I was okay. On their roof rack on top of the dog boxes lay a lion, the head propped up on the rack to make it clearly visible, the sleek body as long as the truck bed, the tail wrapped around the powerful hind end. The cougar looked at me with dull, dead eyes. I hope the lion hunters don't end the lineage of a species the way cowboys in the area ended the grizzlies and wolves more than a hundred years ago.

As chronicled by Howard E. Greager in *In the Company of Cowboys*, in 1893 Henry Knight spotted three grizzlies in Disappointment Valley: a sow and two cubs, one of which was pinto—large white spots on the grizzly's flanks flaring toward his back. Easily recognizable, though rarely seen, the "pinto grizzly" stayed in the area, while the mama bear and the other cub seemed to have vanished. Two years later, a huge old bear charged a couple of trappers, who killed her with a single-shot carbine after multiple repeating-rifle shots barely slowed her down. "A large female grizzly; the bear's skull measured eighteen inches, ear to ear," reports Greager. They figured she was the pinto grizzly's mother.

For twenty-two years, the pinto grizzly roamed the country around Disappointment Valley, North Mountain, Lone Cone, and Wright's Mesa, surviving cold winters and summers of heat, sometimes by feasting on calves or cows to maintain his thousand-pound weight. Surely he ate wild game as well, but the loss of cattle riled ranchers and cowboys, so when three cowboys spotted the old pinto bear, they gave chase. One cowboy veered off to get reinforcements, and when two additional men saw the griz loping across the mesa they raced their horses after him, pelting him with bullets and killing him.

Wolves roamed Disappointment and neighboring valleys in those days. Lots of them, according to Greager, until bounty hunters killed them off. Twenty-five dollars per animal—even pups—the hunters found dens and seized and killed the offspring. Because wolves also were found gnawing on cattle and sheep.

The thing is, the number of cattle in southwestern Colorado and southeastern Utah near the turn of that century was preposterous, which meant sparse feed for the elk and deer, which in turn meant fewer prey animals for wolves and the pinto grizzly. In *Sagebrush Empire*, Jonathan P. Thompson says that more than seventeen thousand head of cattle lived in San Juan County, Utah, in 1890, according to the U.S. Department of Agriculture census. Plus a hundred thousand sheep. What forage did they leave for the wildlife? No one seemed to think about what overgrazing would do to the future of ranching, let alone the future of the land.

Cattle numbers in Disappointment Valley today are fewer by the thousands than a hundred years ago. No sheep except the desert bighorns occasionally spotted near Slick Rock. Once when driving with my mother and Terry a ram stood in silhouette on top of a huge boulder beside the road. I slowed to a near stop so that my happy mother could see him longer.

A golden eagle picks at something near the base of a juniper, magpies hopping around on the outskirts. My approach causes the eagle to pause, then lift into flight, and I look for the morsel that tempted the golden. A fresh-killed Merriam's turkey, feathers stuck to the body and in the snow. Later Terry said I should get the feathers, which I did, leaving them on the dash as I hiked off to look at cows. Sunlight through the windshield warmed the dash and the feathers, cooking the meat and gristle on the shafts. The cab smelled like death for days.

Another morning, near McDermott Arroyo, a rafter of turkeys perched on the branches of a piñon pine. Odd, I thought, as the alarm clock of the rising sun should have already stirred the turkeys from roosting to feeding. Suddenly another large, low-flying bird dove toward the tree, and the turkeys as a flock flew over the arroyo and across the flat to land in another place of piñon pines. The incoming bird: a golden eagle. The turkeys having thwarted its attempt to snag one of them from the branches, the glorious, still-hungry golden lifted on an invisible spiral of air, floating, flying, leaving.

I went back to the elk still clinging by her stuck leg to the fence. She had turned from a large, healthy, wild, free animal into a ravaged carcass. Snow crunching, field glasses in hand, I stopped and glassed her. Movement in the bushes just beyond. A head pushing through the sagebrush to get a bite of meat, hunger an anchor as eyes peered at me through ribs of sage and elk, and then the cat backed up, looking huge as it retreated. It paused, thinking itself hidden, and indeed it almost was. I inched forward and the cat moved again, and I watched with naked eye as it slunk behind sage and then the whole animal stood broadside in the snow.

The kitten. Fuzzy coat with receding spots and the tail all fluffed out again down to its black tip, and I wished Tyler were with me with his quick eye and camera because I have only the photographs of memory. I can see the face through the stems of sage and the parts slinking away and the movement behind brush and the broadside. But I can't pause the images or focus in closely on details of coat and paws and face and tail, although I could see that the paws looked huge as it leapt away, followed by that long, lovely tail.

I have gone every day in hopes of seeing him hunkering in the bushes, peering out for moments, and returning to fevered mauling of the carcass. Last evening he did acrobatics—head and front paws trying to loosen the hide and bone from branches, frozen ground, and fence—his whole butt lifting in the air and then twisting around, his tail like a monkey's offering balance as he worked so hard to free the elk, which I had also tried to do—work it free so the cub could follow instinct and drag it away.

He could be a he or a she; sexing a mountain lion is nearly impossible on the fly, or when it's camouflaged by sagebrush. It is a kitten. Last year's. Spots fading. Seven months old?

Heading back to the cabin I saw some heifers on the section between the foundation of the old Lavender schoolhouse and the creek. This morning Jessi and I walked across crisp yet melting snow to bring them to the rest of the herd. The lead heifer dropped off the bank and headed upstream, so I moved along the edge of the frozen creek to get around her. Topped with an inch of snow, in that powder-on-ice appeared a long strand of *huge* mountain lion tracks—each one perfect and distinct and bigger than any I've yet seen. Made in fresh snow, then frozen to solid, they were so huge I thought they could be the front paws of a bear. Which they weren't.

Moments ago wild turkeys bustled past the cabin porch where I sit writing. They pecked at the soil around saltbush and rabbitbrush that the plants' thermal wicking has exposed—bushes and bunchgrasses drawing warmth from the sun and melting the snow at their base like a candle flame melting wax. The turkeys wandered across to the rim and along it, glancing at the dogs and me and not startling. Just moving the way they do when not startled—hunched over, pecking slowly, stepping one foot at a time toward the next plant that might harbor seeds or insects. Now they have vanished to my eye, but they're somewhere. I feel flattered by their presence, as if it has anything to do with me. Maybe it does, as I am calm and moving slowly today myself.

The cub ran the first time I saw him. I didn't know he was there and moved at a normal pace. Now I move slowly. The juvenile mountain lion watches me and eats dead elk and watches. I hold my breath, hold the field glasses, hold the phone in case I can video something for Tyler and Ken and the kids. I feel wrongly honored that the cougar cub allows this. Also I worry that my presence could teach him that humans are okay. And we're so not. We're potentially very bad news. Hunters who kill not to eat or protect but to flaunt their balls.

The turkeys run off the road at the approach of even a slow-moving vehicle. The elk in James Woods's big open brushy pasture can barely stay still when they see a vehicle coming. If they're lying down and one gets up, in a movement like swift water they depart. If I can slide past and no one rises, they may keep resting and napping longer.

The deer in these parts see me and run. Except when I travel afoot in the backcountry, where I've heard them blow like mustangs though not as loudly, and have found them standing, poised, watching me. Sometimes they take off. The other day I hiked way back in there and saw two bumps that with binoculars became elk who watched me and didn't rise. And I had Jessi. Since you can only go afoot or ahorseback into the wilderness study area, the elk seem not to see me as danger, whereas when I drive past them they know differently.

The turkeys make another round. I like them here. Their pecking and pooping helps this naturally xeriscaped "yard," and I love their voices, the soft gurgles and squeaks. When they see Jessi, they about-face and keep feeding. One tips her head to swallow snow-water, dipping her beak to a puddle then stretching her neck tall and her head high as she swallows. Like a chicken.

I don't see them here every year. The snow brought them down with the elk.

Hiking alongside McDermott Arroyo to look at cattle one morning, I heard a single coyote howling and stopped to try to locate it. Another answered on the other side of the small valley divided by the arroyo. Soon I saw two coyotes on the west side of the big cut. One sat down right there and howled. Through binoculars I could see the head raised, mouth open, jaw quivering the notes out. As the other coyote trotted through the brush the sitting coyote yipped, and the one from across the valley answered. I found him with my field glasses, no longer singing but trotting. Toward me. My hand told Jessi to stay, and neither of us moved. The coyote kept coming. Then he stopped, startled and staring with yellow eyes at the two-legged before him and four-legged Jessi (three-legged Bow in the Toyota). He didn't ponder long—he pivoted and trotted east up the hill toward the piñons the turkeys had fled to as they escaped the eagle.

The coyotes on the west side of the arroyo, watching all this, resumed their yipping and howling, the deterred coyote answering, followed by two more to the south, coyotes surrounding Jessi and me. I didn't feel fear, but had Jessi traveled alone, fear would have been appropriate.

When Keith and I lived on the coastal ranch, a coyote befriended my cowdog Cotton. As we rode, the coyote would follow us and entice Cotton to play. They romped in circles, chased each other, even roughhoused in the grass. I thought this wonderful and hoped the two would breed and I could somehow have a Cotton-coyote pup.

"Don't let him do that," Keith said. "She's teasing him now but eventually she'll lure him away and the pack will attack."

The coyote still followed us places, but I wouldn't let Cotton go to her.

Recently I heard about a dog seeing a coyote and running after it, a man running after the dog. He found her sitting rigidly in the grass surrounded by a pack of eight coyotes. Holding two branches like clubs, the man charged the coyotes, who retreated. He leashed his dog.

Back in the Tacoma, warming up, I thought about making a scene. I tell my students that scenes include conflict, tension, setting, description, action, dialog. While setting and description abound, the action in my scenes is often in what I observe. Is there tension? Maybe only inside me. When I sit in quiet observation, dialog may be the singing between birds; a nighthawk booming; bear grunting; cow bawling, calf answering; wild horses whinnying or nickering or squealing. The mountain lion cub made low growling noises as he tried to free the elk of fence and freeze.

Most of the critters out here talk, like the coyotes, just not to me. Water and air speak more than I do. If someone calls, my throat clogs as I strain to use it.

⊂⊃-

An elk head rested on a bridge over the drainage near the county line. Spine sawed through at the neck, antlers sawn off, it lay in the joint of cement and guardrail as if someone tossed it out of his pickup, throwing the evidence of a poached elk into an arroyo, but he missed, and it landed on the bridge. When I picked up the head by a stiff ear and put it in the bed of the Toyota, the elk looked at me like the mountain lion on the hunter's truck: with dull, dead eyes. I drove slowly up the road to a place where I could pack the head over the fence and down toward the creek, where the little big kitty or big big kitty might find it and have another morsel of a meal.

⊂⊃-

19. Tyler and Ken looking at Forest Service maps. Photo by the author.

Up at Groundhog, the Forest Service begins clearcutting trees. The Forest Service tells us they will be selective, taking only certain aspens, leaving those five inches in diameter and smaller, but no, the loggers cut *everything*. "It's easier," they say.

As I ride past the slash piles, the downed aspens smell like the windfall rounds I split for winter warmth, only this smell is freshened by rainfall and pungent with the intensity of death. Not just of the trees—where are the birds, the deer, the elk, the bears, the snowshoe hares? Tyler has seen house wrens and mountain and western bluebirds hovering where the canopy used to be and grouse searching among the debris for nests or fledglings. He watched a northern flicker take over a purple martin cavity, probably due to the loss of nesting sites.

On horseback we move past the acres of downed forest carefully, the ground cluttered with logs and sticks and stobs that could cripple a horse or dog.

In my completely one-sided love affair with the cougar kitten, I realized I feel that love in this valley of mustangs and mountain lions and also in the high country. Here *wild* can mean calm observation or the quiver of sensing and presence, a visceral thrill from skin to intestines, scalp to the pads of my feet. I equate this thrill with wonder, joy, and maybe fear. And I think for me that's what wild means: alert, full-body awareness in response to the surprises of the Great Mystery. The Unknown, as J. Drew Lanham says.

In the summer evenings in Disappointment I'm reminded of this, the desert air like silk on my skin, no one about except maybe mustangs and other wildlife as the sky shifts through its layered colors toward nightfall, the mixed scents of dried grasses and tangy creek like peace filling the air. I find this in some form every day I'm in Disappointment Valley or on the mountain, though elation dissipates when I see a gut-shot coyote, fence-trapped elk, trees mowed down or dying due to the shortsightedness of humans.

16
After Birth

Aw, hell—it's easy to be miserable, hard to live in joy.

—Luis Alberto Urrea, *Wandering Time*

Disappointment Valley, Colorado, Winter to Spring 2022–23

This winter we had snow and cold for months. Three-degree mornings in February, March, even into spring. We don't like the cows calving in icy air onto frozen ground, the calf wet for minutes as the cow's rough tongue licks it clean, which removes the slick of amniotic sac but leaves the calf damp as it staggers up into the wind to get its first drink. The extremities sometimes get frostbite, but you can't tell that a calf's ears have frozen until suddenly the tips or tops disappear.

Today it's still February and we're feeding in a blizzard, number 345 the first cow to the trailer with the three-quarter-ton hay bales on it. She's one of the biggest Angus cows, tall and wide and gentle, the hairs of her black coat curling with moisture in the sideways-blowing snow. Ken feeds the cows off the back of the trailer while I drive in a big circle, the pickup in granny gear and four-wheel-drive low, the slowest a manual transmission can go. The window open so I can hear if Ken yells for me to stop, hay duff blows in and sticks to snowflakes melting on my cheek. I swab at the exposed skin with a gloved hand and peer through the white blur to avoid hitting cattle or running over greasewood and puncturing a tire.

After Ken finishes, we walk among the big black bumps of cows. Mother and son, sixty-eight and thirty-eight, our chins tucked into our collars, caps pulled down over our ears, we look at broad bellies and bags and vulvas. Number 346's belly is huge, her bag full, her vulva elongated and swollen and loose; numbers 587 and 6112 also.

"They're close," I say to Ken, who nods. Back in the truck, Ken driving now, heater on high, I write in a small notebook: 346, 587, and 6112 springing (when the cows' sides get so big their bellies bounce as they walk, but not like when they're full of water; this is the calf moving toward the birth canal and means they will calve in one to three days).

The cows start drifting with the storm, white snow blanketing their backs as they move away from the hay even as we do, shelter the more important need right now for all of us. The best shelter in this 1,425-acre Nichols Wash pasture of few trees is the wash itself with its banks and brush and ribs of last year's willows, and as a force the cows head toward it.

"I'll look through them again tomorrow," I tell Ken.

Tomorrow turns as cold and miserable as the preceding day. When I get to the cows, 346 is missing, which probably means she calved. Snow drifts thickly and shrinks my world—I can't see much beyond the hood of the pickup. The two roads in this pasture too wet and muddy to drive, I would have to search afoot up and down the banks and around the bends of the meandering wash, and then march across, fence to fence in any direction, peering through snow, and still I'd likely not find cow or calf.

"Tomorrow," I say again, to myself this time.

We don't usually calve this early in the year but one of the bulls jumped fences last year and bred some of the Angus cows on his schedule, not ours. The Criollos, on the BLM allotment in upper Disappointment Valley, got bred later, when we intentionally turned the bulls in.

This winter we also separated the cow herds, to simplify and minimize feeding: the Criollos again in upper Disappointment and the Angus cows downvalley at Nichols Wash. At headquarters in Dolores live the bulls, the finishing steers, and some yearling steers who will go up to the mountain in June with the cows when we all head to the high country.

Tomorrow came again, and again I went to Nichols Wash. Number 346 showed up without her calf. Clearly she had calved—full bag, bloody tail. I couldn't tell if the calf had nursed—I couldn't see a slick teat, or the curly hairs at the base of the teat where a calf's mouth had gripped, or one milk quarter less full than the others. Busy nosing through the hay to get at better hay, 346 didn't bawl. She didn't even look off the way cows will do, gazing into the distance as if they can see a lone calf hiding under a greasewood bush far away.

Like deer, cows hide their young babies, usually near something that can provide cover—greasewood or sagebrush on this big flat, or willows by the creek at the cabin, or the downed branches of one of the many dying junipers. The calves, fawnlike, hug the ground the best they can, heads and chins and bellies and legs folded to the earth, and they won't rise until their mothers drift near. When I come upon hidden calves, they often won't even raise their heads. If I have to pick one up, it's heavy in its cling to the earth and it won't unfold, which makes grasping and lifting it hard to do.

I would have to tell Ken about 346. Meanwhile, 6112 arrived with a red bull calf, and 587 had calved, though I didn't see hers either.

In winter I watch the Criollos on the Salt Arroyo Allotment and gather them off in mid-February, the off-date designated by BLM. This year I will move them to the mustang cabin, where I'll have to feed them, but I'd have to haul either hay or water anywhere this time of year. Especially this year, our world under snow. At least the creek runs, even if under ice.

With Jessi I found cows in draws and on ridges and plateaus and pushed them down to the road, this afoot in the snow. Then from the pickup I called them through the first gate and the next. By that time dark had landed. I did a rough count. Five head short.

Randi calved the next day, the first of the horned cows, throwing a red Angus-cross bull calf. Huston calved three days later. (These are two of the cows we got from New Mexico cowboy singer Randy Huston.) Ken had come from headquarters with hay, and we watched Huston leave a shelter of trees to feed, fresh afterbirth hanging, the calf stashed somewhere. I thought number 8 might calve next. And then Texas Paint showed up with a smoky-gray bull calf, and number 8 showed up alone.

I know the Criollos by name or number, their names following a loose lineage going back to the first cows. Some Corrientes came to us as one bunch two summers ago and we numbered them 1 through 21. The 186 Angus cows we bought to comply with Forest Service requirements had ear-tag numbers with no sequence my brain could follow, except for the oldest among them, born between 2008 and 2010. With fewer Angus cows—

because we sold many—individuals started distinguishing themselves. Like 345, first to the hay every time.

Number 8, a small black Corriente, has long, widespread horns, tapered to a point I wouldn't want to feel. Her swollen udder, the blood on her tail, and her gaunt flank told me she had calved. She bawled long and loudly, and walked from the hay to the creek, across the creek and back, along a trail through the coyote willows, peering through the dry stalks, and back to the hay. Jessi and I searched, too, crossing the creek multiple times, Jessi leaping and splashing through water that ran almost to the tops of my insulated Muck boots, the tangy smell reminiscent of the Mancos Shale formation that underlies much of the upper valley. I peered at the bases of piñon pines and junipers, and through stalks of chamisa and willows and cattails. Looked at calf-size rocks.

And called Ken once inside. "I can't find her calf. And neither can she."

"It'll be okay," he said, "but look again first thing." Calves awaken hungry after sleep, the cows ready to relieve the pressure in their full bags, so just past the dawning is the best time to check for pairs.

The Criollos like to sleep near the cabin itself, tucked under living and dying piñon pines and junipers. I like this too—not the skeletal trees but being embraced by a half circle of sleeping cattle—I who still have stuffed animals on my bed (mountain lions, bobcats, lynx, some the twins of Lacey's "stuffies"). In the early mornings I peek out the windows. Often no one's up yet, and I watch the process of awakening. The cows lift their heads, look around in the twilight, and then tuck their heads back in like dogs curled in sleep, or they stretch their necks out and rest their chins on the ground. Some, heads up, start chewing their cud, eyes half closed. Eventually someone will rise—a calf pestering its mother into standing—and then another cow might stand and stretch, and another, calves butting udders and pulling at teats.

I rose before first light, peering through the windows at the gray of early dawn. Watching through glass as I dressed in winter layers, I saw a little calf I hadn't seen before. She popped up from the sleeping cattle and started running in circles like a puppy, racing around and bucking, her little tail straight up behind her like a pronghorn's. I grabbed the field glasses to see her up close—black with roan butt, tail, and belly, white tip on her tail.

Three other calves jumped up to nurse and play. Their mothers I knew; I didn't know to whom the roan-butted heifer belonged. No one rose to meet her. Instead they gently pushed her away as she went from cow to cow, checking.

A cloudy, thirty-six-degree morning (warm!) met me when I stepped outside. I told the dogs to *stay* and moved among the cows, some still prone; they didn't bother to rise even with me close. Not all the cows were there. Number 8 was not there.

Four cows—Mouse, Texas Black, and another black, but no number 8—nosed through yesterday's hay on the flat we have designated for feeding as even cheatgrass doesn't grow there. We don't feed on top of good grass, instead adding hay to the soil most in need—the cows' hooves work feed, manure, and urine into the ground, making compost, adding nutrients, capturing carbon.

Cows followed me down the hill, hoping that I might have a huge hay bale strapped to my back with which to feed them—not hardly, those bales weighing more than half a ton—when suddenly the little heifer shot out of the trees, running downhill and bucking and circling back up and racing down. If animals besides humans and dogs can express joy (and they can), that was it.

More cattle came down. The heifer went to each cow—no luck. Then a long, low bawl broke through the early morning. The heifer stopped. Looked up the hill, as did I. The bawl came again, but no cow. I knew the voice though: number 8. The heifer emitted her own little bawl and raced uphill as the big, wide, tapered horns of the black cow emerged from the trees.

As sunlight traced the rim of eastern mountains, I texted Ken. The text didn't go through. AT&T had stopped working in a fierce gust of wind the night before. I counted cows and watched calves, and when the sun itself peeked over I saw something new highlighted behind the gray camouflage of a downed juniper.

Ears straight up. Pointed tips, gray trimmed with black. Nose as black as Jessi's. A coyote. Another popped up on the rise, a pup about half grown. It didn't bother to hide, just sat down in the open, watching the cattle. The first coyote moved closer. Cows lifted their heads and pointed at the coyotes with their ears and horns. The mama cows gathered their calves close. A third set of ears showed up—the dog, or male, coyote. Randi brought her calf to within six feet of me, where she watched the trio of coyotes as her calf nursed.

Several two-year-old steers wintered with these cows. One had his head in a protein tub, oblivious. Another steer moved away from the herd toward the coyotes, who moved away from him. He followed at a purposeful walk, head low. The dog coyote disappeared, but the mother and pup rounded the hill, moving away from the steer but closer to the group at the hay. A young cow lowered her head and horns and charged, followed quickly by the steer and three more cows who had yet to calve. They ran the coyotes off, or at least out of sight.

In the midst of this, Huston's afterbirth came out, and when everyone settled I picked it up with gloved fingers and carried it far enough away from the hay that Jessi and Bow might not find it. Let the coyotes feed on that, I thought. Cows usually eat their afterbirth shortly after birthing so as not to draw predators and scavengers. Cows also eat it for the nutrients. But this stringy afterbirth had been dragged through the mud. Huston wouldn't want it now.

As number 11 wandered off to look for a place to calve, I smelled my gloves where I'd gripped the dragging placenta. Only the faintest of scents, a hint of ocean breeze.

I recalled pulling one of Lightning's calves. The cows on TJ's that spring, I checked the cattle and found Lightning in labor. I then found TJ, who grabbed some old towels from her house, and we walked to Lightning, who stood up and lay down without trying too hard to push. TJ sat near a tree with her camera. At Lightning's hind end, a nose and hoof showed. Not knowing how many minutes had passed since Lightning's water broke, I decided not to wait, and using a towel to help me grip I grabbed the two slippery front hooves and pulled with Lightning's pushes and Lightning lay down and I pulled the calf out. Freed the little heifer's nose of remaining sac but she wasn't breathing so I lifted her wet nose to my mouth and breathed into one nostril while covering the other and massaged her lungs, and when her chest heaved, Lightning took over. I stepped away. And spit. And spit again. This before I realized there was no taste. None. Not blood or salt or whatever else—from amniotic sac or heifer, there wasn't a taste I could detect.

Later Ken said what I did was old-school—these days you pick the calf up by its back legs and swing it in a slow circle to free its lungs of moisture. But I am old school and did what I remembered from Ken's dad.

When the calf got up and fumbled at Lightning's full teats, I held the little heifer's damp head to one and squirted a stream of fresh cow's milk into her mouth. She took the teat, TJ and I left, and today I wondered at the lack of smell on my gloves.

I'd watch for coyotes. And text Ken again, once they fixed the AT&T tower on North Mountain.

This winter has worn long, either Ken or me having to drive every other day to haul hay from headquarters to the Disappointment cows. My anxiety works overtime as each morning we check the weather, the road conditions, how many wrecks: semis off the road on their sides or jackknifed in ditches; cars, even four-wheel-drive SUVs with Colorado and Utah plates (meaning drivers who should know better) sliding sideways or about-face on the highway.

Ken also has a contract job with San Juan National Forest. Deep in the mountains, he and another man push through ten feet and more of snow with their bulldozers to open up back roads so logging trucks can access cold decks, load the logs, and haul them to the Navajo Nation, part of the Wood for Life program serving the reservation. The ponderosas in the San Juan National Forest suffer from mountain pine beetles and roundheaded pine beetles, the first working feverishly in July and August, the second in October and November, which gives the trees no time for recovery in between. The Forest Service thins the smaller pines and those tormented and killed by beetles, a side benefit of which is supplying wood to people in need.

This winter, cold, hungry families have had nothing but fence posts to burn—including the elders, who like their woodstoves but are unable to get to the forests to gather wood. A power company found people starving; now Ken risks driving the highway and the bulldozer to break through the snow so the families can at least have heat.

TJ comes with me to feed the Angus cows one day in Ken's absence—to drive the GMC pulling the trailer as I fork big flakes off the three-quarter-ton rectangular bales and push them toward the cows. Number 345 arrives first, grabbing mouthfuls from the bale before I can undo the straps securing it to the trailer, my fingers cold and clumsy in insulated gloves.

"She's always first," I tell TJ, who also struggles with a strap.

A week later I feed alone, stopping the truck every few feet and wrestling with the big, heavy flakes and spreading them around, then driving a few more feet in the blowing snow and doing the same. No 345. It takes more than an hour, whereas feeding with Ken takes about twenty minutes. Finished, I sit in the warm cab, Bow and Jessi on the folded-down backseat, and check cattle through snowy windows, looking for new calves, calving cows, trouble, and 345. After jotting down two new calves born this morning and one from yesterday, I spot 345 standing off by herself, looking across the field as if she's thinking. She has ignored the pickup, the hay, me. I watch her through binoculars. Her tail sticks straight out, or swishes at her sides, and she butts her sides with her head, signs of imminent calving.

Then she's down. She's going to calve. She's calving *right now*.

But she's not. She's up, she's down, she's looking around. Not unusual—from the tail-switching and irritation, it can still take an hour or more.

I want to see better but don't want to risk disturbing her, so I watch from the warmth of the pickup. And call Ken. "Just wait," he says.

Long minutes pass; still no calf. In my gut I feel as if something's wrong and call Ken again. "I'm on my way," he says. Miles between his dozer job and this pasture, and it's snowing.

"Be careful," I say.

Number 345 has moved farther away. I brave the cold, walk through a foot of fresh snow, stopping between steps to glass 345. As I near, I see her cervix like a volleyball outside of her, bobbing as she walks.

"She's prolapsed," I tell Ken on the phone.

"Shit," he says. But prolapse isn't necessarily horrible. You can push the cervix back in—sometimes it takes both hands and all your body weight—and sew the cow closed except for a slit so she can pee. I watched Ken's dad sew a cow up with baling wire. "Call the vet," Ken says. "Let her know we might be bringing 345 in."

I'm setting panels up around the stock trailer when he arrives. We jump on his four-wheeler, and he speeds through the frigid air to the cow. Her cervix has disappeared. In its place a long string, of placenta? We herd her toward the pen, Ken on foot, me on the quad, 345 not wanting to go until she reluctantly yields, then jumps in the trailer willingly. A break from the wind, the snow.

I've taken a picture of her hind end and the long strand of what looks to me more like intestines than placenta and send it to our vet, Kelleen, then I call. "Her cervix went back inside as she walked," I tell her.

Pulling the trailer, I follow Ken's Dodge through the snow and listen to the vet. "It could be calf intestines," she says. "Her uterus could have torn and the calf fell into her abdominal cavity. We'll have to do a C-section tomorrow." I lose service as I drive carefully up the S-curves of Slickrock Hill.

When we get to the ranch I call Kelleen again and start the story from the beginning, and she understands that 345 was in labor when she prolapsed, by now several hours ago. "I'd feel a little better if you could look at her tonight," I say. "Actually a *lot* better." I doubt Kelleen knows how much her presence has helped me through horse and cattle traumas—she's quiet and shy and we don't talk much, and her calm, methodical ways settle my insides.

Ken and I feed and water 345 in the trailer, me holding the door so she can't jump out as Ken pushes hay and a bucket of water through the opening. She shakes her head at Ken but doesn't mean it. Another cow might have charged.

When Kelleen's husband gets home to watch their three kids, one not yet walking, we head to their place. It's early March, still cold, our ranch headquarters with three feet of snow over everything. Kelleen's place is lower in elevation, more mud than snow. Her husband had set up heat lamps in the calving shed—three stalls with warm cows and calves—another lamp over the squeeze chute, along with lights Kelleen can maneuver. Number 345 unloads quietly and walks around shadowy corners, the trail of someone's innards hanging out of her.

"Definitely intestines," Kelleen says. She gets a halter on the cow and Ken runs a soft cotton rope around a back leg, which he'll hold so 345's attempts to kick won't connect with Kelleen's shins. I wince as Kelleen gives 345 a numbing shot in the vulva.

She brings buckets, needles, syringes, scalpels. My job is to hand over implements. My job is to not freak out. Not cry. Not even feel. Get as numb as if that needle went into me.

A long plastic glove on her right arm, Kelleen stands behind 345 and starts pushing into the cow's vagina. Number 345 lets out a long, low moan, and I hear my own breath releasing. Kelleen has to push her arm in to her shoulder, her cheek leaning against the cow's flank as she reaches. Number 345 wants to push the arm out. Wants the calf out.

The cow in the adjoining stall chews quietly as Kelleen and Ken, who are near the same age and both went to Colorado State University, swap stories of professors they knew, and Kelleen strains harder, and 345 strains, Kelleen reporting what she feels: the calf's head, a hoof, neither of which she locates in the right place, and then she says, "It's inside out."

I look at Ken, his set jaw, his tired eyes. "What is?" I say.

She pulls her arm out, pulls off the plastic sleeve. "The calf is inside out. It happens. Rarely. I can't remember what it's called."

"Inside out?" I don't understand.

Kelleen is tired too. It's past her kids' bedtime. And the snow and mud and cold of this winter have worn us all down. "It's caused by a recessive gene on the bull's part," she tells us, "which can join a recessive gene from the cow, and the calf develops kind of backward, not fully forming over the intestines. When she went into labor she pushed the calf's intestines out."

Ken holds the rope loosely on 345's fetlock as the cow rests, and I get quiet again like the other animals in the shared space. Kelleen readies for the C-section, which can't wait until tomorrow.

I hand Kelleen the scalpel, and we all tense as she slices into 345's side. The big cow groans. The scalpel goes through the outer hide, so tough, then through the inner skin and membranes into the uterus, where Kelleen's gloved hands enter as if reaching through an open window. She finds a back leg and loops a pulling chain over it but the calf is too big and bent for Kelleen alone, who is my size and strength. I put the implements down as Ken hands me the rope and he puts another chain on the other hind leg inside the cow and has both hands on the chain, Kelleen with both hands on hers, their bodies leaning toward the ground with weight and exertion, and I watch 345's hoof, her head, ears, my son and the vet as they strain to pull the calf out through the cow's side, pulling as hard as they can, and when finally the calf bumps out, his intestines slide through the cow's vagina and out her side.

Ken sets the calf out of the way because Kelleen needs to sew 345 up as quickly and cleanly as possible, and I'm back handing her supplies—needles, sutures—and Ken has the rope and the hoof, and the curl of calf lies in the corner of the stall, inside out: a curve, but instead of backbone at the back of the curve it's the exposed belly. The calf is otherwise fully formed.

"She probably went into labor when it died inside her," Kelleen says. "If it was dead for more than a day it would already be rotting."

At the university Ken saw rotting corpses inside cows. They talk about it.

I'm still making my stomach numb, but when Kelleen has finished and leaves to rinse off and Ken leaves to set gates, I step to the calf, touch the wet black fur, curly like 345's, and lift an ear, a leg, tugging the tiniest bit at understanding and feeling the rigidity of the inverted spine.

At headquarters during this long, cold winter, Ken has some horned cows: Lightning, in case she has problems calving, and Old Paint, whose worn teeth say she might be older than fifteen. I won't let her go to the sale barn; I'd rather Ken shoot her and bears and mountain lions feed on her. Meanwhile, she lives with free-choice hay and close water and other cattle.

Ken also has number 856, another old cow, a black whiteface, thinking winter on the open range might get too hard for her. At headquarters she only has to walk on paths through snow to the hayfeeder, to water, and back to a sheltered spot under junipers where Ken spread more cornstalks to make dry beds in this pasture.

At the ranch for a night to do laundry and see the family, I didn't notice 856 springing, but when I pass her in the morning on my way out, I see a still bundle at her feet. I can't tell if the calf's ears or chest move. Stepping out, leaving engine and heater running, I climb the fence and approach the cow, and I know what the stillness means. Standing on the opposite side of the tree from the mother, who has lowered her head at me as she bawls to her calf, I reach to lift a hind hoof to make sure. The calf seems small, like the Criollo calves, though it is Angus.

Leaving 856 to her licking and lowing in her attempts to give life back to her baby, I decide not to tell Ken just yet. Driving the snowy highway to cut roads through more snow to help get heat to the reservation, he doesn't need to hear more bad news until later.

Later he checks the calf I left for him. *Premature*, he texts. Nobody's fault.

Despite our plan, nothing this winter is simple. And we're going through hay like crazy. The Nichols Wash cows are almost calved out, but only half the Criollos have calved.

I saw the last five Criollos on the allotment upvalley several times. Three had tiny calves, which I'd first seen as day-olds. The small group stayed within about a two-square-mile area with plenty of feed and water. Heading out to bring them in, my plan entailed walking up each drainage toward the backcountry until I figured out which drainage or valley they occupied. Tracking difficult in the mud the snow the mess, I needed to move cross-country until I found fresh tracks.

Parking on the road, leaving Bow in the Tacoma, I headed up alongside the first big arroyo slicing the small valley. McDermott. There's no way to get beyond that arroyo without going through it; in its bottom I would figure out which branch to take out the other side. Starting down a trail, I found that the snow had turned to mud.

Often when heading down something steep and slick, like the side of a deep arroyo, I ski on my big feet in my big boots, planting them in front of me in the right direction and just sort of following them down—I've never skied, but to me it looks as if that's basically what happens—and that's what I did that day, except one foot went straight down and the other . . . didn't. Part of me heading downhill, part of me not. When I managed to stop the slide, the not-moving part stuck out to the side and behind me, my thigh bent at a ninety-degree angle off my hip, my calf making a forty-five off the knee.

As Jessi looked at me with a *now what are you doing* expression, I assessed the damage. My knee hurt but nothing had broken, so I gathered my breath, lifted my leg with both hands, put it back in front of me, didn't bother to stand, just sat in the mud and slid the rest of the way down until I hit bottom. On my bottom. An inch of mud coated everything on my right side: my right buttock, my thigh, my boot, my jacket. My gloved hands muddy, my field glasses, looped around my neck, muddy, my knee hurt, and I had a couple of hours of hard hiking ahead. I couldn't guess how many miles because mileage in terrain that goes up and down and back and over and around is impossible to figure out—nothing lies flat out here—arroyos cutting through every sagebrush and greasewood "flat." And I had to keep going. Because that's what I do.

Guessing and going up the wrong drainage first, climbing then rimming out on a narrow ridgeline, I could see my tiny truck on the distant road, and no cows. Down I went, skiing and sliding carefully into a slim valley, then trudging up the far side—no way to get there but down and up—where I found a fresher track in the mud. Today's, not yesterday's. Topping out on the next ridge, I saw more tracks working toward a stand of piñons in a swale, where the Criollo cows lay chewing their cud. Three pairs and two yet to calve.

The sun had stepped beyond the Glade and darkness lurked as I pushed the cattle out of there, the cows going downhill until we crossed McDermott Arroyo, and when we got to the road and they headed in the right direction—toward the pasture at the mustang cabin—I limped to the pickup. Jessi in, we said hi to Bow, and I hoisted my muddy butt up onto the seat, lifted my knee in, and drove slowly behind the cattle, the young calves dragging, tired from days of traversing the steep, rough country following their mothers.

Once through the gate I didn't dillydally, my knee stiffening with the cold drop toward nightfall. Stripping on the porch, my clothes not just muddy but wet, I shook off what mud I could, slapping my jeans against a porch pillar, and left everything outside. Took a quick, hot shower, got into comfy clothes, and by the next morning the outside clothes had dried, so I slapped off more mud flakes and put most everything back on. Because I was just going to go out and get dirty all over again.

I had to feed alone, a pain in the ass in the mud in the rain in the snow, no one to drive—no place to drive, really, at the cabin—that bale of hay like third-cutting hay, short pieces, hard to get the flakes off, so I had to pull armloads at a time from the bale and carry them through the mud, and it took two hours to feed half a bale—these are the big bales—which means I fed about six hundred pounds of hay by hand in a two-hour stretch. My knee hurt, my shoulder hurt, I got cranky, and finally I finished. And left to check the Angus cows at Nichols Wash, so not until late did I take off all those same muddy and wet-again clothes, only this time I thought to wear some of them into the shower.

Sometimes to save water at the cabin I wash clothes in the shower—if I'm soaping up arms and legs and torso I might as well wash something clinging to my upper body, like tank top and bra. I did this and when I peeled the tank top off to rinse it better, the water at my feet ran nearly black. I didn't know I

20. Night photo of the mustang cabin. Photo by Tyler Lausten.

was that dirty, or that my clothes were that dirty, and I kept wringing out the top, not saving water at all, until finally the rinse water turned mildly brown.

Mud from the fall had worked from outside in and I didn't even know. Wearing the same mud-caked clothing two days in a row is what I do out here when I see only cattle and wild horses and elk and deer, the cattle equating me with hay, the rest of the animals basically ignoring me.

When I told my friend Suzanne this story, she reminded me what my kids said when they took my chainsaw away. Actually, they didn't say it; they implied it, implied that I might do something foolish while cutting firewood alone in Disappointment Valley, where anything could happen and no one would know, until someone did, and by that time, well, you know what I'm saying. I've been pissed about the chainsaw—as Terry said, "If they don't want you cutting wood then they should cut wood for you"—but when I told Suzanne about this latest fall, she said, ever so gently, "Maybe that's why your sons took your chainsaw away."

I wondered what would come next. My trucks? Horses? Ah, the cows.

All the Criollos now at the cabin, each morning I wake and watch them rise. Randi is usually off grazing before her red bull calf gets up; when he does he bawls like a baby because he can't find her in the dim light. Texas Paint's gray calf rises before her every morning, butts her belly and rump and head, and tries to nurse while she's still lying down—Texas Paint likes to sleep in. Curlie Q (Curlie's daughter) sleeps near the middle juniper with her calf, and Rabbit has chosen a bed near two fallen trees, her heifer tucked against a trunk. The cows who have yet to calve sleep farther away, as do the steers.

One morning I watch for only a minute before my cell phone rings. Ken and I have paperwork to do and plans to make, and we do this over the phone when I'm at the cabin. It takes a while, so I don't get out with the calves until mid-morning.

Right away Jessi barks: something's up. Her head points toward the source. As I peer through the trees, the shadow of a coyote evaporates like mist. My gut clenches and I follow Jessi, who follows the trail of something. While healthy placentas and newborn calves may not have much scent, fresh raw meat does. Even I can smell it, and soon Jessi stands at the site of death. A calf turned as inside-out as 345's, only this one from the coyotes feeding on it.

I look for the cow—black with a white stripe like a skunk—whom Ken named Cruella Deville. She was springing yesterday, her vulva looking large enough for the calf to simply fall out, but I don't see her as I move through the cows. Jessi often finds what I'm looking for, as if she knows; I follow her down to the creek, where we see Cruella with a black cow and a tiny black calf near the willows. Clearly Cruella doesn't understand that this calf is not hers.

I call Ken and tell him about the coyote. "Cruella's calf is dead. And Cruella is mothered up to number 19's calf."

"Where's your gun?"

"In the safe." While the boys took my chainsaw away, they have left me armed.

"Get it," he says.

I remember the combination and grab the pistol. Load it. This one has no safety—no hammer to cock, just a trigger to pull. I put it in my jacket pocket and go back outside to herd Cruella and the black pair into the pen. They go willingly, but once inside, Cruella gets on the fight, snorting and charging at me through the panel fence, and I can't separate them. Or, I don't want to, even though Cruella won't let the calf nurse on its own mother—I don't want to get chased, attempt to leap the fence, fall, get stuck by one of Cruella's horns. And Ken is on his way. From the road he will glass for coyotes. While we're not supposed to love our cows, Cruella is one of his favorites. I like her too, that wide, white skunk stripe on black making her easy to spot, which helps me locate and identify groups of cattle in the backcountry, but right now I'm just kind of mad all over, like she is.

Ken and I both know what this situation means for the cow. Coyotes, and the expense of feeding her without a calf to show for it, have determined her fate.

I am tired of what this winter has taken. I haven't slept a night through since Cruella's calf died, my ears working the dark to hear anything amiss, even my skin on the alert. Wishing we still had Money the protector, each morning I patrol the dawn like a soldier, holding a loaded .270 in front of me, the .38 in my jacket pocket, listening above the creek for yipping or howls, searching the shadows, watching Jessi, and watching carefully the next cow who's getting ready to calve.

Walkabout calves on the other side of the creek, and coyotes bark and cry. Jessi and I cross and enter the willows near Walkabout and her calf, not an hour old, and the mother leads the wobbly, leggy thing to the creek and through it, the water running low due to still-freezing temperatures up on Lone Cone.

I have never even shot *at* a coyote, and I'd likely miss anyway, but I damn sure want to scare them off, even though I can't say that coyotes killed Cruella's calf—she could have stepped on it as she fought to protect it, or maybe she got confused because the other cow calved near her and she abandoned her own, leaving it for the coyote family, or something else happened—I'll never know—but the calf is dead, and 346's is dead, and 345's and 856's, and one day we take a few panels and the trailer out into the pasture at Nichols

Wash and set up a little pen, because we have seen that 587's calf has a hard time getting around.

Snow falls and sticks as I single 587 out from the feeding cows and push her toward the trap. Ken spots the heifer resting in a shelter of greasewood, gets her up, and tosses a loose loop over her head in case she decides to run. Neither cow nor calf fight us, 587 going through the opening into the pen because she knows that's what she's supposed to do, and Ken leads the limping heifer like a puppy through the snow. We load 587, close the dividing gate, and she complains in a deep voice when Ken lifts the heifer into the trailer. We leave quickly as the dirt road is getting slick again, then Ken heads to the ranch with the pair and I drive back up the white valley of Disappointment.

Sometimes, like frostbite, we don't immediately know the effects of a season, yet this year the depleted bank account from all the hay we've had to purchase already mirrors the death loss and our own physical, mental, and emotional wear. And it's not over. When we gather the cows on the Nichols Wash pasture—no new snow, just wind—Ken rides his quad to the distant corners while on foot half a mile away I push calves from the brush. He calls me. With binoculars I spot him standing beside the quad.

"I found 523," he says.

Back in the middle of things I thought I had seen her springing, then I didn't see her again, and I told Ken but by that time other dramas distracted us.

She lies dead in one of the farthest corners of the pasture, a place where I wouldn't have found her unless I stumbled upon her, as Ken did. A place I should have searched, as I should have searched the wash in the snowstorm when 346 showed up to eat alone. As I should have searched for coyotes every morning after I saw the three together, *before* Cruella's calf died. The loss of 345's calf had nothing to do with me, but maybe if I had paid more attention I would have noticed 856 ready to calve and maybe I could have saved it, even if it was premature.

Number 345 would have died in the field trying to birth the inside-out calf. We saved her but lost her anyway—because of the genetically defective gene she carried and the surgery she endured, we couldn't risk her spending a last summer in the meadows of the high country and getting bred. Too dangerous. Along with Cruella, 345 went to town.

Half of each ear fell off of 587's heifer, and half of her tail, and her frostbitten toes prevent her from standing long. She and her mother occupy the stall in the barn where 345 convalesced—even without heat lamps they stay warmer than on the open plains of the Nichols Wash pasture, feed and water just steps away, but those few steps hurt the little heifer, who was born in the same icy snowstorm that killed 346's calf and froze the ears off 6112's.

Later we will hear that someone near Dove Creek lost ten calves in that storm, and in the late spring, when pairs start heading up to the forest from their winter pastures, we will see lots of cropped ears and short tails on surviving calves.

C⊃-

Ranchers and cowboys trudge ever onward, one step at a time—either theirs or their horses'—through snow and mud, drought and debt and heartache, to the joys. Sunlight on green grass. A gentle rain—or any rain. The wonder of a little black newborn calf with a white quarter moon on his face, reaching for the teat and latching on.

The Criollos are at TJ's, and I stay mostly at headquarters—irrigation has started, which requires different daily work. The Angus cows now on a leased pasture near the ranch, we feed the Criollos in Disappointment every two or three days.

We're down to 1,250-pound round bales, which I have to rock to the end of the flatbed trailer, slice through the webbing and peel it back, then with every bit of strength I have, roll the bales off and hope they keep rolling. Yesterday the bale stopped as if it had brakes—a big chunk of hay fell off at the front and I could not get the bale over that hump. As I forked hay off to shrink the bale, Randi hooked me in the butt accidentally. The hit of her horn hurt, and this is when I wanted to cry in my flannel shirt in seventy-eight-degree weather because I don't know how to dress anymore with heat followed by quick blizzards or rain or hail and heat again and I had hay poking my breasts inside my bra and there's still no grass growing after the cold winter. So I did cry and muscle and cuss and finally got the bale to roll, a mat of hay following like turf, which meant the younger cows could get to feed away from the older dominant ones, and while doing all this I watched for the few cows yet to calve. Like Mouse, who gets fuzzy in winter along the sides of her face and looks like the cute end of a mouse.

"You're finally going to calve?" I said to her.

Two days later, Mouse had left the premises. Even bred to an Angus bull Criollos throw small calves and usually don't have problems unless the calf is breach or otherwise misaligned. They may calve and not show up for a day or two, hanging out in a protected place, resting, the calf nursing, growing, getting stronger. I thought I looked everywhere, but Mouse eluded me for a week, then one morning she stood among the other cows with her cute little black bull calf as if nothing was wrong. Because, this time, nothing was.

17

Between You and Me

> Even to mention such a thing puts me—both as a storyteller and as a character in my own story—in way over my head. Yet if deeper truths do indeed dwell in the depths, there would seem to be no other way to reach them without some risk of drowning.
>
> —David James Duncan, *My Story as Told by Water*

Disappointment Valley, Colorado, Spring to Summer 2023

I open my eyes to look at the time, 3:47 a.m., but before I open my eyes I see Savanna's gray head, her left shoulder, my saddle as she tries to launch herself out of the creek. I'm downstream of her looking upstream and trying to stop my own flow in the cold, fast water, but the current has me, and Savanna too. I work to watch her as she tries to stop. To climb out. Her lunge up the steep bank fails. A log over the creek like a bridge, several logs actually, a tangle of logs, is the next thing coming and if Savanna hits that and the saddle or her head get hung up, she will die before my eyes. Except the current sweeps me away and I can't see her anymore; all I can do is try to get myself stopped. My shins bang rocks, I feel my flannel shirt ripping, roots scratch my arms as I grab at them and they break or pull out or I lose my grip and I'm doing it all wrong, for a boater—if I rolled over and floated feet downriver as we know to do I'd be better off but my horse flounders upstream and I need to see her and somehow help her . . .

She floats under the log bridge and then manages to get out, I don't know how, don't see her do it as I tell myself to grab a root and *hold the fuck on*, and finally I do. Manage to hold on. The current still tugging at me.

My boots have major holes because I haven't made it to town to go boot shopping, and the water passes through the boots and out, so they haven't anchored my body. But I'm wearing chaps—chinks actually, or chinkaderos, which hit me mid-shin instead of going clear to my ankles—and as I grasp that root and cling, I have all that weight, soaked leather boots, soaked leather chinks, jeans, flannel shirt, everything wet, but I hold on and the root holds and I drag myself hand over fist up the root like a rope and pull myself all the way onto the bank, gasping and lying prone to get my breath, then struggling onto my hands and knees, and Jessi licks my face, once, and watches me closely. When I manage to stand despite the wet and the weight I see Savanna. On the opposite side of the creek. Her reins looped under her leg. She stands still, dripping, not about to move. Jessi watches me.

What I see before I open my eyes in the night: Savanna's gray head, her struggle.

This time I deliberately wait a whole day before calling Suzanne. She's my writing buddy, a boatwoman, a single mother of grown sons. Not ag at all, but she understands me. She has worked with PTSD and trauma; now she's the conservation field organizer for a local river advocacy nonprofit. Fences, canyon walls, and riverbanks rim our worlds; within those parameters we find common ground.

I have already fed Savanna, adding Bute-Less, an anti-inflammatory, to her timothy-alfalfa pellets, thinking she'll need it today. I have popped three ibuprofen myself, adding to the lingering effects of last night's four. That's all I get and all I want, other than to crawl back in bed and pull the sheet over my head. Which I do. At the mustang cabin, no one will interrupt me. No one sees me here. No one besides Suzanne will hear this story. Until now.

Usually I call Terry. Like when a sheep slipped into an icy pond and couldn't get out and I found her. Drowned. Her shape stayed in the ice for a day after I pulled her out. I tell my sister about the cats who go missing, the calves who die. She had a farm and knows the losses nature gives us. She calms me, even when I call to say that Ken is mad at my cows again. How that hurts, watching a dream slip away. Unable to pull it from the ice of its doom the way I tugged that poor ewe free by her horns. Will the shape of this life stay for a while after the life itself has passed?

In my bed under the sheet I think about what it all means. And about eating chocolate. Instead I reach for the cell phone charging on the nightstand and call Suzanne.

C⊃-

Disappointment Creek ran high with snowmelt from our big winter, but not like a flash flood. Savanna and I had crossed it the day before and several times that morning. I just chose the wrong place this time. Savanna willingly went in and instantly her legs got swept out from under her and she struggled for footing, panicked a little, and I tried to turn her so she could maneuver better and suddenly only her head showed above water. I bailed off to make it easier for her, thinking naively that I could get to shore holding her reins and pull her to a good spot to get out, but as soon as I let go of the saddle horn the current took me. Not underwater. I didn't go underwater because I kept trying to swim upstream—I needed to see Savanna, the logjam coming—we'd gone in well above it and the current swept me under it, but at 3:47 a.m. when I opened my eyes I knew what would have happened had I still been on Savanna.

A dead horse is worse than a dead cow. A big animal lying that still before you seems impossible. I have seen too many dead horses. Death by heart attack. Lightning. Bullets. Disease. But not drowned. Not my Savanna.

It hurt to walk in my soaked boots as I searched for a wider spot to cross the creek to get to Savanna on the other side. Jessi bounded through. Not me. Facing downriver I stepped side to side, step by close step, anchoring each foot before taking the next step, like in some of the side streams in Grand Canyon, everyone linking arms and moving slowly, deliberately, the guides keeping the people safe, but this was only me and I had to get to my horse and I was astounded at the strength of the current pushing at my legs.

Savanna stood where I had last seen her; she hadn't moved at all. I talked to her, standing close, and she reached her face around and nudged me and let me hug her and drip into her wet neck before I lifted her hoof and slipped the reins over it and then checked her all over. She had cuts from the rocks but not deep and not many. When I turned to look at the river she turned with me. I couldn't ask her to enter it again, not yet, so I led her through some Gambel oak, which snagged my hair and scratched my face and I didn't care, and my boots squeaked as we angled upward toward the ridgeline, slowly ascending the steep, high side of the old riverbank. Snaking back and forth, resting, climbing, we made it to the top. Breathing hard, we walked along the ridge, me in front, Savanna following, and Jessi.

My wet chinks threatened to pull my pants down; my wet boots, wet socks rubbed my heels and toes raw. At the head of the steep trail down, which leads back to the river, we rested again. Then, still shaky, I led Savanna down like I do on parts of the Cowboy Trail, Jessi close behind. At the bottom we wove through scrub oak, serviceberry, and blooming wild rose bushes, stopping near a cottonwood to face the water. Heavy in my wet clothes, and cold, shivering, I stood on a rock and climbed into my saddle. Savanna did not want to enter that water. Way upstream of our wreck, I'd seen cattle cross here and knew it was okay. But Savanna didn't, and it took words and a willow tap on her butt, because we *had to* cross—no way back to the truck and trailer and home without crossing that creek. Finally she stepped in.

That's what I told Suzanne on the phone that had miraculously survived its swim in the leather pocket of my chinks. And, "My braid didn't get wet."

"How is that possible?" she asked.

"Because I didn't flip over onto my back and float the way I should have? I kept trying to swim upriver."

After unloading Savanna at the mustang cabin and removing my wet saddle and the soaked blanket and pad, placing all that and the wet bridle in the sunshine and feeding my poor mare before stripping on the porch, again, I had headed for the shower, more to get warm than clean, for the story still held the chill tightly around me. I rinsed in hot water without undoing the braid until the next day, when I finally got out of bed after talking to Suzanne, well after eleven. Then I unraveled the braid that reaches to my belt and could tell by its kinks and bends that it had in fact gotten wet. I could still feel the wet at its core.

"My biggest fear," I told Suzanne, "*after* I got back to the trailer and loaded Savanna and Jessi, was that my phone wouldn't work and I'd have to find another way to contact my kids. They would ask why I called from TJ's phone, or Cliff's, and they would know."

They don't know. Only Suzanne and now you. And because my sons don't read my work, this is still just between us.

Two weeks later, I drove over the top of the Glade from Dolores and down the switchbacks to Disappointment Valley with two new, young, red Angus bulls and Savanna in my trailer, Jessi in the cab with me, dark skies hovering to the north. Driving toward that darkness, I knew what might or might not await. Gambling on the *not*, I kept going, because turning around and backtracking on an *if*—*if* it rains—seemed a waste of fuel and time.

The bulls needed to get turned in with the Criollo and Corriente cows, at the section for their last weeks before going up to the mountain. Ever since we got the Forest Service grazing rights and bought the forced-upon-us Angus cows, I've had to accept Angus bulls crossing with the Criollos—because bulls aren't selective, and a Criollo bull would not only breed his cows but anything else he could find. He would have the horns to fight off Angus and trespass bulls, which made me wish even more to use Criollo bulls, but they could throw horned calves, which get docked majorly when sold. And the processing plant we use, known for its low-stress handling of cattle, will no longer take horned animals. The whole business is skewed, cattle buyers having decided what's the best beef, even though it's not.

A big black Angus bull had already infiltrated my herd. While I worked hard after the disastrous calving season we'd just had to not let the cows get bred until later, a neighbor's bull jumped the fence, or crashed through it. I spotted him following Punkin Pie—I didn't see him breed her but either he already had or he would—and took phone photos of his brand, which Ken sent to Danny, who told us to whom the brand belonged. Ken called. The owner said he'd get the bull. Which he did the next day.

The bigger bull would have fought the younger, smaller bulls off the cows, so I'd waited. Now they needed to go out. We wanted to do something different with the Criollos, like using these red bulls from Redd Ranches in Paradox Valley; plus they would be easier on the younger, smaller cows than bigger bulls, and even though all the cattle would end up together on the mountain in a month, I wanted the young red Angus to breed what they could before everyone went to the high country.

The sky darkened. I drove through the gate, parked near Little Cojo, jumped Savanna out, and didn't bother with chinks or spurs, wanting to get this done before the storm hit—I had to gather cows to the trailer before letting the bulls out so the cows would greet the newcomers and show them around.

Thunder rolled off the rimrocks; lightning brightened the sky. I started Savanna at a trot, and we headed for the creek, me hoping the angst in my belly didn't travel down the reins to Savanna to remind her, and she hesitated and balked, and I had to circle her and tell her, *We're going! We have to!* and she stepped into the gray current, which rocked her for a moment before she plunged across, Jessi following. On the far side we maneuvered around low-hanging cottonwood branches and thick Utah serviceberry toward the steep trail, drops beginning to fall. Fresh tracks going up, fresh cow shit, and Rabbit stood at the top, breathing hard like Savanna from the climb. *I'm sorry girl,* I said as we bowed around her. I stopped to watch the storm for a second—the lightning—thinking maybe it would sweep to the west.

Spread across the roll of basin to the south, the rest of the cows grazed or lay around pre-storm. And smack-dab in the middle, the big black Angus trespass bull. In case you haven't noticed, *fuck* is my word of choice for such situations, and I followed it with *fucking bastard* and *motherfucker* as rain fell harder around us. At a constant trot we got the herd up and moving, Savanna shaking her head at the rain, then hail, my ball cap and shoulders and jeans wet, lightning flashing near the trees, half of which are dead. Tinder. Kindling. The cows, smarter than I, did *not* want to move into the piñon-juniper forest, did *not* want to go back down the trail they'd just come up as they moved away from the pending storm—no longer close but on top of us, we were in it, in the trees, lightning penetrating the dark shadows, the cow Lightning refusing to go anywhere as I kept pushing. Hollering. Cussing. Trotting Savanna back and forth. Signaling to Jessi to get them out. Ducking my head under tree branches and white flashes. Finally some cows started the descent. Rabbit, who'd just made the climb. Bobbi, Walkabout, Randi, Huston—the older cows. Lightning, despite her stubborn self. And their calves. And right in the middle, the bull. I didn't want him but couldn't waste time fighting him. I had to get some cows to the trailer. Fast.

Bobbi and Rabbit led the others down the trail to the creek, where they balled up on the near bank. Lightning-the-cow snuck downstream. I must have said *fuck* at least forty-seven times; Jessi, Savanna, and me everywhere, trying to get somebody across. Anybody. Finally Randi went, bawling for her chunky red bull calf, thinking he was over there though I knew he was behind us. More crossed, including the bull, and Savanna and I pushed them toward the trailer. They went willingly then, wanting out of the tall cottonwoods as badly as I did, though I didn't relish being in the open either, lightning still flashing, thunder taking no pause—and I jumped off Savanna, both of us raining onto the ground at our feet, swung open the trailer door, urged the bulls out, and Curlie Q came toward the truck, probably thinking the trailer looked like decent shelter, so the two young bulls went right to her and I didn't even watch as I saw the two-track to the gate and the road full of running water.

Quickly haltering Savanna, loosening her cinch, and loading her, I ran to the cab with Jessi, put the old pickup in four-wheel-low and first, the lowest an automatic can go, and drove like a mo-fo up the two-track toward the dirt-gravel-mud of Disappointment Road, hoping I wouldn't get stuck and have to ride through lightning and rain to Cliff's to have him pull me out with the backhoe, this mud so difficult to navigate even in boots and I had truck and trailer and Savanna and Jessi and me and I had to get us the fuck out of there.

At the gate I had to stop, open it, then roar up the slick berm to the slick road, and jump back out to close the gate, my boots already hosting an inch of mud, Jessi smelling like wet dog and shivering on the backseat, the windows fogging up completely. Heater and defrost on high, a six-inch-wide frost-free zone appeared in the windshield, and I peered through it and adjusted buttons and knobs trying to get the defrost to work better and opened windows and could see little to nothing through the rain. Except water. Running. Everywhere. Across the road. Down the bar ditches. From the sky.

Hopefully the big trespass bull wouldn't hurt the little ones, I thought as I gripped the steering wheel. Hopefully one of the red Angus bulls would breed Punkin Pie and his seed would take. Hopefully the calves and cows separated by the river would reunite quickly so no one would have to ford the flash flood I anticipated coming. Hopefully I would stay on the road.

The rain let up a little, the lightning and thunder behind me now but still with the cattle at Little Cojo, and I drove slowly along on a patina of mud, aiming for a place where I could get cell service and call Ken. Rolled to a stop. "Fucking bull was back in there," I said.

Like mother, like son: "Fuck. Did you turn the other bulls out?"

"Yes." I told him about the rain but didn't mention the lightning. Or fear. "I'm soaked. Thinking I might go to the cabin to get dry clothes."

"Keep going. You don't know what's coming. You don't want to get stuck out there."

He's right, I thought; I might not be able to drive to the cabin anyway, with its long, steep, muddy driveway. "Okay. Should be back within two hours." Depending on the road, we both knew. Depending on if this was just a cell or if the storm blanketed the whole valley.

Easing onward, still peering through the small frost-free area of the windshield, praying I wouldn't meet anybody on the road, I drove past TJ's and yearned to stop but not until close to the paved road did I do so, after twenty miles of slip-and-slide. I had to pee. And to peel off my wet vest and shirt and tank top and put on a dry sweatshirt, which was all I had in the pickup, my Wranglers and boots almost as soaked as the day we swam the river, Jessi still shivering, and Savanna too.

Back at the ranch, inches of hail filled the shadows of houses and trees. "I didn't know if I should run out to the vehicles and move them to shelter or stay put," Tyler said.

"I'd rather hail damage a paint job or dent a roof than dent your head." I told him how the storm had hit the section, but did I mention that I passed two cattle trucks as I drove toward Slick Rock? Didn't mention it to TJ when I emailed her later. My fingers still wrapped tightly around the steering wheel though my tires gripped pavement by then, I had hoped that the cattle trucks were going on through Gypsum Gap toward Naturita, Nucla, Norwood, anywhere but heading farther up Disappointment Valley.

"I wondered if that was you," TJ said in response to my email about the storm.

"The truck thermometer read forty-seven degrees—it was high sixties when I got to the section—but I didn't dare stop." Besides, fear clung to me like my wet clothes. Stopping at TJ's, I might have had to acknowledge it. To keep driving was an act of hope.

The next morning TJ wrote to me about the wreck. The driver of the first cattle pod slid off the road like all those semis in the snowstorms that winter. "Ten cattle killed," she said. She had watched as emergency vehicles, wreckers, and others rounded the turn past her house and headed upvalley fast as they dared go, which wasn't very fast. Then she saw our county-road maintenance guy, who told her.

Ken ran into Cliff in town later that day. The driver had walked the two miles to Cliff's house, where they called for help—Cliff has a satellite phone. Cliff's helper, Ben, drove Cliff's backhoe to the wreck. A mile west of the gate I'd fled through, the pod had slid sideways in the mud, the back tires going over the edge and the whole heavy, loaded trailer following, the cab the last to tip sideways and slide down the twenty-foot bank, the driver miraculously unhurt.

With Ben on the backhoe, they cut open the trailer roof to get to the cows. Some climbed out. Others couldn't. Either already dead or shot because of broken legs, or worse. At least twenty cows died. Calves too. Hard to know how many, Cliff said, as the backhoe kept hoisting dead animals into a dump truck, Cliff and Ben there past midnight with the truck driver and rescue people, trying to save what they could. The wreck happened maybe forty minutes after I passed that same spot.

Ken told the owner of the trespass bull that the bull had returned, and we went to the section to check on our bulls and cows and to see if he had retrieved his bull a second time. We met the owner and his wife riding toward their pickup.

"We're looking for a bull," the man said, as if we were out for a pleasure ride.

"Are you Rick?" I asked. "This is Ken."

"Oh," the man said. They might have shaken hands but for the deep cut of an unnamed arroyo separating us. He didn't introduce his wife.

"We haven't seen him," the man said. "We have three other riders looking."

"We'll go across the creek and up that steep trail," I told him, gesturing. "From that ridge we can see down both sides. That's where I found him two days ago. In the storm. Before the wreck. I left him on the north side of the creek." The side where we now sat on our horses.

The guy looked at me blankly. I wondered if he would have believed Ken had he spoken instead of me, a woman. Ken and I rode off.

Topping the steep trail, we saw a few cows, and Ken rode one way while I rode the other to circle around them. Right away I saw the bull, just as he reared up over Little Pretty.

Ken saw him too. "Take them all," he said. We started pushing cows and calves toward the trailhead, the trespass bull among them. They moved much more easily than the last time, in the storm. I did as well.

Often when I step into the stirrup and swing up into my saddle, everything just feels right. My boots in the stirrups. My chaps hugging the stirrup leathers. My seat in the saddle, reins in my hands, Savanna beneath me. This was one of those days, despite the recent storm, despite the bull owner's doubtful look, despite Ken's annoyance that we had to spend another day dealing with somebody's trespassing cattle. The bright yellow prince's plume stretched feet high, the grass higher too. The sagebrush had flourished with the rain and scented the valley. I knew the country, knew my cows, knew how to herd them, where to push, when to pause, when to stop completely as they contemplated the steep rocky trail. Knew where to trot through the trees as the cattle balked at the creek. How to encourage the cows, through pressure and voice, to step into the flow, and how to crowd the calves together so they'd move as a bunch, leaping like lemmings into the current.

As we pushed the bull and cows toward the trap where the bull would get loaded into a trailer, Ken saw the cowboys of the bull owner's group heading back toward their rigs, apparently intending to leave. Ken waved his hat and they stopped. And watched. And finally figured out that, yes, that guy and his mother had the bull they couldn't find.

I smiled. Cowboying with Ken, and sunshine, made things easier, for sure; at the same time I figured I could have found that bull and trailed him to the pen myself.

The Angus bull went into the trap with a small group of our cows. As the owner rode in to sort the cows off and load his bull, his wife rode over and introduced herself. We shook hands. The three cowboys on the ground ignored both Ken and me. They were in a hurry to leave, having wasted a morning looking for something they couldn't find and didn't actually believe was in there: the big black Angus bull Ken and I drove down the trail.

Later, after seeing our young red Angus bulls comfortably snoozing with a group of Criollo cows, Ken drove us downvalley and we passed the site of the wreck. Most of the debris had been cleaned up, but in the dried mud the tire tracks remained where the semi had slipped off the road and slid down the embankment, along with huge dark stains on the shoulder and at the bottom of the slope where motor oil and blood had pooled.

The trespass bull didn't hurt our young bulls (but he did sire Punkin Pie's 2024 calf and a couple of others). Little Pretty didn't conceive until a red Angus bull bred her. The river didn't flash that day. I didn't have to catastrophize—it was bad enough as it was.

The first time I herded the Criollos past the place of the wreck, they bawled low and deeply the way bulls do and pawed and on their knees put their faces to the ground, butting and rubbing their horns and jaws in the dry but once blood-saturated earth, though it had been six months.

When I told Ken, he said, "They knew something bad happened there."

18

The Last Fall

Cut the ties you have to failure and shame.
Let go the pain you are holding in your mind, your shoulders,
your heart, all the way to your feet . . .
Ask for forgiveness.

—Joy Harjo, "For Calling the Spirit Back from
Wandering the Earth in Its Human Feet"

Disappointment Valley, Colorado, Summer and Fall 2023

It's officially summer and Jessi and I lounge beside Disappointment Creek, fairly close to where Savanna and I swam. The water has dropped significantly, but the tangled mess of logjam bridge remains. Several young cottonwoods, loosened by the constant tug of water at their roots, have also fallen across the creek. The high-water marks carved into the bank show how much higher the river ran. Exposed roots of narrowleaf cottonwoods dangle above today's flow. Rocks, every size, everywhere, but no big logs right here—the high water from the high snow level took them farther down—just clumps of dried mud and cow shit and rocks and sticks strewn about. Water even took the last skeletal remains of the Hereford cow who got wrapped around the Fremont cottonwood our first year here. Her bones will embed in the bank downstream, where someday someone might find a piece, and wonder.

As I walked the mostly dry creekbed one fall evening several years back, looking for pockets of water to see if the cows could use the pasture, a glint of white in a last ray of sunlight on the bank caught my eye. I couldn't reach it but wanted to see it better and found a long stick of driftwood, stood on a stone, and started excavating, dirt raining down on my head until I could poke the stick through an exposed eye socket and pull.

Bear! I knew by the extended snout bone and the teeth, and I took it back to the cabin to compare it to the skull of a black bear I found in California, Tyler in a stroller, Kenney racing along. We had crossed a shallow stream, I saw white, and Kenney and I dug the skull out of that creekbed, the skull much larger and less brittle than this one, which has dried for how long in its desert tomb?

I kept both skulls. The way I do windrolls from mustang manes, freed and fallen to the desert floor. Turkey feathers. Some sheds of elk and mule deer I keep, others not, depending on uniqueness and location of the find (BLM has a shed-hunting season), because, as Ken reminds me, sheds, like bones, put minerals back into the soil. Antlers need protein, calcium, and phosphorus to grow, and additional minerals on a smaller scale. These minerals leach back into the soil from slowly decomposing antlers and bones. Also a source of minerals for small animals, they offer calcium and phosphorus to racoons, skunks, and mice, and to plants through the deconstruction process that returns the minerals to the earth. But a bear skull . . .

Today from the bank amid cow pies and the cows themselves the two red Angus bulls look bigger, as if in a week they grew muscle from baby fat and height from rearing over cows. One stays at Roanie's side, the other shadows number 1. The trespass bull has not returned. The cows doze in the shade of cottonwoods or browse the tender extremities of greasewood, the calves playing or sleeping in clusters all around.

Again I think about my grandmother and Sister, matriarchs who have passed. And my own mother, elder of our family of four generations. We celebrated her ninetieth birthday in April: my mother, her three daughters, four grandchildren and two spouses, and two great-grandchildren congregating at Terry's place on the coast. So that Ken and I could both go, Kathy's brother, Lane, stayed at Cachuma to feed cats, dogs, chickens, Lucas's guinea pig, horses, and cows. I got home first, flying while Ken drove with his family. Pushing past tired, as soon as I got back Lane and I hauled hay to the Disappointment cows.

Unbeknownst to me, for the first sixteen years after the ectopic pregnancy I had hepatitis C. From the blood transfusions. Doctors didn't recognize the symptoms ("I'm so tired it scares me," I wrote in a journal in 1997); even

21. Texas Black and Apple (Criollos). Photo by Tyler Lausten.

bloodwork that showed elevated liver enzymes didn't alert them. Finally in 2003 a Maui doctor figured it out. Six months of chemotherapy killed the virus.

When I look at my behavior during those sixteen years, I see a pattern. No matter how tired and sick I felt, I pushed through the challenges and exhaustion. Of single motherhood while teaching and getting a master's degree. Of running rivers and racing outrigger canoes. In relationships. Stubborn and hard-headed, as my first husband said (my second one too), I believed I could *make a relationship work* if I worked hard enough. That in itself is a sign that something's not working, and despite my efforts, some things ended.

Stubbornness and determination also led to good things. I can't believe I'm about to tell you this: for seventeen years—in a row—I applied for a certain literary award. At my mother's ninetieth-birthday family gathering, I received the coveted phone call.

Because all my family was present, I gathered them on the grass near the giant redwoods in Terry's yard. "I want to make an announcement," I started.

"You're not pregnant?" Terry said.

When they stopped laughing, I said, "That would definitely be immaculate conception." Then, "I just got a call from the Ellen Meloy Fund committee . . ."

Terry gasped. My mother grinned.

"Yes," I said, "I fucking won!" I told my family about my friend Ellen Meloy, how she died too young (fifty-eight), how the next year this award for desert writers began in her honor, how I didn't know about it the first year and have applied every year since.

For seventeen years.

"The proposed project," I told them, "is a book called *The Last Cows*." I looked at Ken, who I thought might worry about what I would write, told him how much money the award included, and in that moment everything felt okay.

But. Am I repeating the stubborn-and-determined behavior, pushing to keep the Criollos, to keep cowboying, despite the signs? I do get more anxious after swimming the creek with Savanna. Maybe that was a sign. Well, it *was* a sign. That's what happens: things line up. The boys pilfer my chainsaw. I tweak my knee sliding down a bank. I swim a creek, afraid I'm about to see my horse drown. Those are all indications. But of what?

I met a rancher from the Montrose area in Kathy and Ken's bakery, and he told me about a friend who had turned one hundred years old in February, and in May he was on a horse, pushing cattle with some other cowboys, when something happened. He fell. In a coma in the hospital, he died five days later.

"He was still on a horse at a hundred?" I said.

One day Tyler turned to me. "Mom, you should think about stopping." He didn't say it meanly, yet I felt he lacked compassion.

"Cowboying? I'm going to ride until I can't ride anymore."

Right now I can still ride, I can still cowboy, I can still make mistakes, and I can still do it right. I'm not ready to hang up my spurs and give my saddles away. I'm nowhere near a hundred. But. Something's changing.

Ken and Kathy opened a bakery in a building in Dolores—built in the 1890s, it's way over a hundred years old. It began as a supply house for the railroad and has held many different shops—last a bakery, before that a frame shop, from the 1950s to 1980s it was an emporium with a pinball machine and rocks, artifacts, and animal parts for sale. Danny remembers riding his bike from Summit Ridge as a teenager, the emporium the only place in town where he could buy chewing tobacco. The building was a Forest Service office with a still-existing vault, the heavy door in place and the original, puzzled-together sandstone-slab walls still visible.

Ken and Kathy secured the lease, purchased some of the bakery equipment from the previous operator, and Kathy started baking while Ken set up a rock shop in a corner. He sells rocks, gems, and jewelry—jewelry he makes, which he started doing several years ago. He might pick up a piece of jasper in Disappointment Valley and see a pendant in the stone. Later he will bring it out, cutting, shaping, and polishing until that raw piece of chert becomes a shining star. Ken does the silverwork himself—self-taught silversmith.

Kathy leaves the house and gets to the bakery early, making dough and baking cinnamon rolls and gluten-free brownies, and the place smells great whenever I step inside. Ken takes the kids to school and then stops at the bakery.

I see how much he enjoys talking rocks and geology, selling pendants and rings he's made. It's not that he wants to stand on his feet and talk all day every day—that's not his nature. Yet he has discovered another aspect of his nature—one I saw in glimpses in his growing-up years: doodles of (horned) cows, signs and logos, a journal of Africa, gifts like a spike antler with my name carved into it, horseshoes welded into our brand. As a mother I have watched and wondered.

Tyler's creative trajectory was easier to follow. Building LEGO constructions beyond any instructions, making model airplanes, then flying model airplanes. Then making custom surfboards from scratch, beginning with air and thought and ending with sleek lines and polished color. And now, his photographs.

Once Ken moved to the Four Corners region of the Colorado Plateau, he took to the rocks. He'd liked rocks since childhood (as did Tyler); now Ken looks rocks up in books and online, researching, retaining what he reads. I have loved the geology of the Colorado Plateau since first seeing House Rock Valley those many years ago, but I struggle to remember the layers and certainly don't retain composition.

Ken does. He takes knowledge and passion and his artistic and visionary self and makes something beautiful. My grandfather, the painter David Park, raised his two daughters while painting and teaching; my mother, Helen Park Bigelow, raised her three daughters while making pottery for a living, and now she writes; I raised my boys while writing and teaching. That Ken is raising his kids while ranching, cowboying, *and* making jewelry thrills me no end.

When we got the Groundhog Allotment, we thought we'd keep only enough Angus cows to show the Criollos around—the seasoned cows knew the mountain terrain, locations of water, fences, gates, good feed—and then cattle prices went up and the Angus calves made money, so we didn't sell as many Angus cows as we meant to, feeling financial pressure to raise what sells well—the cattle-buying world decided long ago that horned range cattle aren't worth much, and it doesn't know the difference between Corrientes and Criollos.

When I talk with Matt Redd of the Canyonlands Research Center at Dugout Ranch in Utah, he says that marketing the calves is the biggest challenge. The research project that started in 2019 has the participating ranches crossing Raramuri Criollo cows with Angus bulls (the Chihuahuan Desert Rangeland Research Center crosses the Criollos with Brangus, like Ruby and many of the cows Keith and I raised). Canyonlands Research Center now has forty Raramuri Criollo cows. Matt crosses them with red Angus bulls from Redd Ranches in Paradox Valley, like the two we bought, and sells the crossbred calves. "Those calves just bring more," Matt says. Criollo-Angus calves can bring more in the commercial market than a full-blood Criollo *cow*.

Although I love the purebred Criollo *calves*, if the Criollo-Angus crosses bring nearly double the money and that gives me a way to keep the Criollo cows, maybe that's a workable solution. We still raise and sell natural, hormone- and antibiotic-free, grass-fed-and-finished beef. Which is so much better for you, the Earth, and us than commercial, grain-fattened beef.

For a while Ken wanted a large herd of Criollo cows. We kept the replacement heifers and bought a few more Criollos each year, and we had Sue, the full-Criollo bull. We kept a young bull for the heifers. Then Ken got mad at the horned cows. If we sold them all because of the aspens, would I then fall in step with the commercial ranchers who raise big Angus, Hereford, and Charolais cattle because the market supports it, despite what's best for the land? What of my ethics? Thwarted by aspens and the dominant market, I yield?

We have eliminated the most behaviorally challenged cows—including Money and Mango's Mom. Trouble is, others learn, and calves learn, especially on the Forest Service lease where the fences are so bad. Ken is right—we need to eliminate any cows who don't respect even the shortest fences. In other words, I need to practice being a practical rancher.

Which means I'm supposed to be directed by my head not my heart. My head says replace more shitty fences. My heart says *get more Criollo cows!*

Once, driving to New Mexico, we saw cowboys moving a large herd of horned cattle near the state line. Ken said, "That's what I want someday. A big herd like that. All those horned cows." But somewhere along the way the hope and joy of building this herd of cattle seems to have withered. I look for those other cows whenever I cross the state line. They're still there.

Ken developed our business with the farmers' markets; the Farm Bistro in Cortez, which sells Cachuma Ranch burgers; the Mancos Brewery; other venues; and Cachuma Ranch beef occupies a freezer at the bakery—people can pick up their orders or buy spontaneously. We started with that first little bunch of cows we got in New Mexico, which included Lightning and Roanie, and then we got Old Paint.

Old Paint weighs 790 pounds and always has as a mature cow. She's lived everywhere—in really rough country, in aspens at 9,800 feet, in irrigated pastures, in desert pastures, and through winters like this last one. She has given us great calves: the first organic, naturally raised beef we sold; a breeding-stock bull; finishing steers; replacement heifers now cows dropping calves of their own. Pretty and Little Pretty, whom by God I do not want to get rid of.

22. Old Paint's daughter, Pretty (Criollo-Corriente cross), grooming her calf. Photo by Tyler Lausten.

Old Paint *is* old. And tired. Maybe she's the metaphor. I feel tired too. I have pushed this forward like a relationship, wanting badly for it to work, unwilling to give up. Give in. Maybe not listening enough to my sons (or listening too much). Perhaps, as Linda Hogan says, *listening* to the "way that nature speaks, that land speaks," and, as Ken says, *listening* to my intuition, will get me closer to the answers already inside me. I wish also to talk with other women, like Heidi Redd, in her early eighties, and my longtime friend Pam Ewing, women who know this lifestyle and have faced aging and decisions. I wish I had talked to my great-aunt Sister about this, but back then I only thought about her getting old, not me.

Ken said, "You don't just do that," when I asked to buy Old Paint. But I had already done it. We have already done all this. The land. The cattle—this beautiful herd of horned cows that matches that herd at the state line.

I don't know what's next, other than going to the high country in a couple of weeks, later this year than our usual summer solstice on-date. Because of the record-breaking winter snowpack and the lingering cold, the grass hasn't yet grown while an abundance of larkspur, deathly toxic to cattle, carpets the meadows in purple. We'll push the Angus pairs, with their bulls and the yearling steers, from the lease in the lush redrock-and-ponderosa-rimmed Fish Creek valley to the Groundhog Creek Pasture. From the section we'll gather and haul the Criollos, the two red Angus bulls, and five big three-year-old Criollo steers. We sold the replacement heifers when we knew we would run out of hay, and winter and fate took those cows: 523. 856. Cruella. And 345. Cattle prices have run so high that we can't buy more Angus cows (okay by me) or steers. And Ken resists buying more Criollos. Another puzzle to solve. We're working on it.

The losses accumulate, and so do the joys. Maybe that's why I covet finds like bear skulls, like the huge white cannon bones of my grandmother's Shires found so long ago. Why I covet days like this, riding quietly through the cattle at the section, checking that cows and calves are all here (which they are), then tying Savanna in the shade of the trailer and returning to the creek. Sitting on the warm earth, Jessi curled at the base of a coyote willow, Bow at the ranch with Tyler, whom Bow adores, the smell of cow shit maybe not appetizing but so familiar, the susurration of the creek running past my boots sounding like peace. Or like love, as the silty water caresses and shapes the rocks over which it rolls, and the cottonwoods slurp life through their roots into branches of heart-shaped leaves that twirl above me in the breeze.

When we take the cattle up to the mountain, the Criollos behave—maybe they have learned, as Danny said they would. And now even the Dressel Pasture has open space: vast acres of clearcut directed by the Forest Service. We ride around those acres, but the cattle, if unhurried, will go into the maze and graze—until the new growth of saplings rises into a thick, tightly woven, impenetrable twill of young trees.

Lightning calved on her own. Old Paint moves with the herd on the mountain. So does 587 and her sweet, recovering-from-frostbite heifer. Our bulls cover the country and the cows. Ken and I do fence work together and cowboy together often. We don't have all the answers, but the Criollos staying in the right pastures helps Ken remember why we got them in the first place.

The other day some *Angus* cows pushed through a wire gate into the wrong pasture, and when Ken and I gathered them to drive them back, they balked and didn't want to go. A three-year-old full-Criollo and her calf—on the correct side of the fence—stepped up and took the lead, and the Angus followed her over the saddle to Saddle Pond (I didn't point this out to Ken).

Criollo-cross calves may be a solution for Criollo ranchers. At weaning, full-Criollo calves are too light for rodeo and the commercial market. The steers mature for the grass-fed market at around thirty months. Studies at Jornada Experimental Range using tracking collars on cattle show that crossbred steers raised by Raramuri Criollo mothers still exhibit the traits that earned the breed the handle *desert friendly*—the Criollo-cross steers browse, travel farther from water, spend less time at water and more time exploring than straight Angus steers, and certainly than Angus cows. Overall, in my book, Criollo cows, heifers, and steers take first place, and Criollo-Angus steers place second, as they still have a lighter environmental footprint than their straight Angus cohorts.

It's all an experiment, really. A heritage breed of beef cattle that fits desert lands. Hope that more desert ranchers will follow suit. Crossbred calves that may keep us in ranching while my ethics remain intact. Working *with* my sons. Not arguing about a chainsaw, instead going to Norwood with TJ and getting another, albeit smaller, one. Even the bakery is an experiment.

For me, I *must* learn to manage anxiety, stubbornness, and catastrophizing. Each time someone around me gets angry doesn't mean it's the end. And if the Criollos want to leave the thickly forested pastures, it doesn't mean the Criollo experiment failed.

It means the cows don't like the aspen forests. Because (my perspective) they can't see long distances, can't fight predators or easily protect their calves from danger, can't run—they have to maneuver not only their bodies but their horns through the thick stands of trunks and branches, which makes them vulnerable.

One day near what I call the purple martin pond, which is located at the bottom of a big open hillside, I found the cows restless and alert. In a stance I hadn't previously witnessed, Ivy stood rigidly, her neck taut, arched, head and horns angled toward something I couldn't see. She moved forward stiffly, along with several other cows, same posture, and I followed their urgent, pointed looks. Hunkered down in a willow thicket, a yearling black bear peered out. The cows kept stepping purposefully in his direction, and finally he bolted. When more cows arrived at water, they could smell the bear and took the same stance until they were sure he was gone.

This experiment has shown me that Criollos are smarter, more protective, and more desert-adapted than I thought. Which germinates another thought: maybe leasing from the Forest Service is the part of the experiment that didn't work out so well for our desert cattle.

In California, members of the Chumash community paddle in tomols, traditional canoes once made of redwood driftwood and sealed with pine pitch and asphaltum, the tar-like substance seeping up from the deep to mark the beaches. Today Chumash paddle from the coast of Santa Barbara to Santa Cruz Island. To Limuw. Through the cold and dark, with escort boats nearby, and sometimes sharks, and often dolphins, the descendants paddle home.

The Nature Conservancy invited my sister Terry to the Cojo, the ranch that for me felt not so much like a childhood home as an anchor. To the land. Animals. My grandmother, although I never saw her there. Sister. So I invited myself. Terry needed an escort, I said. A chaperone. A sidekick.

The night before the event, we dined with our Uncle Jeff and his lovely partner, Susan, in a Santa Ynez I hardly recognized. The Italian restaurant sat beside the Maverick Saloon, and even that old, wild bar (frequented by Ken when he was still underage) looked gussied up.

In a wonderful turn of events, Jeff and Susan moved into the same senior residence in which my mother lives. Uncle Jeff is my father's younger brother: the young man retrieving a cowboy hat off the arena floor from the back of his horse, checking on his nieces when we were little, and now that we are "mature" and our father is gone. He remembers so much about the ranches, and Sister and Ed and his mother—our grandmother.

In a huge gesture that supports my life of horses, cattle, and ranching, Uncle Jeff gave me my grandmother's silver-trimmed saddle with silver-concho breast collar, and a bridle with spade bit, silver headstall, and latigo reins. Running my hands over horn, pommel, seat, and the silver of the cantle helps me think. On the wall I have a copy of a painting of my grandmother at Mount Diablo, the plaque beneath once marking the site of her ashes: "I will lift up mine eyes unto the hills, from whence commeth my help." I lift up mine eyes to her.

Terry and I headed toward the Cojo the next morning on the curvy road that passes through a big chunk of Jalama Ranch—through live oaks and poison oak and memories—then we drove through a big open gate, the large metal Cojo brand still welded in place though the Cojo and Jalama are now called the Jack and Laura Dangermond Preserve.

We knew the road through the Cojo by heart, and the embracing views. I kept checking in with myself: how did I *feel*? *Dull* was all I came up with. We parked under a eucalyptus tree at Cojo headquarters, noticing that the pepper trees that mark many an old California rancho had vanished. That's when the grip of sadness found my stomach. Joining Uncle Jeff and Susan as TNC staff ushered us toward the "cookhouse," which had been converted years before to a house for cowboys and their families, we saw that it had been converted again, this time to offices and a room with bunkbeds for TNC employees and guests.

I questioned Uncle Jeff. "Didn't the room run this direction, with the kitchen over there?"

"Yes," he said, "it did."

We reminisced about breakfasts in the original cookhouse sixty and more years ago. "I remember sitting at one end of the long table, the cowboys at the other, hats removed, smiling at us three little girls. Maybe the way they smiled at Aunt Katharine and Sister and our grandmother when they sat with the men before they all headed out to gather cattle."

The Nature Conservancy staff moved us along on a tour through other renovated buildings—the old house where we stayed during the cowboy-breakfast days, and the adobe house where Sister lived when she ran her own herd of cattle on Little Cojo (her horned Herefords). With our parents, Terry, Peg, and I had stayed in that house uncountable times, as we did later with our own children.

When we entered what was once Sister's home and then a guesthouse for four generations of family, something struck me beyond bedroom and bathroom remodels: the kitchen floor, tiled with Saltillo. The family had

23. Mother and three sisters. From left: Helen, Peg, Terry, Kat (we can't remember the horses' names) on a Cojo beach. Photo by Edward B. Bigelow. Courtesy of Helen Park Bigelow.

remodeled the kitchen a few years back, pantry eliminated to make the room larger for all the food prep that happened there. Still small, the expansion helped as there existed no dining room, just a long, heavy wooden table at one end of the living room (like in Sister and Ed's house, it occurred to me). Did Sister's Cachuma Ranch also have Saltillo? And those red tiles at Mount Diablo—Saltillo? Or something close to it.

If we can be imprinted at a young age by the bad things, why not the good as well? In Flagstaff I found a spec house (so cheap back then) and toward the end of construction got to add touches of my own. Saltillo tile went into the kitchen and bathroom. In the old house at our Cachuma Ranch headquarters, the hundred-year-old foundation (stacked rocks) required attention, and I took the opportunity to tile the mudroom floor and woodstove hearth with . . . Saltillo.

The old, 1,500-square-foot farmhouse has twenty-eight windows downstairs, including glass in the doors, from a previous owner's remodeling job, which means that every room has views: La Plata Mountains. Mesa Verde. Sleeping Ute. The Chuska Mountains on the Navajo Nation, which span the New Mexico–Arizona state line, and the Carrizo Mountains in Arizona. Closer views of horses, cattle, elk, deer, birds. A great blue heron taking an hour to circle the pond one slow step at a time, swallowing minnows and crawdads along the way. A scrub-jay dancing in branches with a red-naped sapsucker.

Through those windows I can watch cows calving. And cows coming to water.

I love the mustang cabin and all I see and feel and hear in Disappointment. I have not loved being in the barn house; even after adding windows, it felt like dark and wasted space with just me floating and cold and alone in there. Both my sisters came to Colorado to move me back into the old house of many windows, as if they knew something I didn't.

At the Cojo, we dined on barbecued ranch beef in a new courtyard while listening to TNC employees talk about projects such as removing ice plant and returning those thousand acres to dunes and coast chaparral. The Preserve director, Ben Miner, answered one of my questions before I asked it. "Working with the Chumash to protect and conserve cultural resources at the Preserve is one of our top priorities," he said, and explained that TNC has a Memorandum of Understanding with the Santa Ynez Band of Chumash Indians.

Michael Bell, senior advisor to the Preserve, spoke of the first Chumash settlements of eleven thousand years ago; of Spaniards sailing past and naming the point La Punta de la Limpia Concepción; and of Fred H. Bixby's 1913 purchase of Rancho el Cojo, followed by the Jalama. "This land served as a working cattle ranch, which preserved it, and kept it from development," says The Nature Conservancy.

In 2007 the nonprofit tried to buy the Cojo-Jalama Ranch (unbeknownst to my sisters and me). Instead, the powers that be chose the hedge fund partnered with the developer.

Michael told us of a late night on Santa Cruz Island, drinking wine and talking with a friend, and my mind slipped back to the California cowboys and whiskey campfires on the island. In Michael's case, the friend offered to introduce him to a hedge fund higher-up. Thus began TNC's second attempt to purchase the property; this time Jack Dangermond stepped up and offered the bulk of the funding, sealing the deal in 2017.

"This week," Michael said, sounding giddy as a boy, "we're blowing up a dam." I imagined how my sons would respond to the prospect of blowing up dams. "This will open a mile of Jalama Creek for steelhead passage." A second dam removal, he told us, will free twelve more miles of habitat for the critically endangered Southern California steelhead.

The practice of blowing up dams for the native fish lured me. As did the assurances that TNC would continue using the land-management tools of prescribed burns and grazing cattle (Terry and I had seen some of Jimmy Poet's Angus cows on the way in). And the Preserve will be involved with the proposed Chumash Heritage National Marine Sanctuary, if it gets approved (it did!)—the first Native-nominated national marine sanctuary in the United States.

After lunch we strolled barefoot on the beach, spying sand dollars and avoiding tar. With a wry smile Uncle Jeff said, "I've never seen so many people on my beach," a sentiment most family members could echo, an echo that might resound back through generations, although Chumash might have said, "I've never seen so many white people on this beach."

Terry and I sought shade, and second cousins came to sit with us. Somehow the topic of the initial sale came up (was I the one to raise the subject?) and a discussion ensued. When I mentioned wanting to give the ranches to The Nature Conservancy back then, I was told that the ranch company had talked to TNC, but the nonprofit simply didn't have enough money.

"We could have settled for less," said I, thinking *like Heidi Redd and her family did.*

The wind must have come up, truncating the conversation.

While TNC conducts vital research and actively restores ecosystems, it can't undo the damage caused by the interim owners any more than I can fix broken hearts. Yet the future looks promising. More than one thousand students have visited the Cojo and Jalama, and 6,014 (and counting) coast live oaks have been planted. Mountain lions and black bears are being studied, feral pigs removed, and the cattle remain. Prescribed burning will continue. Life will continue, even without cowboys living at headquarters and horse smells in the barns. In a few years, the land may look more like what Sister and my grandmother knew, if not the original human inhabitants. With proper range management (smaller cows?), it could look better yet.

Arriving back at my own ranch headquarters at two thirty in the morning (after three extra hours of waiting in airports), in bed by three, I slept until a phone call from Ken brought me awake. "Calves at Groundhog are showing signs of sickness," he said, not knowing I'd come in so late. "I'm taking a horse up today."

"I'll go too."

As I stood in the barn currying Savanna, floating hairs tickled my nose—her smooth summer coat had started shedding to make way for the coming winter fur. I wiped the hairs off my face, inhaling that rich warm-horse smell, and Savanna turned her head toward me and gave me a hug. Horses saddled and loaded, and Ken's dogs and Jessi, the hungover feeling of little sleep passed as Ken drove us up to cow camp and I told him all about the visit to the Cojo.

Fall chill crept under the morning, yet once astride Savanna I felt the sun warming the surfaces it touched—my shoulders, the leather on my thighs, Savanna's neck. Riding with Ken at a slow trot through grassy meadows and grazing cattle, saddle and Savanna fitting not only my body but my heart, felt like the most cleansing, rejuvenating work I could possibly do.

I can't fix the loss inside Ken or Tyler. I can't replace the Cojo and Jalama with our Cachuma Ranch, which is not the ranch I saw in my dreams in those early days when the boys' future father and I searched across the Southwest—a ranch with headquarters connected to winter and summer range like the Kane and Two-Mile Ranches in northern Arizona (now called North Rim Ranches)—but we *are* running cattle, and growing our own family story. My movement between the mustang cabin and the old house, with its touch of Saltillo, windows, and views like my grandmother had at Mount Diablo and Sister had at her Cachuma Ranch, has me thinking—and again, this is just between us—that even when I do have to stop cowboying, maybe I will stay.

Epilogue

Landing

They [Fred H.'s daughters] loved it, but it couldn't last. College, marriage: one by one they dropped out . . . Sister stayed the longest.

—David Lavender, "Rancho Los Alamitos" manuscript

Disappointment Valley and Dolores, Colorado, Fall 2023

Tyler shows me the pristine beginnings of water, and I write. Coyote sings across the canyon, and Jessi barks and I answer in words. The air distills to a crispness so precise I can *hear* the big black boar bear drinking from the puddle left behind by the fleeing summer creek, his tongue making rings of water-sound that rise up to the mustang cabin, and I write.

I write because I want it known that fertility control works for mustangs, and each foal not conceived is saved from helicopter roundups and a lifetime in captivity; because I hope we think about where the food we eat comes from, and if we eat beef, eat grass-fed-and-finished beef, buy local, stop at the farmers' markets, and get to know the local rancher who produces food in the most humane way possible, and learn that that same rancher loves her cows and her horses and we may love the same land beneath hooves and grass and rocks and junipers and our own boots equally, both you and that rancher ultimately wanting the same thing: health for the Earth and health for each other; I write to be part of that conversation. Because if we share heart-to-heart what we know, then maybe we will all become better people, cowboys and ranchers no longer the enemy but truly better stewards of the land, and maybe we will all hear Coyote singing and nobody will want to shoot her.

Sometimes I mistake the petroglyphs of claws in white aspen bark—which I can see at eye level from my saddle—as threat, and fear rises in the small hairs on the back of my neck, yet claws and hair and skin and fur and bone and words are all part of animal language. Bison belong here and so do wild horses and so do their predators and friends, wolves and mountain lions and common cowbirds, and so do grizzlies at the top of the heap. And may that heap not be the garbage of human dumps but a shoulder of the Earth rising in the distance as the pads of bear feet move toward it, massaging soil and salmon into story.

One of George Floyd's last words was *Mama*, a force we all know—the calves in the pasture, elk in the trees, grizzly bear and her cubs, Coyote and Jessi and the fawn at the edge of the highway where his mother lies still in her forever. We have all known that word, that love—cannot love of Mother be our common ground?

Ken has the bakery to return to each day, so we spend less time at cow camp; even when I ride out alone, which I do often, I go back to headquarters at night. Fall filters through the days. The kids have returned to school. The U.S. Fish and Wildlife Service has agreed to scientifically evaluate the decline of piñon jays to determine if they qualify for endangered or threatened status under the Endangered Species Act. Todd 1, who has kept in touch about the pup I gave him, texts to tell me that Todd 2, his best friend since high school, has died. Cancer.

I work to balance the bad news with the good as I work to balance the seasons of my life. Now it's weaning time, all the cattle off the mountain and onto the eighty-acre leased pasture near ranch headquarters. Well beyond the corral fence, Wisuv Káruv, the high peak of Sleeping Ute Mountain, angles up out of the land. Ken and I gather the cattle on foot with the dogs—this is the prairie-dog-hole pasture, and I won't ride Savanna in it. In the corrals, sorting cows from calves, and long-yearling steers from calves, we then sort the Criollo-Angus-cross calves from the full Angus. I work the gate, and only one animal gets by me.

Kathy at the bakery, Tyler brings the kids mid-morning. Lucas goes with Ken to haul the full-blood Angus calves to the new sale barn a mile away. The day has warmed with the sunshine despite its November date. The remaining calves have quieted, their mothers grazing on the other side of the fence. When Ken and Lucas get back, I ask my grandkids to come into the pen. They climb the panel fence and drop down beside me.

"What colors do you see?" I ask Lucas.

He studies the calves. "Black. Red. Tan. White."

"What kind of cow is the white one?"

"Charolais."

"And what is your favorite kind of cow?"

He doesn't hesitate. "Charolais," he says.

"Would you like to have this heifer? For your first cow?"

His brown eyes shining, Lucas looks from me to his dad, who grins. "May I name her Angel?" Lucas asks. Ken nods, and smiles grow.

We had planned this, holding the Charolais heifer back for Lucas. Like me with first-heifer Ruby, these kids will start their herds with one heifer apiece. But I won't tell them not to fall in love with their cows.

I feel Lacey beside me. She looks up at me with those starry eyes, in them a question.

"Now we have to pick one for you," I tell her, and her eyes get bigger. "Let's look at red heifers. The desert is easier on them."

As we move among the calves, Lacey says, "I like the fluffy ones." Unk Ty reminds her that they get fuzzy coats in preparation for winter. She nods solemnly. "Is that one a heifer?"

"Look at the belly," I say. "If the belly is smooth, it's probably a heifer."

She looks. "It is a heifer! I want that one."

"Bobbi's." I show her Bobbi out in the field. "Bobbi is one of my favorites."

Lacey likes Punkin Pie's calf. Little Red's. Rabbit's. For years Lacey has been able to pick Rabbit out of the herd—dark red with darker trim, including big black brushstrokes around her eyes—Rabbit is my favorite. "I have yet to keep a Rabbit heifer," I tell Lacey.

She shows me number 8's calf. "She's black but she has white on her belly and tail"—the roan-butted heifer who scampered so playfully at the mustang cabin the second day of her life.

Ken looks the heifer over. "She's a really nice one."

"One of my favorites," I say. And, "You don't have to decide today."

Lucas goes with Ken to watch the sale, and Lacey, Tyler, and I head home. Ken calls and has Lucas read me the amount of the check for the Angus calves. "Please read it again," I say. He gets through the number twice without stumbling. "Oh, thank God." The year, almost over, started looking better when snow turned to green grass on the mountain and the Criollos stayed put, and now it looks better yet.

After supper Ken calls again. "I saw Danny when we were leaving." I wait for the story. First Ken tells me that Danny asked Lucas what he'll call Angel the first time the heifer kicks him. "Devil!" Lucas said without pause. Then Ken says, "Danny told me he wants to run horned cows. A herd of a hundred just came up for sale."

"Do you know whose they are?"

"Danny said they belong to a friend of his." Ken pauses, drawing it out. Then, "He said they're from a ranch near the New Mexico state line."

"They're *those cows*?" I hold my thoughts. Hold my breath.

"Yep," Ken says. "He was surprised I knew them."

I exhale. This is when I want to cry, but in a good way—another local rancher, someone we know, running horned cattle.

The next evening Lacey calls me. "We just fed the calves," she says, her voice sweet and young and eager over the phone, "and I have some questions I want to ask you." She has written down ear-tag numbers, and as she says them I tell her who the calves' mothers are, which she also writes down (Ken told me later that she had a big whiteboard on her lap on which she took notes as we talked). I tell her how Rabbit hopped about as a calf, earning her name; about what a good lead cow Bobbi is. "What about number 48?" Lacey asks. The roan-butted heifer.

Ultimately Lacey chooses Rabbit's calf. "Because I like her," Lacey tells me. "She's fluffy. And because you've never kept a Rabbit heifer."

The world keeps spinning. Soon Tyler will head back to California for winter work and swells; soon I will head out to the mustang cabin. Friendships with my valley neighbors will resume where they left off when the cattle went to the mountain, I will cut and split and stack firewood, and on the BLM allotment my Criollo cows will get fluffy as we ready for winter and wonder in Disappointment. Sometimes things line up just right.

Sister stayed the longest, wrote David Lavender. She did. She stayed until the end.

24. Lacey, Grandma Kat, and Lone Cone. Photo by Tyler Lausten.

Acknowledgments

I am heartfully and forever grateful to Clark Whitehorn, senior acquisitions editor at the University of Nebraska Press, who saw a future for this work and whose enthusiasm, council, humor, and prompt responses kept me afloat when the raft of my confidence sprang leaks. To the rest of the crew at the press, and copyeditor Jennie Swanson, thank you for making this a better book. To peer reviewer and fellow rancher Bob West, I found your insights and encouragement invaluable.

Huge gratitude goes to the Ellen Meloy Fund, which graced this project, and me, with an Ellen Meloy Award for Desert Writers in honor of my friend Ellen Meloy. And to the Rancho Los Alamitos Foundation for support and help with archived photos.

To Joe Wilkins, J. Drew Lanham, Janisse Ray, and David James Duncan, thank you for the words and chapters you inspired, and hugs to Joy Harjo for granting me permission to use lines from the poem "For Calling the Spirit Back from Wandering the Earth in Its Human Feet."

Thank you to sister author Rebecca Lawton for being my friend these thirty years; to TJ Holmes for reading, editing, neighboring, and befriending me in addition to a hundred mustangs; to Suzanne Strazza for guiding me on currents of words and rivers; to Amber Clark for taking me along; and to Orrin for glimpses.

To Judith Selby for surprising me with a copy of *In the Company of Cowboys*. To Pam Ewing, Amy Hale, and Heidi Redd, cattlewomen all, for their examples of living a life with cows.

To Emily Campbell and Jamie Knight, you know what for.

To Ina Leonard and Debbie Millennor, who, along with my sister Terry, have listened to much raw material and helped me decide what to include (and what to leave out!).

To Jeff Green, who helped me untangle family history and offered more than I knew. To Ken and Tyler's cousin, Hunter Kelly, who for three summers stepped into his stirrups to cowboy alongside us.

Mahalo nui loa to my mother, Helen Park Bigelow, and my sisters, Terry Tobey and Peg Pierce, primary readers, primary supporters of my writing, my kids, and me. Reading through these pages I realize how often you have come to my aid. When I say I couldn't have done it without you (this book, this life), I mean it. And mahalo nui to Tyler for sharing your photographic eye, talents, and treasured perspective.

To Ken, Tyler, Kathy, Lacey, and Lucas Lausten, thank you for participating in the creation of this ranch and this story. Sometimes we struggle, yet we keep coming back together at a rock table in the shade of aspens at the end of a day. And Ken: I *love* the pendant you made for me out of Little Cojo garbage glass!

Lastly, I am forever indebted to this land, its earliest and longest caretakers, and the animals upon it: the wild horses, deer, elk, bears, bobcats, turkeys, piñon jays, canyon wrens, marmots, mountain lions, and all the rest of the wild ones in the neighborhood, and to the horses, cattle, cats, and dogs who give me a life. Especially Savanna, Jessi, and one-eared, three-legged, big-hearted Bow, who made it to the end of the story and not beyond.

Some of the preceding chapters, or parts thereof, appeared previously in slightly different form. Many thanks to the editors and publishers of the following publications, starting with the late Michael Steinberg, who selected "The Last Cows" as the winning essay for the Editors' Prize way back in 2007—an essay that stayed with me all these years, in want of the rest of the story. The earlier version of chapter 1 appeared in *Fourth Genre* 10, no. 1 (Spring 2008): 1–10.

A small portion of chapter 5 appeared in "The Weight of It" in the "Open Range" column of *Contra Viento*, 2019. https://contravientojournal.org/the-weight-of-it/.

Part of chapter 7 appeared as "Getting Ready" in *Deserts: The First Five Years of the Waterston Desert Writing Prize* (Bend OR: Waterston Desert Writing Prize, 2019), 51–59.

A tiny portion of chapter 8 appeared as "Withdrawal" in the Torrey House Press blog *That Thing with Feathers: Hope and Literature in a Time of Pandemic*, April 22, 2020. https://www.torreyhouse.org/single-post/2020/04/22/that-thing-with-feathers-hope-and-literature-in-a-time-of-pandemic.

Part of chapter 9 appeared in *Terrain.org*, February 16, 2023. https://www.terrain.org/2023/nonfiction/in-the-rut/.

A version of chapter 10 appeared in *Fugue*, no. 61 (Summer/Fall 2021): 131–37. It has also appeared in *Four Corners Voices: Stories, Poetry, Essays* (Cortez CO: Four Corners Writers, 2024), 156–64.

A version of chapter 12 appeared in *The Gulch*, no. 18 (Winter 2021–22): 18–25.

An earlier version of chapter 16 appeared in *Missouri Review* 27, no. 1 (Spring 2024): 131–46.

Thank you all!

In the Our Regenerative Future series

The Last Cows: On Ranching, Wonder, and a Woman's Heart
Kathryn Wilder

To order or obtain more information on these or other University of Nebraska Press titles, visit nebraskapress.unl.edu.

www.ingramcontent.com/pod-product-compliance
Lightning Source LLC
Chambersburg PA
CBHW031236070925
32137CB00004B/6

* 9 7 8 1 4 9 6 2 3 9 1 6 7 *